TALL MEN,
SHORT SHORTS

TALL MEN, SHORT SHORTS

*The 1969 NBA Finals: Wilt, Russ, Lakers, Celtics,
and a Very Young Sports Reporter*

Leigh Montville

DOUBLEDAY
New York

Jacket photograph: 1969 NBA Finals, Boston Celtics Bill Russell (6) in action vs. Los Angeles Lakers Wilt Chamberlain (13), Inglewood, CA, by George Long / Sports Illustrated Classic / Getty Images
Jacket design by John Fontana
Book design by Michael Collica

Library of Congress Cataloging-in-Publication Data
Names: Montville, Leigh, author.
Title: Tall men, short shorts : the 1969 NBA finals: Wilt, Russ, Lakers, Celtics, and a very young sports reporter / Leigh Montville.
Description: First edition. | New York, N.Y. : Doubleday, 2021.
| Includes bibliographical references and index.
Identifiers: LCCN 2021000519 (print) | LCCN 2021000520 (ebook) |
ISBN 9780385545198 (hardcover) | ISBN 9780385545204 (ebook)
Subjects: LCSH: NBA Finals (Basketball) (1969) | Boston Celtics (Basketball team)—History. | Los Angeles Lakers (Basketball team)—History. | Chamberlain, Wilt, 1936–1999. | Russell, Bill, 1934– |
Montville, Leigh. | Sportswriters—United States—Biography.
Classification: LCC GV885.515.N37 M665 2021 (print) |
LCC GV885.515.N37 (ebook) | DDC 796.323/640973—dc23
LC record available at https://lccn.loc.gov/2021000519
LC ebook record available at https://lccn.loc.gov/2021000520

MANUFACTURED IN THE UNITED STATES OF AMERICA

1 3 5 7 9 10 8 6 4 2

First Edition

To all the other cool kids who worked at
135 Morrissey Boulevard, Boston, Massachusetts 02125.
It was great fun.

Looking out at the road rushing under my wheels. Looking back at the years gone by like so many summer fields.

—Jackson Browne, "Running on Empty"

Contents

TALL MEN,
SHORT SHORTS

Introduction

I wrote much of this book during the 2020 NBA playoffs. It was an odd process. At night I watched the Los Angeles Lakers' step-by-step journey to yet another title on television in what was called a "bubble." The month was October, the time for baseball and football, not basketball. All games were played in an antiseptic gymnasium next to an amusement park in Orlando, Florida. By day, I spent my time in another bubble, 1969, where it was spring and the Lakers were trying to win their very first title in Los Angeles.

All games were not played in an antiseptic gymnasium next to an amusement park in Orlando, Florida.

There were fans in my bubble.

There was actual noise.

Loud noise much of the time.

An organist—John Kiley in Boston, Gaylord Carter in Los Angeles—played music during the timeouts.

Hot dogs were sold.

Beer.

Yes, there were tall men.

Bill Russell.

Wilt Chamberlain.

Jerry West.
John Havlicek.
Elgin Baylor.
Yes, there were short shorts.
Canvas sneakers.
No instant replays.
No commercial breaks.
Big stories.
Little stories.
Injuries.
Details.
Interviews.
Phone calls from phone booths.
Cigarettes.
Basketball.
Basketball.
Basketball.

I spent time in buildings that no longer exist.
   I worked with people who no longer are alive.
   I traveled across the country, back and forth, on airplanes.
   I ate in restaurants.
   I drank in bars.
   I talked to friends, sometimes late into the night.
   I rode in cabs.
   I talked to strangers, some of them famous, face-to-face.
   I bought three newspapers every day, first thing in the morning, read them with a tactical and discerning eye, looked for news I had not heard. Worried. Analyzed.
   I went to the games.
   Yes, I did.
   I pushed through crowds.
   I shoved.
   I stayed up late.
   I woke up early. (West Coast time.)
   I stood in lines, everybody close together.
   I hustled.

The rush of it all, the colors, the emotions, the deadlines, the locker rooms, the quotes, the typing, the worry, worry, worry.

My heart sometimes seemed as if it was going to explode.

I was young.

I was younger than I thought I was.

I was 100 percent alive.

The games at night on television from the 2020 bubble were very good, interesting, congratulations to everyone involved, but they seemed to be played in a laboratory or on a space ship circling the moon. I looked at the big NBA logo on the Disney World hardwood floor, the most familiar figure in the production, appreciated the talents on display, acknowledged the results—congratulations to L.A.— and the next day, very early, returned to the other bubble in my notes, in my memory, in my mind.

Hello, Wilt.

Hello, Bill.

Hello, Jerry.

Nobody had to wear a mask.

Chapter 1

FLYING

The bright young man is dressed pretty much the way I am dressed today, right now, as I type these words on my MacBook Pro. Jeans. Polo shirt. Sneakers. Maybe a sports coat for the trip. Maybe not. More likely that yellow zipper jacket, one of those Baracuta jackets with the Scotch plaid lining, in case the day is cool when he gets off the plane. They were popular back then, the Baracuta jackets. Kids in Charlestown and South Boston wore them inside out to show the lining and the label. Irish kids. Tribal. Local. The bright young man wears his the regular way since he is much older than those kids, twenty-five, not from South Boston or Charlestown, married and all, but the collar is up. That is the way everybody wore it. I still wear the collar up on my zipper jackets today.

Because. Just because.

The bright young man's red hair is longer and fuller and brighter than mine. That is for sure. He has a pair of modified muttonchops for sideburns. Hasn't added the mustache yet. That will come on his thirtieth birthday. ("You should have grown that years ago," some-one will say. "Yes, I should," he will reply. Never will shave it off.) He is smoking. There is no doubt about that. He always was smoking back then. Lucky Strikes. Unfiltered. No bullshit. Same brand as Mom and Dad. The Luckies put Dad in the ground two years earlier, emphysema, but Dad was old when he died. Sixty-seven. No need to worry. Twenty-five is a long way from sixty-seven.

The day is a wonder.

California awaits.

April 21, 1969.

The bright young man smokes all the way across the United States. Boston to L.A. The little ashtray in the armrest is filled by the time the plane passes over Cleveland. He grinds the butts into the pile, one after another, compressed proof of his addiction. He hopes he doesn't start a fire. Something seems to be sort of smoldering right now, so he clicks the little silver cover back in place. Could he, should he ask the stewardess to empty the nascent conflagration somewhere over Iowa or Kansas or wherever they are? Doesn't know. Doesn't ask. Keeps grinding. The smoldering seems to stop.

The stewardesses—and that is their 1969 job description, their title—are young. Pretty. The same age as him. They have a movie star quality with their long hair and high heels and tight skirts and their beauty. He has an aisle seat and watches the young women take cans and miniature bottles of liquor from the beverage cart. Yes.

Time will dilute this experience. I have been watching these same women reach for those cans and miniature bottles for the last fifty years. We have grown old and wide together. The stewardesses of then have married and had children and their children have had children. Somehow the women have never left the airline. There is no romance, no mystery. They are doing the same job, same as forever, and can't wait to get home and soak their feet.

Except this is fifty years ago.

And they are babes.

All of them.

A portable typewriter in a carrying case is underneath the seat in front of the bright young man. Sometimes he puts his feet on it. The case is baby blue with a two-inch black leather stripe down the middle. The typewriter inside is an Olivetti Lettera 32, a brand and model that have become the favorites of serious journalists around the world. This is the Louisville Slugger of his profession. Red Smith uses a Lettera 32. Jim Murray. Frank Deford. No doubt Hemingway, Dashiell Hammett, and Shakespeare would have used one, too, if they could have. The bright young man is very proud of his Olivetti Lettera 32.

He is a journalist of sorts, a writer, at least in his own mind, a sportswriter for the *Boston Globe,* off to cover the first two games of the best-of-seven National Basketball Association finals between the Boston Celtics and the Los Angeles Lakers. He is not afraid to share this fact with whoever might have the fortune to sit next to a sportswriter for the *Boston Globe* who is off to cover the first two games of the series between the Celtics and the Lakers. (God bless that person.)

The assignment is the biggest the bright young man has had in fifteen months at the newspaper, the biggest of his short career. He is scheduled to cover the whole shebang, a possible two full weeks of athletic bloodletting. Games will be played every other day. Time zones will be flipped and flipped and flipped again. Circadian rhythms will be dismantled and left in late-night coffee shops and airport lounges.

> April 23—Boston at Los Angeles
> April 25—Boston at Los Angeles
> April 27—Los Angeles at Boston
> April 29—Los Angeles at Boston
> May 1—Boston at Los Angeles (if necessary)
> May 3—Los Angeles at Boston (if necessary)
> May 5—Boston at Los Angeles (if necessary)

There is the promise of melodrama, suspense, transcontinental electricity inside this schedule. The bright young man can feel it. He has been traveling with the Celtics since the start of these playoffs, has chronicled the team's successes in Philadelphia and New York to reach the finals. He has latched onto a show that has become much better than it was predicted to be.

The Celtics were supposed to be dead by now. They had finished an embarrassed fourth in the Eastern Division of the NBA with a 48-34 record, nine games behind the first-place Baltimore Bullets, six games behind the third-place New York Knicks. No matter that they were defending champions, had won nine NBA titles in the past ten years, had dominated their sport for an entire decade, the Celtics were supposed to be finished. Done.

The universal judgment was that they were too old. Every year another piece had fallen off the juggernaut, another part that had made the basketball machine function. Bob Cousy and Bill Sharman, Frank Ramsey and K. C. Jones, Tom Heinsohn and celebrated coach Red Auerbach, all future members of the Basketball Hall of Fame, had peeled away, one after another. A host of supporting players like Wayne Embry and Jim Loscutoff, Gene Conley and Willie Naulls, also had departed.

Sam Jones, master of the jump shot, thirty-five years old, would be the next to depart at the end of the playoffs. A Sam Jones Day already had been held at the end of the regular season at Boston Garden, complete with a proclamation from the City Council, a cake, a dinner, a standing ovation from 13,555 fans, and a gift of the shell of a prefab home that would be built in Silver Spring, Maryland, at his new address. All that was left was for the playoffs to end before he could move.

Bill Russell, the six-foot-ten foundation of all of the success, same age as Jones, also was thinking about retirement. He was in his third year as a player/coach, Auerbach's replacement. He was in his thirteenth year in a green uniform. As a young coach at thirty-five, he knew the limits of an old player at thirty-five. His body gave him reminders every day. He couldn't run as fast, couldn't jump as high. His arthritic knees ached. He had his moments, but, man, he had to spread them out. He had to survive on bursts of energy, rather than the constant flow of high-grade performance that had made him the winningest player in the history of American professional sports.

Bursts were how he had led the team to a tenth championship in 1968, a year ago, lifting the Celtics from a 3-1 hole against the Philadelphia 76ers in the Eastern Division championship, then to a six-game triumph over the Lakers in the finals. Could he do it again? There were positive signs in the first two playoff series this year, both mild upsets, but not enough to change the minds of the actuarial thinkers in Las Vegas.

The Lakers are a 9–5 favorite, which pretty much translates to

2–1, large odds for a championship series. This is not a new evaluation. Despite their loss in the finals last year, despite their loss in all six finals they have played against the Celtics in their history, the residents of the Fabulous Forum, 3900 W. Manchester Rd., Inglewood, CA 90305, have been the favorites to win this title since July 9, 1968, three months before the season even started. That was when their owner, Jack Kent Cooke, laid out an astounding $260,000 for the first year of a five-year contract to secure the services of seven-foot-one Wilton Norman Chamberlain. Ranked everywhere except, perhaps, Boston Massachusetts, as the biggest, bestest, most stupendous basketball player in the history of the world, Chamberlain was added to a lineup that included certified superstars Jerry West and Elgin Baylor.

No team like this ever had been assembled in the NBA. It was as if the roster had been cut from the pages of comic books, Superman pasted together with Batman and, oh, the Incredible Hulk or any one of the Avengers in an effort to rid Metropolis of the dark forces that had ruled for so long. The move was unprecedented. There was no such thing as free agency in the NBA or any American professional sport in 1969. Players like Chamberlain simply weren't available on the open market. They were chained to their employer, indentured, locked into servitude at their latest stop until their owners chose to send them elsewhere.

And yet, here he was.

The word "destiny" seemed appropriate on a bunch of levels for the Lakers and for Wilt. This was the final test before it could be fulfilled.

Stories bounce through the young man's head. Angles. They are there when he wakes up in the morning, there when he goes to sleep. He makes a mental list, changes it, adds or deletes. He conducts imaginary interviews that he hopes will happen. He will be ready for anything. He will make the readers see what he sees, hear what he hears, feel what he feels. The matchups sing to him.

Celtics vs. Lakers

Perpetual Winners vs. Perpetual Losers

Bill Russell vs. Wilt Chamberlain

Fate vs. Jerry West

Sam Jones vs. Age

Age vs. Elgin Baylor
John Havlicek vs. The Four-Minute Mile
Red Auerbach's Basketball Knowledge vs. Jack Kent Cooke's Ownership Money
The Athens of America vs. Hollywood
Defense vs. Offense
Running vs. Walking
Teamwork vs. Celebrity
Good vs. Evil (Parochial View)
The Boston Garden vs. The Fabulous Forum
Truth, Justice, and the American Way vs. High Gloss and Big Money
Boston vs. Los Angeles
Yes!
Yes, indeed.

This is an important trip for the bright young man. Excuse, if you can, his self-absorption. Ambition pumps through his body in a daily systolic beat, always there, threatening to explode from his body in inopportune moments. He is young enough to believe that anything can happen. This is a chance to make people notice.

A simple game story will not be sufficient—"The Boston Celtics defeated the Los Angeles Lakers, 110–109, as John Havlicek scored 42 points and Bill Russell pulled down 28 rebounds, blah, blah, blah . . ." The stories of today must do more. They must be different, provocative, but also must read like a page or two from a novel, tell the background of what took place, describe the characters involved, their thoughts and emotions, their answers to the toughest questions. Details. Details. Details. There never can be too many details.

The term that is peddled on the most literate streets in 1969 is "New Journalism." Tom Wolfe and Truman Capote and Gay Talese are prominent New Journalists in the real world. They not only report the news, they report the colors, the sounds, the brands of cigarettes and automobiles, the contents of the subject's imagination. *The Kandy-Kolored Tangerine-Flake Streamline Baby* (Wolfe), *In Cold Blood* (Capote), "Frank Sinatra Has a Cold" (Talese). This is revolutionary stuff. Musical. Funky. The dull informative clatter of the

Associated Press, say, or the *New York Times* has been replaced by stories that read like good fiction, stories that talk about thoughts and motivations, reasons, and memories of home and Mama.

The sportswriting business has a different name for the would-be practitioners of this approach to writing. They are called "chipmunks." Young, mostly under thirty-five, they are irritants to the older generation. Too noisy. Too demanding. Too . . . everything. Jimmy Cannon, the longtime standout columnist in New York, age fifty-eight, grew impatient with these new people and their incessant questions. He said, "They sound like a bunch of chipmunks." The name stuck. A famous moment came when Ralph Terry, a pitcher for the New York Yankees, won a game in the World Series and said afterward that his wife was home feeding their new baby. "Bottle or breast?" a sportswriter asked. That was a chipmunk question.

The bright young man considers himself part of the revolution. He works for the evening edition of the *Globe,* so he has later deadlines—pretty much no deadlines at all—and will be able to stay later in the locker rooms, ask his questions, then take time to write his story. Bottle or breast? He will have that story behind the story. He will write it for what he is worth. Breast would be more exciting.

When he first moved to Boston, fifteen months ago, before he was married, he lived in a rooming house on Marlborough Street. Dead asleep one night he was awakened by an alarm and noises in the hall. An orange glow was outside his only window. The Unitarian church on the corner, First Church of Boston, was on fire. The glow was a reflection on a wall of another building.

Half-asleep and panicked, he put on some clothes and grabbed the Lettera 32 in the baby-blue carrying case with the two-inch black stripe down the middle. He went outside and stood on the street. He watched the fire with residents who had grabbed cats and dogs and family photos, antiques, and other treasures. He had grabbed his typewriter.

Somewhere in the flight, the beverage cart is replaced by baskets filled with headphones wrapped in plastic. The glamorous stewardesses walk through the plane with the baskets. A movie will be shown. (Is there a charge? Can't remember.) The fine young man accepts the offer, plugs the power end of the headphones into the armrest, careful to stay away from any possible inferno in the ashtray, inserts the appropriate plugs into his appropriate ears. Small television screens drop from the ceiling in a choreographed entrance, all of them at once. There is a screen at every fourth or fifth row, the entire length of the plane. The movie is *Bullitt,* starring Steve McQueen.

I watched this movie again on Netflix two nights ago. This was maybe the seventh time I have seen the thing in my lifetime. Holds up well. Steve, if you never saw it or don't remember, plays Bullitt, of course, the headstrong detective who gets things done, no matter the cost. Jacqueline Bisset is the love interest.

The inescapable fact of this seventh viewing is that I know Steve McQueen will be dead on an operating table in Juarez, Mexico, in twelve more years at the age of fifty. He will try a long-shot operation to combat the many cancerous tumors in his body, but will die of a heart attack. (I looked up the dates and circumstances.) In the movie, Steve still is thirty-eight years old, thirty-eight forever, handsome in that hard-edged way that appeals to both men and women. He takes no shit from anyone. He outwits the bad guys. His face crinkles in all the right places when he smiles. His blue eyes stare into the future that he doesn't know exists.

The fine young man is entranced. He hasn't traveled much, certainly not long distances like this, and never has seen a movie on an airplane. The decadence of the experience is wonderful. Smoking. Drinking a Pepsi. (Real Pepsi, not diet.) Stretched out. Watching a movie. Steve McQueen must do this all the time. Fly in a jet. Probably a private jet. Maybe with Jacqueline Bisset at his side. Drink. Smoke. Maybe watch himself on the screen.

Who wouldn't want to be Steve?

Nobody.

A voice asks everyone to buckle their seat belts, return their seat backs and tray tables to an upright and locked position, make sure all their carry-on luggage is stowed under the seat in front of them or in the overhead bins. The stewardesses prepare for landing.

California!

—

I am going to say the plane flies out over the Pacific Ocean and turns around to land at LAX. I don't know if this is true, can't remember, but I'm going to say it does for dramatic purposes. The bright young man looks out the window. (I'm also going to say he has a window seat.) He is spellbound by the sight of the Pacific. There it is. Son of a bitch. He never has seen the Pacific Ocean. He never has been to California. He never has seen a palm tree, except in pictures. There is a lot he never has seen.

In the army, finishing up basic training with the National Guard, he hitchhiked from Fort Leonard Wood to St. Louis once with a guy from New Albany, Indiana. After they drank a lot of beer and went to a baseball game, they visited the famous arch, then went down and spit into the Mississippi River. The guy from New Albany, Indiana, said that a man had to spit into the Atlantic and Pacific Oceans and the Mississippi River to prove that he was a true American male. It sounded like a proper Code of Life. Something important. This will finish the process for the bright young man. Spit into the Pacific.

Will he go to Hollywood, see the names of the stars in the sidewalks? Will he see any stars in real life, doing their shopping or going to the dry cleaners? Will he recognize them? Will he go to a beach? Will he see any surfers? Will he see a Beach Boy? Brian Wilson would be good. Will he see a Dodgers game? Probably not. Will he go to Disneyland? Probably not. Will he go up to Griffith Observatory where James Dean kicked ass in that knife fight in *Rebel Without a Cause* and captured Natalie Wood's heart? Rodeo Drive? Venice Beach? Will he ride on a freeway? What's that like? Will he eat a California orange?

He heads through the terminal confusion toward baggage claim with no problem. All he has to do is follow the heads sticking out of the crowd, the Celtics' heads, taller than all the other heads. There's Russell. There's Tom Sanders. There's Bailey Howell. The players will lead the way, then stand around, then pick their bags off the luggage carousel, same as the bright young man. They will grab a cab to the Airport Marina Hotel, same as he will. Often the same cab.

There will be no air-conditioned luxury bus. There will be no preferred treatment. Joe DeLauri, the team trainer, also handles the travel arrangements. He will hand out keys at the hotel. All the players except Russell will have a roommate.

The bright young man will follow along. The trainer also will give him a key. His roommates will be those Lucky Strikes and that Lettera 32. The room will be filled with smoke and that clackety-clack noise, a bell at the end of each typewritten line. An ashtray will always need to be emptied. There will be great internal debates about choices of words and phrases, quotes to use and quotes to leave out. Plot lines will evolve. Drama will develop. The characters on the Celtics and Lakers will play their parts, working through a series that will be as memorable as any in NBA history. The bright young man will play his part, clackety-clack, in the room.

He is the twenty-five-year-old me. I am the seventy-seven-year-old him.

He knows nothing about what will happen next. I know pretty much everything.

Chapter 2

PRACTICE

By Leigh Montville
Staff Writer
LOS ANGELES—The drill was simple.

Three members of the Boston Celtics would thump down the long basketball court at the University of Loyola. They would weave and pass and run, pell-mell, with the final step being a layup. Then they would come back the other way. Same thing. Another group would follow.

"Twenty layups in a row," said Bill Russell, sweat-less and without a tee shirt on one side of the court.

The troops responded—after a while.

For a long time, they would make double-figure assaults at the 20 straight layups. Then a Don Chaney or a Mal Graham would flub a shot.

"One," Russell would say as the next three-man group rolled down the court. Sometimes, like an aggravated drill sergeant, he wouldn't count too well and 14 straight layups would be numbered as "six" in Russell's delayed cadence, count cadence, count.

The drill, one hour after the team had stepped from a 5½-hour plane ride, had a purpose. The Celtics are

going to have to run and run—using their familiar
success formula—if they hope to win National Basketball
Association championship No.11.

The Los Angeles Lakers, the opposition in the finals
for the sixth time, have played different basketball this
year. The difference has been noticeable. Its name is Wilt
Chamberlain.

The seven-foot, one-inch center has slowed down the
Lakers. He has forgotten the quick outlet pass and made
a team with Jerry West and Elgin Baylor conscious of
working plays. On defense, he has done a Russellesque
job, blocking layups and forcing jump shooters into funny
jump shots.

His defense is the main reason the Celtics have to run.

"You have to run the Lakers some," said the Celtics'
Bailey Howell, the man who finally scored the 20th
consecutive layup. "If you don't get any fast break baskets,
you don't get close shots at all.

"You can't let Wilt get set up all the time. When he sets
up, he forces you outside. You don't ever win with outside
shooting."

"And once Wilt sets up, we can't move him," said John
Havlicek, whose basketball gospel has involved foot racing
as much as foul shooting. "A center like Zelmo Beatty of
the Atlanta Hawks can do it, but Russ can't.

"Beatty, who is a good outside shooter, can hit that
little 15-foot jumper all day. Wilt has to come out.
With us, he knows he doesn't have to worry about Russ
shooting from the outside."

The game plan for the opening of the best-of-seven
series Wednesday night at the Forum in Inglewood will
be made today. The Celtics plan a closed practice at the
Forum this afternoon. Changes will be made.

"Every series is different," Russell said while taking
a whirlpool bath after throwing the team into a seven-
basket, losers-take-20-laps scrimmage. "This is an entirely
different team from the one we played last year.

"At the Forum we will try to prepare directly for the Lakers. Today we were just running."

Russell said Howell would probably draw the defensive assignment against Baylor with Emmette Bryant against West. Both choices, however, were subject to change this afternoon.

And after the Wednesday night opener.

THE NOTEBOOK—The Lakers held an informal workout—shoot if you want to shoot—in the morning at Loyola . . . Thus far, in six playoff dates they have drawn 2000 more people than Bill Sharman's LA Stars team in the American Basketball Association drew all year.

"I'll tell you this," Russell said with a whirlpool-bath smile, "the two best teams in the league are in the playoffs . . . All the has-beens, the third and fourth-best centers in the All-Star balloting."

Russell declined to call this the best Laker team the Celtics have faced in the playoffs . . . "We'll have to see what happens and I don't mean who wins and who loses, but how the games are played," he said. "You have to remember that our team is not as strong as it has been in other years. Years when people like Sam and K.C. (Jones) were coming off the bench."

Boston Evening Globe
April 22, 1969

So this is the bright young man's first dispatch from the sun-drenched western front. I give it a B, maybe three out of four stars, 7.5 out of 10. I wanted to grade harder, no more than a C, two stars, a pedestrian 5.5 of 10, but decided to assign extra credit for youth and obvious ambition. Perhaps my relationship with the writer factored into the decision.

You can see that he is trying. He has dumped his bags at the Airport Marina and hustled to the practice at Loyola Marymount. This is worth points by itself. The usual sportswriting procedure after a cross-country flight, especially east to west, three-hour change in time, was to submit a formulaic advance, a can of stale quotes saved from the back pages of a reporter's notebook. Going to the practice was not seen as necessary. The bright young man (TBYM) is the only Boston writer in attendance.

His idea is to capture the look and feel of what he sees. Remember that there is no such thing as ESPN in 1969. The all-sports network will not arrive for another decade. No radio sports talk shows are in need of a high-calorie diet of clichés to survive. The clichés are available, but the shows haven't been invented. Local television, one station or two, might send a crew to cover the run-up to an event like the NBA finals for a spot on the evening news, but probably will not. Television does not travel lightly or easily with its lights and sound and awkward equipment.

The level of show business excitement measured here against future mega-noise, megawatt, great gargled exultations, is low, if not nonexistent. There are no podiums for speakers, no backgrounds against a wall with advertisements to promote automobiles or banks or energy drinks as the stars grant group interviews. There are no group interviews. (There are no energy drinks, either, except coffee, black.) This could be a basketball practice at the local YMCA, young-ish accountants and plumbers, bartenders and schoolteachers, getting ready in obscurity for the Men's League finals. These would be tall bartenders and schoolteachers, to be sure, much more competent in the layup lines, but this would be the same quiet scene.

The description of the normality of the workout is what I like best in the story. TBYM has hooked onto that, describing Russell's all-business approach. The coach is not wearing a shirt while he conducts the drills, punishing his players for mistakes by recalibrating his count. He is not a participant, either, a testament to his workload as a player. He gives his post-practice interview from the whirlpool bath, naked famous man surrounded by bubbles, breaking down the series, making a little joke at the end about how both he and Wilt were disrespected in the All-Star balloting. (Wes Unseld of Baltimore and Elvin Hayes of San Diego were selected this year in front of the familiar one-two finishers.) Who, the coach wanted to know, were the big men here at the end?

TBYM, I am sure, went back to his hotel room and wrote his story surrounded by the nicotine cloud. A basketful of balled-up failed beginnings no doubt was part of the scene. Finished, he had to find a Western Union outlet somewhere in the area. Western Union was the recommended way to transmit a newspaper story across the country at that time. Friends might tell people now that the bright young man had to attach his work to the right leg of a carrier pigeon and send the bird on its way to Boston, rest stops in Utah and Kansas, but that is not the truth. Western Union was the favored method of transmission.

That meant he had to look in the phone book, the Yellow Pages, to find a Western Union office in nearby Inglewood. (Note to Generation Z: The Yellow Pages was the business side of the phone book. The phone book was a fat printed listing of all local phone numbers. The phone was that contraption with the dial on the desk in the hotel room. Dial 9 for an outside line.) The office he found sometimes was an actual office, but often was part of some other business like a drugstore that also featured a Western Union machine. I seem to remember a drugstore here in Inglewood.

TBYM no doubt took a cab, handed his typewritten words and instructions to the nondescript operator/pharmacist, who then retyped them on his or her Western Union machine and sent them hurtling across the country to another machine in what was called "The Wire Room" at the *Globe*. A bell would ring on the *Globe*'s machine when the story arrived, and the machine would retype the words. Bing-bing-bing. Back in his hotel room, TBYM would call an hour later to make sure everything had worked.

The process seems medieval and clunky compared to modern computer technology that pretty much takes a thought from a writer's head and zips it into common knowledge in the speed of a hiccup, but this was magic at the time. The *Boston Globe* daily circulation was 443,037. On Sundays, it was 564,083. In talking to advertisers, the newspaper always would mention a "pass-along factor" of 2.5 for the daily edition, more than 3 for Sunday. That meant well over a million people would read the paper during the week, well over a million and a half, closing in on two on Sunday. The words mattered. No ESPN. No talk-show radio.

The bright young man is the man.

—

An entire year—minus nine days—has passed since the Celtics finished off the Lakers on May 2, 1968, in six games at the Forum for their tenth title in twelve years. That final game was a 124–109 pounding, a rout that was another affirmation of the Celtics' superiority in the NBA cosmos. This was the fifth time they had beaten the Lakers in the finals in five tries.

Twelve months.

"We talked about being just a bunch of old guys doing the best we can," Bill Russell reported after that game, trying to describe a bit of humility during one timeout in the carnage.

"What part of the game was that?" a reporter asked.

Russell laughed.

"When we came over to the bench and we were ahead 17 points," he said.

Twelve months.

Both teams returned to the beginning to start a new season, made adjustments, and started all over again. Both have survived the Chutes and Ladders game board of their sport. Here they are. Same time. Same place. They each have played eighty-two regular-season games plus eleven more in two rounds of playoffs. Injuries, inconsistencies, and incidental contacts have been brushed aside. Back again.

Tumultuous events have taken place in other parts of the newspaper during this time. Martin Luther King was assassinated twenty-eight days before that final game in 1968. Robert Kennedy was assassinated thirty days after that game. The Democratic convention in Chicago in August was a string of demonstrations, arrests, all in a cloud of tear gas. Hubert Humphrey was nominated. Richard Nixon, chosen as the Republican candidate in Miami in August, won the election in November, was inaugurated as president in January. The Beatles released *The White Album* in November, played a concert on top of the Apple Records headquarters building at 3 Savile Row, London, in January then broke up, never to play again. John and Yoko staged a "Bed-In" in Toronto in March. North Korea, which had seized the USS *Pueblo*, finally released the crew two days before Christmas. Sirhan Sirhan confessed to killing Kennedy and was found guilty and sentenced to death. James Earl Ray confessed to killing Dr. King and was found guilty and sentenced to ninety-nine years in prison. Apollo 8—with astronauts Jim Lovell, Bill Anders, and Frank Borman—became the first spacecraft to orbit around the moon. Plans were announced for Apollo 10 to land on the moon in the summer of 1969. The Boeing 747 made its debut. Dwight Eisenhower died. Tommie Smith and John Carlos protested racial injustice in Mexico City. Arthur Ashe won the U.S. Open at Forest Hills.

The news from Vietnam was an industrial whine in the background, start to finish, the war machine grinding up lives without rhyme, reason, or cogent explanation. More than fifteen thousand U.S. soldiers died in the twelve months. Demonstrations against the war were everywhere, especially on college campuses. Administration buildings and classrooms were occupied at Harvard, Columbia, MIT, UCal-Berkeley, assorted schools across the map. The ghettos bubbled with civic discontent, remnants from the riots after Reverend King's death. The Black Panthers were a vibrant force in Oakland.

The hijack of jets to go to Cuba was a trend. Eastern Airlines Flight 7 was diverted from its normal route from Newark to Miami and landed in Havana. Allen Funt and a crew from *Candid Camera* were on the flight. Passengers first thought the hijack was a stunt, but it was not. China detonated its first thermonuclear device. The Zodiac Killer began his grim work in Benicia, California. Jim Morrison was arrested for indecent exposure in Miami. Yale University admitted women in New Haven. The politically incorrect Hong Kong flu killed 33,800 Americans, which seemed like a lot.

Hair was long, skirts were short. (Everybody said that.) Marijuana was everywhere. Plans were made for a large musical gathering during the coming summer at Max Yasgur's farm in Bethel, New York. Marilyn Manson, Andrew Breitbart, and Jennifer Aniston were born. Tallulah Bankhead, John Steinbeck, Boris Karloff, Gabby Hayes, and the *Saturday Evening Post* died. Elvis appeared on a comeback special. *Oliver!* won the Oscar for best picture for 1968. *Butch Cassidy and the Sundance Kid* and *Midnight Cowboy* were major contenders for the next year. *Laugh-In* was the top-rated television show, with Artie Johnson appearing from behind a potted plant, Goldie Hawn smiling, and Judy Carne asking everyone to "Sock it to me." *Gomer Pyle, Bonanza,* and *Mayberry R.F.D.* were Nielsen winners. Cronkite delivered the news from one network, Huntley and Brinkley from another, and the third network never could find the right guy. *Hair* was the big Broadway musical. *The Godfather* by Mario Puzo was a big book. *Slaughterhouse Five* by Kurt Vonnegut was another one.

The minimum wage was a buck sixty. The average price of a new house was $14,950. Gas was thirty-five cents a gallon. January in Los Angeles was the wettest month in the city since December 1889, with 14.94 inches of rain. The "100-Hour Snowstorm" from February 24 to 26 was an all-time record in Boston, with 25.8 inches of snow. Sonny and Cher were officially married after the birth of their daughter, Chastity. The number-one country song was "D-I-V-O-R-C-E" by Tammy Wynette.

Anything else?

Wilt became a Laker. Russell and the Celtics became a year older.

Twelve months.

Same place. Same time.

The NBA finals, it must be said, are not the dominant story of the news cycle. (Is there such a term in 1969? News cycle? Probably not.) They are not even the dominant sports story, even in the cities where the games will be played a day later.

In Boston, the refusal to report to the Cleveland Indians by flamboyant outfielder Ken (The Hawk) Harrelson, owner of many Nehru jackets and a famous round waterbed, after a trade by the Red Sox is on the front page of the *Globe,* along with a proposal to build a $91 million football stadium over the Massachusetts Turnpike that will keep the Boston Patriots from moving to Seattle. (The stadium never will be built. The Patriots will never move to Seattle. The Hawk will, however, move to Cleveland. No report on the status of the waterbed.)

On the front sports page, the finish of the Boston Marathon, won by Yoshiaki Unetani of Japan, the fortunes of the Boston Bruins hockey team, and a scheduled start for Red Sox pitcher Jim Lonborg all are given more prominent positions. The Celtics are fourth in importance.

In the *Los Angeles Times,* columnist Jim Murray does write a sweet blank-verse ode to veteran Lakers forward Elgin Baylor, but the predominant sports page story is the Los Angeles Dodgers' 7–5 win over Juan Marichal and the San Francisco Giants. A story about STP salesman Andy Granatelli's eight-car assault on the upcoming Indy 500 also is in a more prominent spot. The Lakers are third.

Baseball is the undisputed king in both cities. Hockey is second in Boston, football or horse racing second in Los Angeles. The colleges are strong in both cities, stronger in L.A. with UCLA and the University of Southern California, but spread across more schools in Boston and New England. Various other constituencies like boxing, high school sports, fishing and hunting, and golf argue for time and attention.

Basketball, professional basketball, still is in a fight to clear out more space for itself. The residue from the early traveling-carnival days of the sport—teams in Syracuse and Rochester and Fort Wayne, regularly scheduled games in places like Providence and Dayton and Evansville—is stronger than any apparition of what is to come. The Lakers, with their year-old arena and the big-bucks pretentions of owner Jack Kent Cooke, perhaps offer a first glimpse of the future, but the Celtics are a strong look into the past.

Four employees—that's all—staff the Celtics team office, one flight up from the pinball parlor and the train station at the base of the Boston Garden. Those four employees are Red Auerbach, the Hall of Fame coach, now general manager; his secretary, Mary Whelan; publicity man Howie McHugh; and Jeff Cohen, who is twenty-five years old, son of Red's best friend. Cohen is listed as "assistant general manager," but also is someone sent for donuts and coffee. ("'You want to be assistant general manager?'" Cohen remembers as the conversation about his promotion with Auerbach. "'That's great. You're assistant general manager. There's no more money, though. Understand? You're not a player.'")

A new owner of the team is Ballantine Beer, based in Newark, New Jersey. The Celtics have become a commodity, an investment, since the death of original owner Walter Brown five years earlier. The brewery has replaced the previous owner, real estate speculator Marvin Kratter, the investor who bought and then demolished Ebbets Field in Brooklyn for apartments. Marvin had a lucky rock from the Wailing Wall in Jerusalem that he asked the players to touch before heading onto the court. The players are not unhappy that this ritual has disappeared.

In a corporate moment during this present season, Howard Pines, the director of benefits at new-owner Ballantine, had occasion to call the Celtics office to talk to the director of personnel. There was a question about a check from a player that had bounced. He was surprised when Auerbach answered the phone.

"I'm sorry," Pines apologized. "I didn't mean to bother you. I was looking for the director of personnel."

"Howard," Red replied, "I am the head of personnel, the head of public relations, the head of operations and the general manager. So you have no choice but to bother me."

Pines eventually would include this anecdote in his book *The Case for Wasting Time and Other Management Heresies* as an example of a pared-down operation. This was a good choice. Anything less would reduce this pared-down operation to one man working from his basement.

Everything is low-key. The budget for scouting college talent for the NBA draft famously is the price of a Street & Smith's Basketball Annual for the new year and the bill for some long-distance phone calls between Red and his basketball friends. If the timing is right, a potential season ticket holder—and there aren't many—can be accompanied by the general manager himself for a view upstairs of the new seats. If Red is not available, his secretary or the assistant general manager will show the customer the potential new seats.

The NBA, itself, is a cozy operation. The office might have been moved from the eightieth floor of the Empire State Building to Suite 2360 at 2 Penn Plaza, part of the two-year-old Madison Square Garden complex, but the league still has only six employees. They would be the commissioner, Walter Kennedy, the assistant commissioner, Carl Scheer, a PR director, an office manager (who doubled as league statistician), a secretary, and a telephone operator, who handled the six phone lines. The number, remembered by a former employee, was (212) 279-1535, which was as nondescript as something your mother might have in her studio apartment on the Upper East Side.

"We didn't even have a number that ended in '00,'" the former employee says. "That was the NBA."

The best indication of the NBA's place in the 1969 world is that none of the first four games of the series (which would be all the games if there were a sweep) will be shown on television in Boston.

Channel 38, which won the bid for the local rights, had a clause in the contract that the station would not cover games on the West Coast due to cost. That eliminated the first two games in L.A. The second two games, one of them a Sunday afternoon national broadcast on ABC, will be blacked out in Boston in order to protect the live gate, a common procedure for most sports at the time.

The Lakers also will black out their home games. Closed-circuit telecasts will be available at the Warrens and State Theatres in downtown L.A. and at the International Ballroom at the Beverly Hills Hotel. Tickets are $5. For the first two games, except for these theater outlets, no one in either of the two cities will be able to watch the action live.

Radio still will be king. Forty-five-year-old Johnny Most, his gravel-throated voice brought to the breaking point again and again, will broadcast the action on WHDH in Boston and along the Celtics' network. Chick Hearn, fifty-two, smooth and cool, insightful and witty, will be on KNX 1070 in Los Angeles, also across the Lakers' network. Reports from both sides will be biased and overdramatic, especially in Boston, but loved by the local audiences. Most and Hearn will be as important as any player on either team, including Russell and Chamberlain.

Television will be a flickering blue light on the horizon.

"Equal to 800 sold-out Orange Bowls or 400 times the population of Plato's Athens," William Oscar Johnson proclaimed in wonder about the sixty million television viewers in January for the New York Jets' 16–7 upset of the Baltimore Colts in Super Bowl III, a vision of the television future. He described the bulk of America hunkered down in "darkened parlors" and "a million dim basements with knotty pine nailed over cement blocks . . . No butterfly, no snowflake, no street fight or car wreckage at the corner could fight for attention."

The image here will be quite different. Radio. Words still will be more important than pictures.

The players in the series will not be millionaires. There might be good money for the big stars, for Russell and Chamberlain, Baylor and West, contracts between $200,000 and $300,000 that could be prorated to over a million dollars in twenty-first-century dollars, but nothing to compare to the status of LeBron James and Kevin Durant and a host of future NBA potentates. Auerbach still boasts that he never has dealt with an agent, although he sorta has because Bill Russell brought along a lawyer just this past summer for contract negotiations. Salaries make a precipitous drop after the top couple of names on the roster. The NBA minimum for the 1968–69 season is $10,000, which is an increase under a newly revised basic contract.

A number of players still work in the off-season. Many run camps or perform in barnstorming tours or have other careers. Tom Heinsohn, an All-Star for the Celtics in the past, sold life insurance. Bob Cousy once said he was making more money driving a truck in the off-season than he made with the Celtics. Frugality is seen as a basic.

"Those Celtics were all good guys, but they were the cheapest group of people I met in my life," guard Mal Graham says. "You'd go to lunch and they would figure out the check, who ate what, to the penny. Nobody wanted to spend anything."

A good look at the basic-level NBA existence is provided by Rick Weitzman. As the final man off the bench, twelfth man on the Celtics roster, he scored the final basket in that 124–109 rout to finish off the Lakers in the final game of the 1968 finals He played the entire season as a set of embedded eyes and ears, a rookie, a twenty-one-year-old student of everything happening around him.

Drafted in the tenth round as a six-foot-two shooting guard from Northeastern University, mostly as a tip of the hat to a local school, he surprised everyone, including himself, by making the team.

"The day before the season opened, we still had thirteen players for the twelve spots," he says. "Someone had to go. We all knew it. At the end of the last practice, Bill Russell said, 'Wait a minute. Before we leave. I want to see a two-on-two game between the four rookies.'"

Easy as that, drama entered the gymnasium. The rest of the team and Russell and Auerbach stood around to watch. The most physical game Weitzman ever had seen then took place. He was in the middle of it. Everyone knew the stakes. One of the rookies—Mal Graham, Nevil Shed, and Johnny Jones were the other players—would be eliminated.

Weitzman's best friend in training camp was Graham, the first-round pick from NYU, another shooting guard. On the first play of the two-on-two, Weitzman decked him. Knocked him to the floor. Graham bounced up and tried to slug Weitzman. Everything proceeded from there. Fouls were not called. Hands, arms, legs, bumps, outright pushes and shoves were everywhere. Baskets were almost impossible to make.

The game—if that was what it could be called—did not end until Shed, one of the names from Texas Western's grand NCAA tournament final upset of Kentucky in 1966, landed wrong and blew out a knee. Russell called an end and everyone went home. There was no phone call to Weitzman that night, no congratulations, but also no good luck message, see you later, enjoy the rest of your life. He didn't know what to think.

He went to the Boston Garden the next night, opening night, uncertain if he should, and entered the locker room. The white home uniforms with the green word CELTICS across the front were laid out at every locker. Weitzman had worn number 25 during all of training camp. There was no number 25 ready to wear.

This was the answer?

"You're number 26," equipment man Walter Randall said. "K. C. Jones was number 25 and we're going to retire that number."

This was the answer.

Averaging 1.3 points per game, appearing in only twenty-five of them, Weitzman lived the life, watched a lot of games, saw what he saw. The final audition, the gym-rat decision on who stayed and who left (Shed underwent surgery, never played an NBA game) was a beginning. Few frills were involved.

The rookie mastered the basic six Celtics plays, each of them with three options, a total of eighteen possibilities that could take place from a set offense. He learned to run and run, run some more, a freelance foundation of all the past success, fast breaks with trailers and more trailers, options. He learned the way to play defense with the best defensive big man of all time behind him, ways to switch to cover the defensive big man's dance partner when his own man broke free.

Practices were held in a string of everyday places. The Boston Gar-

den was not available most of the time, hockey always the favored
tenant, so the team ran those six plays, those eighteen options at the
Cambridge YMCA, at the Tobin Community Center in Roxbury, at
Melrose High School, and at Brandeis University in Waltham. Where
was practice this time? Check the blackboard. The Cambridge
YMCA later fell off the list because local thieves would break into
the players' lockers while the players were getting ready for, say, the
Cincinnati Royals.

There were no practices on the road. Almost none. Travel and
play. That was the routine. There were no shootarounds on the day
of the game. (Shootarounds had not been invented.) There was no
weight training. (Training with weights was discouraged. Hurt flex-
ibility.) Travel and play. Film was available to watch, black-and-white,
if a person wanted, but not many persons wanted. Scouting reports
were rare. Everybody kept his own scouting report in his head. There
were twelve teams in the league, 144 players. Every team played every
other team at least seven times. Everybody pretty much learned the
idiosyncrasies of everybody else pretty fast.

The white uniforms were for home. Finish a game and you handed
your shirt and shorts, jock and socks, to Walter Randall. He would
have everything for you, clean, for the next game. Green uniforms
were for the road. Finish a game, and you would put your uniform in
your suitcase and bring it to the next game. Clean or not clean, that
was up to you.

Sneakers were all black, different from the white worn by every
team in the league. This was Auerbach's longtime innovation. His
idea was if a player were dribbling with his head down and had to
make a quick pass, he would be able to spot a teammate by sneaker
color alone. Black sneaker, pass. White, do not pass. The brand of
choice in 1968 was Converse, Chuck Taylor All Stars, canvas tops and
rubber bottoms. Actually there wasn't much choice. Russell wore a
different sneaker, made by a struggling company from Bristol, Rhode
Island, but everyone else wore Converse Chucks. No endorsement
checks were involved for everyone else. (In 1968–69, Adidas replaced
Converse in supplying free sneakers.)

Travel was commercial, players in coach on the airplane except
for the playoffs, when veterans rode in first class because the league
took care of the expenses. Rides from the airport were shared in the

cabs ordered by trainer Joe DeLauri. A rookie had to be in each cab because rookies had to pay the driver at the end, then track down DeLauri for reimbursement. Rooms, again, were shared.

Weitzman's first roommate was five-year veteran point guard Larry Siegfried, twenty-eight, an intense character from Ohio State. This relationship did not last long. Siegfried would return from the games with adrenaline still at work in his body. He would want to talk. This was not an unusual situation for athletes in the afterglow of competition, a rehash of the night's adventures, except Siegfried would not stop until daybreak.

"The sun would be up and then he'd go to sleep like a baby," Weitzman said. "I would stumble through the day. I had to get out of there."

The most important chore for the twelfth-man rookie was to carry a bruised yellow suitcase to every game. Known to everyone on the team as "Ol' Yeller," named after the 1957 movie about a boy (Tommy Kirk) and his dog, the suitcase contained Bill Russell's green uniform and sneakers. Weitzman had to make sure the suitcase and uniform arrived for every road game. It was something like carrying the nuclear codes from town to town with the U.S. president.

"Never forgot it once," the rookie reported. "That would not have been good if I did."

The finish for that 1968 rookie season was the fifteen-footer for the final basket of the final game of their championship run. The payoff was his piece of the modest $80,000 winners' playoff money. This was more than Rick Weitzman made for the entire season.

In the training camp for this 1968–69 campaign, alas, Weitzman battled a string of injuries and the usual group of new arrivals. Russell told him to "go see Red when we get home" after the last exhibition game, and that was the answer. That was how Weitzman learned that his tour of the league was finished. He played the 1969 season for the New Haven Elms in the Eastern Basketball League.

Rich Johnson, a thin six-foot-nine forward from Grambling, rookie at the end of the bench, has been responsible for transporting Ol' Yeller back and forth across the country for this 1969 year. He also does not want to make a mistake with the nuclear codes.

—

The journalistic traveling party from Boston is small. Sportswriters from Worcester, Providence, Lowell, Quincy, assorted dots on the New England map, will cover the games at the Garden, but their editors and publishers do not spend the money to send anyone as far as Los Angeles, especially with the three-hour time difference that destroys East Coast deadlines. Three other sportswriters from Boston have made the trip with the bright young man.

Bob Sales, thirty-five years old, also is employed by the *Boston Globe*. He covers the Celtics for the morning edition of the newspaper, which is separate from the afternoon edition. Eddie Gillooly, thirty-five, covers for the tabloid *Boston Record-American*. George Sullivan, thirty-five, covers for the *Boston Herald-Traveler*. All three writers will pump out stories, same as TBYM. Ten years older, certified grown-ups, family men with kids, all of them know more than he does. They have seen more games, been to more places. They are the same age as Bill Russell and Sam Jones, older than all the other players. They have stature, experience, the inside track. They can relate.

The bright young man does not care about any of this. In his mind, experience is not an asset for these older writers; it is a lounge chair of indifference. They do not see the new things he sees, feel what he feels. This is not something he would say to any of them, God forbid, but he believes it to be true. New eyes see best. Working with a quiet combination of ambition, overconfidence, and ignorance, he is certain he can handle anything.

In truth, TBYM is here due to circumstance more than ability. He would argue that he is the perfect choice for this job, the perfect New Journalism voice from the *Boston Globe* lineup, but facts intrude. The back of his mind contains the truth. He is a replacement part.

Herb Ralby, a longtime sportswriter at the *Globe,* is supposed to be on this trip, supposed to be staying at the Marina, recording (or probably not recording) the practice moments. He was here last year for the finals, recorded the Celtics' easy 124–109 sixth-game clinching win at the Forum.

"INGLEWOOD, Calif—For Capt. John Havlicek, it was his sixth National Basketball Championship in his seven years with the Celtics, but it meant more to him than all the others.

"'Because we weren't supposed to win it,' he smiled happily. . . ."

The bright young man holds his journalistic nose when he reads these words. He would point out that there was a better lead buried in Ralby's own notes. General manager Auerbach encouraged the Celtics players to throw coach Russell into the shower, then coach Russell encouraged the players to throw general manager Auerbach into the shower. General manager Auerbach had flown into L.A. on the day of the game and was taking a red-eye flight back to Boston at midnight and did not have a second set of clothes. He had to fly wet all the way home. That was the story. That was the lead.

Humpfh.

Ralby was fifty-four years old, a man-about-town bachelor who started working for the paper straight from Boston Latin School in 1931. He had covered the Celtics through their glory years. Outside of the time he spent with the Coast Guard during World War II, the *Globe* has been the working part of his adult life. He was at the paper on November 5, 1949, when the team and the NBA started local operation under a headline that read "Pro Basket Ball Makes Debut at Arena Tonight." This was the Dawn of NBA Creation. That is how long he has been on the scene.

TBYM, of course, considers him another shopworn old-timer cranking out prose as if it's so much industrial product. Didn't go to college. Isn't plugged into the modern athlete, the modern game. Doesn't know what's happening. Not a bad guy, understand, pleasant enough and helpful in his own way, but caught up in the sportswriting past. Perfunctory and dull.

The most damaging fact about Ralby's ability as a reporter—and don't get the young man started about his fellow sportswriter's wardrobe, straight out of *Guys and Dolls,* with stripes and plaids surrounded by a cloud of too-strong aftershave—is that he has a second job as the publicity man for the Boston Bruins. Has had it for a long time. This is an inconceivable conflict of interest. How can a man cover the local basketball team and work for the local hockey team at the same time? Aren't they in competition for the local sports fan's dollar? The daily ethical dilemmas involved would make a very long list.

"The *New York Times* would never put up with something like this," TBYM mutters often in late-night journalism discussions with his wife, Diane, or anyone who will listen.

"Certainly wouldn't," the cornered Diane or the cornered listener always has to reply.

The good part (for the bright young man) about this dual citizenship for Ralby, these divided loyalties, is that the normal Celtics beat writer can't be in two places at once. Especially not now.

The Bruins, formerly a well-used doormat in the National Hockey League, have become a good team. The emergence of Bobby Orr, a precocious defenseman from Parry Sound, Ontario, has changed their fortunes. They ended an eight-year absence from the Stanley Cup playoffs a year ago and are back again this year. (The eight-year absence was in a six-team league. Four of the six teams made the playoffs every year.) Orr is twenty-one at the end of this, his third season. The future is grand. Ralby is very busy. The playoffs started on April 2, 1969, and the Bruins went ahead and whipped the Toronto Maple Leafs in four straight games for their first playoff series win in eleven years. Now they are matched against the accursed Montreal Canadiens in the semifinals. All of Boston is abuzz with this fact. Ralby spends the bulk of his days explaining that, no, he does not have any tickets for any game.

The bright young man has been with the Celtics since the start of their playoffs. I can't remember anything being said about handling the job, about taking Ralby's place for the duration. The assignment mostly evolved. The work schedules would be posted one week at a time on a bulletin board in the office, and TBYM's spirits would leap when he saw "NBA Playoffs" written in pencil next to his name, an arrow stretching through the prescribed seven days.

None of this was supposed to be a big deal. The predictions everywhere were that the defending champions would be done after the first round in Philadelphia. When that didn't happen, the thought was the Celtics surely would be eliminated by the rising New York Knicks. The final round, the visit to the Lakers and Los Angeles, is the grand surprise. Ralby certainly would have been back in a normal year, but not this year. The bright young man, yes, feels as if he is Lou Gehrig taking over first base from Wally Pipp.

Enjoy the Stanley Cup playoffs, Wally.

I'll take it from here. . . .

One more thing. There is an addition to the *Globe* team for the playoffs. The sportswriter version of Lou Gehrig will be working with the basketball version of Babe Ruth in these finals.

Chapter 3

RUSSELL

By Ernie Roberts
Staff Writer

From a height of 6 feet, 9 inches.

From the unequalled experience of 13 playing years and 10 championships in professional basketball.

From the emotional perspective of the most involved Celtic in tomorrow night's Philadelphia playoff.

And with the candor of a man who tells it as it is, who knows no subterfuge.

That's the viewpoint Globe readers will enjoy when Boston's Bill Russell reports the opener and all the rest of the Celtics' playoff battles exclusively in the Morning and Evening Globe.

The Celtics' coach and center will make his first report Thursday . . . and it will be authentic. Russell will tape record his reactions and analysis, the humorous and poignant sides of playoff basketball. His comments will be faithfully transcribed for Globe readers, with no ghost writer gimmicks added.

The aging Celtics face the toughest playoff of the Russell years. They finished fourth in the Eastern Division and now must struggle against road-game odds and hostile crowds. Follow their uphill battle with the man of the moment, Bill Russell. Starting Thursday in the Boston Globe.

March 25, 1969
Boston Globe

No problem. The most intriguing addition to the *Boston Globe* playoff lineup will finish his forty-eight-minute battle against the big man in front of him, seven-foot-one Wilton Norman Chamberlain, who happens to be the most prodigious scorer and rebounder in NBA history, deliver a locker room postmortem, make sure his team management duties are done for the night (practice tomorrow, 11 a.m.), rattle off his obligatory postgame press interviews, shower, dress in some outlandish big-and-tall outfit that sometimes includes a cape, then provide six or seven or eight hundred words for the good readers of the largest local daily newspaper in New England.

No problem.

The 2019–20 Celtics media guide in the far-off future lists seven basic assistant coaches to help head coach Brad Stevens, then adds a player enhancement coach, a director of player development and personal growth, a coaching associate/director of player development, two strength coaches, assorted scouts, analysts, video coordinators, trainers, rehabilitation specialists, and a director of team nutrition and his assistant. Russell has no assistants. None. He does all these jobs himself, except the ones that have not been invented. Trainer Joe DeLauri wraps ankles and takes care of the travel arrangements. Russell pretty much takes care of everything else, including the center jump to start the game.

One more job?

The *Globe*?

No problem.

The bright young man has been involved in this Russell business since the start of the playoffs. He was thinking he had one assignment—write the greatest articles on the Celtics and basketball and, perhaps, life itself, better than any articles ever written about the Celtics and basketball and life itself, maybe win the first of many Pulitzer Prizes—and now he had two? Two assignments seemed like a lot.

"Make sure Russell remembers to call," sports editor Ernie Roberts said as the 1968–69 playoffs run began. "Remind him after every game."

"He can't remember on his own?" TBYM asked.

"Tell him. Tell him after every game. Make sure."

This second assignment was accompanied by a possible complication. Tell him? After every game? Telling him involved conversation, interaction. The bright young man's relationship with the most intriguing addition to the *Globe* lineup was best described as "distant."

An awkward salesman-client dance had existed in most transactions from the first meeting. The salesman was young, appropriately nervous, measured his words. He was convinced that he said the wrong thing as soon as every question or simple declarative sentence came out of his mouth. The Intriguing Addition to the *Globe* Lineup was in control. Older, famous, either busy or exhausted from his busyness, his moods would change from day to day, minute to minute. He could be charming, aloof, more aloof, really more aloof, contentious, silent. Pick one. Pick a variation. Pick a day. "Distant" would be the overriding word.

There were writers Russell liked, old-timers, familiar faces. He would respond especially well to the New York guys, the famous basketball bylines, laugh with them in that high-pitched cackle that was so different that the descriptions of it in stories seemed to be part of an ongoing theme contest. ("If thunder were played on an English horn instead of a kettle drum, you would have some idea of the pitch and tone of Russell's laughter" was one prime entrant.) The bright young man was not included in this inside writers group. His questions brought about no cackles. He understood. If this were the army, he was a five-foot-nine, redheaded private first class. Russell was a decorated six-foot-nine four-star general. A foot taller. A decade older. Certainly a decade smarter. A busy man.

Did Russell know the bright young man's name?

No. Probably not.

Did Russell care that he didn't know?

No. Definitely not.

Once or twice, maybe three times, the bright young PFC caught the busy, smarter, older, famous general alone in the locker room, time on his hands, and there was a solid conversation. A different question would draw a different response. Russell described moments in his youth, his thoughts about food or movies, his memories of games past against present competition. Fifteen minutes passed. Maybe more. The bright young man would leave in an enthusiastic cloud. Bill knows me at last. I know Bill. The next day, he would see Russell and say hello, and Russell would bluster past with no acknowledgment. Nothing had changed.

It was a bonus that no ghostwriter was involved in this new enterprise. Russell wanted his own words to be his own words. He would call a special number at the *Globe* sports department. An office boy, a "nighthawk," usually some work-study kid from Northeastern University's journalism school, would answer. The kid would click on a Dictaphone machine, a recording device. Russell would speak into the phone at his end, delivering his impressions of the game, which would be recorded at the *Globe* on a floppy blue plastic record.

The nighthawk then would transcribe the words, typing them on a piece of paper attached to two carbons. The paper and carbons would be handed to a copy editor, checked for spelling and grammar, then shipped through a pneumatic tube (whoosh) to a linotype operator who would cast the words in lead and begin the printing process that would finish with Russell's words whirring out in the 443,037 copies of the morning *Globe,* a million readers, 564,083 copies, a million and a half readers, if this happened to be the *Boston Sunday Globe.* The copies would be distributed from the top to bottom of New England, though not so much in the parts of Connecticut near the New York border.

The start of it all, though, would be the phone call. The bright young man had to nudge the famous athlete toward the nearest landline. (There were no cellphones, not even in the most extravagant public imaginations.) The rest would happen as planned.

Or not.

Russell was a complicated character. In this decade of racial upheaval, of marches and demonstrations, of assassinations and strife, he was basketball's foremost representative, the tall one, six feet nine-and-a-half inches. He wasn't a joiner, part of any organization, but still was front and center. He had been to Washington for the march in 1963, refused a seat on the stage and listened in the crowd to Reverend Martin Luther King's speech about having a dream. He had been to Mississippi two months before that to run an integrated basketball camp in the aftermath of Medgar Evers's murder. He had been in Cleveland in 1967 at the so-called summit of black athletes drawn together by football star Jimmy Brown to advise Muhammad Ali about his battle with the United States government and the draft board.

An overcoat of seriousness was an important part of his wardrobe. He was the socially activated modern African American athlete, able to respond to the big events of the time, but also bothered by the daily paper cuts of racism. He was smart enough to recognize slights, subtle as they sometimes might be, bold enough to talk about them. He didn't care who heard what he had to say.

His size made him recognizable at a first glance, but his disposition made him approachable only at a risk. His basic answer to strangers asking for autographs was "no." There was little time for chitchat and bullshit. His basic answer to most of the demands from his celebrity was "no."

"The first thing we (as Negroes in sport) have to get rid of is the idea that this is a popularity contest," he told writer Ed Linn in a 1964 article in the *Saturday Evening Post* titled "I Owe the Public Nothing" that shaped his public image. "I don't work for acceptance. It doesn't matter if the fans like me or not. To me or to them. If they like me and I put up a poor performance, I will still be booed. If they like me and I'm over the hill, they still will say 'Get that bum out of there.' They pay to see production, not personalities.

"What I'm resentful of, you know, is when they say you owe the public this and you owe the public that. You owe the public the same thing it owes you. Nothing! Since I owe them nothing, I'll pay them nothing. I'm not going to smile if I don't feel like smiling and bow my head modest. Because it's not my nature. I'd say I'm like most people in this type of life; I have an enlarged ego. I refuse to misrepresent myself. I refuse to smile and be nice to the kiddies. I don't think it is incumbent on me to set a good example to anybody's kids except my own."

His relationship with the city of Boston was not good. A grid work of neighborhoods determined by ethnicity and class and race put assorted chips on assorted shoulders. The black population, 9 percent in 1960, approaching 16 percent at the end of the decade, was not as large as it was in any number of large American cities. Boston was a tough place for African Americans, a definite minority, a tough place for anyone from the wrong neighborhood. All the words, all the slights, all the machinations, all the flat-out injustices of racism could be found here, especially if you were paying attention.

Russell always was paying attention.

"Boston itself was a flea market of racism," he would write in his 1979 memoir, *Second Wind,* long after he retired. "It had all varieties, old and new, and in their most virulent form. The city had corrupt, city-hall-crony racists, brick-throwing, send-em-back-to-Africa racists, and in the university areas phony radical-chic racists (long before they appeared in New York).

"I had no doubt about those people in Boston because I saw them every day. They constantly surprised me, since I'd thought of Boston as the city where Paul Revere rode for freedom. If Paul Revere rode today, it would be for racism. 'The niggers are coming! The niggers are coming!' he'd yell as he galloped through town to warn neighborhoods of busing and black homeowners. Most of the Irish Catholics in Boston were ready to pick your fillings out if you weren't the right religion or from the right clique, much less from the right race. . . . I had never been in a city more involved with finding new ways to dismiss, ignore or look down on other people. Other than that, I liked the city."

Red Auerbach would preach the philosophy of bad apples. If an incident happened to any of the black players, he would say that the individual who caused the incident was responsible. If a player couldn't buy a house, the problem was the individual who was selling the house. Everyone was not to blame. The individual was to blame.

Russell didn't buy it. He saw an orchard full of bad apples. An ugly incident, a robbery at his home in suburban Reading, helped form his opinion. The robbers wrecked the house, spray-painted "NIGGA" on the walls, smashed a bunch of his trophies, and finished the destruction by defecating in his bed. How do you explain that to your three small children? How do you explain it to yourself?

"The only time we were really scared was after my father wrote an article for The Saturday Evening Post [see above]," his daughter, Karen Russell, wrote years later in the *New York Times.* "He earned the nickname Felton X. We received threatening letters and my parents notified the Federal Bureau of Investigation. What I find most telling is that years later, after Congress had passed the Freedom of Information Act, my father requested his FBI file and found he was repeatedly referred to therein as 'an arrogant Negro who won't sign autographs for white children.'"

Russell decided, early in his career, that he played for the Celtics. He played for his teammates. He played for his coach. He did not play for the city of Boston. He did not play for the fans. He played for the Celtics. In another city—in New York, in Los Angeles, somewhere else—perhaps the situation would be different. The championships would have brought true adulation. He would have been a king.

Not all was bad in Boston. There were moments, tons of them, standing ovations, crowds that carried him off the court at the end, tugging on his shirt, but there were obvious limits to the love. Would there be limits in the other places? He never would know.

"It was Russell who made the Celtics winners in those early championships, but it was Bob Cousy who sold the tickets," Jeff Cohen, former twenty-five-year-old assistant general manager, says. "It was Cousy, Tom Heinsohn, the white guys who sold the tickets. And they didn't sell a lot of them. Six thousand was a good crowd."

That was the sad socioeconomic fact. There were limits to the love. Racial limits. The one time Russell got mad at Cohen was when Cousy retired. Cohen wrote an article at the start of the next season for the program that was titled "How Are the Celtics Going to Get Along without Cousy?" Russell read the article.

"How are the Celtics going to get along?" he said. "They're not going to know who the fuck he was." And Russell was right. He had a great season, won everything again.

Even his selection as coach was wrapped in whispers. Shouldn't the choice of the first black coach in the NBA, first head coach of any North American professional sport in over thirty years, be greeted with some kind of civic applause? Nothing. The stories were that Auerbach had tried Frank Ramsey, Cousy, and Tommy Heinsohn, all without success. Russell was the choice because, well, he could coach Russell.

The stories were half-right. Auerbach's major concern was that Russell would continue to play. Retirement had been mentioned in the past, the star player leaving in tandem with his coach. They could bring down the curtain at the same time. That was Russell's inclination. It was not Auerbach's inclination at all.

He said, look, let's each draw up a list of five names about who would be a good coach. Then we'll compare the names and talk it over. The two men drew up their lists and compared. Not one name was on both lists. This was a frustration to Auerbach.

"What about you?" he said. "Why don't you become the coach?"

Russell said he had thought about the idea. The challenge was intriguing. He accepted.

"Do you want an assistant?" Auerbach said. "You can have an assistant."

"You never had an assistant," Russell said.

"I always thought it would be just another guy I'd have to take care of."

"I think the same thing," Russell said.

Was he really the coach? (Yes.) Did he really do all those jobs? (Yes.) Did he get the credit he deserved? Only when it was wrung out of narrow minds.

"When I was appointed coach of the Boston Celtics the other players accepted me with no antagonism at all," he said in a *Sports Illustrated* article after the summit meeting for Ali. "They respected me as a player and my knowledge of the game and they played as hard for me as they used to play for Red Auerbach.

"For quite a while, though, some of the writers around the league seemed to doubt that I was really the coach. They would go to Red and ask him if there were any changes in the lineup or about the condition of a player on the team. I could not help believing that this was, in part, because I am a Negro. I think that now everyone knows that I'm the coach."

The *Globe* assignment to chronicle the playoffs was one of the few outside commercial opportunities that had arisen for Russell in Boston. He was the owner of Slade's, a restaurant/nightclub at 958 Tremont Street, the club purchased in 1964 with the aid of a $90,000 SBA loan. He had his own model of shoe, designed and built to his specifications by a small company in Rhode Island. ("TRI-ACTION outsole gives skidproof contact. Double shock absorbing sponge insole lessens foot fatigue. Padded tongue stays up and centered." Price: $7.95. Youth sizes available.) He didn't have much more. An investment in a rubber plantation in Liberia didn't count.

Advertisers always seemed to want him at a discount. The hell with that. Other people didn't want him at all. The hell with them.

"The Boston stations got indignant if players like myself refused to go to their station for free to promote their interview shows and newscasts, but I never could get any of them even to discuss the possibility of giving me my own show," he would say in *Second Wind*. "When a television station in Boston wanted to hire a professional player from one of the city's teams as a sportscaster . . . they didn't interview a single black and wound up hiring the placekicker from the Patriots. For these and other reasons, the Boston media seemed to me to represent the city fairly well."

The bright young man, strange enough, had a role to play in this bit of business with the *Globe*. He didn't know so much about the local situation. He wasn't from one of the neighborhoods, didn't know a lot about the boundaries and rules. He had the idea that Russell should write the column. He pushed the idea. OK, he put together the whole deal.

In the playoffs a year earlier, both the *Herald* and the *Record-American* featured As-Told-To columnists as part of their packages. The *Record* had Red Auerbach, friend of sports editor Sam Cohen, on the payroll. The *Herald* had John Havlicek. The stories weren't anything special, sort of a forerunner of the how-does-it-feel sideline interviews in the television future, but they were marketable as inside-knowledge reports. The *Globe* had no one. This did not mean the paper was averse to the idea. It had signed manager Dick Williams and captain Carl Yastrzemski to write as-told-to reports about the Red Sox from this year's spring training. The Celtics did not seem to have a proper candidate.

"We should have a guy there, too, an inside expert from the team," the bright young man suggested to Ernie Roberts as the '69 playoffs arrived.

"Sure, but who would we get?" the sports editor asked. "Everybody's taken. Auerbach and Havlicek probably will be back with the other papers."

(Pause.)

(Double pause.)

"What about Bill Russell?" the bright young man said.

The immediate reaction from Roberts was a quiet version of astonishment. Bill Russell? The thought didn't seem to register. Mr. I Owe the Public Nothing? The civic lightning rod? The ultimate dissatisfied black man? Didn't he hate the Boston press? Didn't he have a lot to do as coach and star player? Would he have any time? A litany of unspoken Bill Russell stereotypes filled the room.

"Do you think he would do it?" Roberts finally asked.

"I could ask him," the bright young man replied.

Negotiations were not long, or extensive. TBYM waited after practice for the one or two other writers and most of the players to leave the locker room at the Maurice J. Tobin Gym in Roxbury. He approached Russell in his usual awkward way. A fidget and a cleared throat were followed by the proposition. Russell heard, nodded, asked what the money might be. The bright young man rolled out a modest figure that had been shipped down from someone important in accounting. Russell nodded again and said he would do it. No hands were shaken. No agents or lawyers were involved. No papers were signed. Done.

(I think the price was $200 per column. Might have been less, maybe $180 per column. I checked with the *Globe*, but no records apparently exist. I do know that the bright young man was making $212 a week, $11,055 for all of 1969. I remember thinking that Russell was making almost as much for one story as I was making for a week's worth of stories. That would be $200. His salary for 1969, after winning those first ten championships, was $200,000. It was a different time.)

Ernie Roberts was pleased. This was a distinctive addition to the sports page. Management in the glass offices at the far end of the Morrissey Boulevard building was more than pleased. The *Globe* was known as the liberal paper in Boston, against the war in Vietnam and for the use of busing to alleviate the racial imbalance of the city's public schools. These were positions that eventually wound up with gunshots fired at the newsroom from the Southeast Expressway and with *Globe* delivery trucks stolen and driven into the Fort Point Channel. Russell fit the paper's image quite well. The people who hated Russell the most also hated the *Globe* the most.

His first journalistic effort came in the March 27, 1969, paper. The Celtics opened their playoff run with a 114–100 win over the Philadelphia 76ers at the Spectrum in Philadelphia. Under a headline that said, "Let's Concentrate on Friday," the player/coach said that he was pleased by the effort and the result, but warned about over-confidence. In a dash of color, he described how he liked to sleep as much as possible on the day of a game, simply to keep his mind under control. He said that outside of installing a plan of both attack and defense, he didn't like to think about what was going to take place that night. Thinking made him nervous. He famously had stomach disorders when he became too nervous. His big disappointment in this game, he said, was his foul shooting. (He was 0-for-6 from the free-throw line, scored only one basket from the floor, but played all forty-eight minutes, grabbed 15 rebounds, and blocked 12 shots.) He said he knew he would take at least a hundred foul shots in the next practice to try to straighten his stroke.

The bright young man, as requested, was part of the operation. Before he wrote his own story—"76ers Get a Look at Celtics' Hole Card—Defense"—he fidgeted, waited again for other writers to leave. Then he stepped up to his new teammate and said in a self-conscious mumble, "Bill, don't forget about the *Globe*." Bill nodded in return.

There were questions that hung around inside TBYM's head. Did Bill have the right number? How soon would he call? *Would* he call? There would be tension for the bright young man until his new team-mate's words were on that blue plastic record. Maybe the coach hadn't thought about the game during the long Philadelphia day, but the bright young man had thought about this postgame transaction for every minute.

The assignment, the experiment, whatever it was, worked pretty well for the surprising playoff run. Russell would write columns after ten of eleven games as the Celtics thumped the Sixers in five games (4-1) and the Knicks in six (4-2). The one game Russell didn't report on was the second against Philadelphia. Perhaps there was a blue-record problem. (That memory seems to beep softly through the cloud of time.) Perhaps the craziness of the game—Sam Jones ejected early for two technical fouls, Russell tied to the bench for sixteen of the last twenty-four minutes due to his own foul problems in a 134–103 Celtics win—was a factor. No matter. The column was scheduled for the Saturday morning paper, anyway, the least-read paper of the week. The rest of his offerings were perfect.

Russell proved to be a unique voice from the scene. (His sources were quite good.) After the third Philadelphia game, a 125–118 win at the Spectrum to put the Celts ahead, 3-0, in the series, he detailed an important moment when Siegfried and Havlicek told him to put Sam Jones back in the game. The Sixers had cut a Celtics lead down to a basket, and the two players thought Jones was needed in the lineup to hit a few jumpers. Russell agreed with the request. Jones immediately hit a jumper.

"The players know I have a lot going on in my mind and I appreciate the help," the player/coach said/wrote. "I've never tried to prove that I'm a big genius and I'll accept all the help I can get from the players. If something's not right, let me know."

A bad game against the Knicks made him confront and reject the possibility of criticizing individuals. ("I don't like to single out guys in public. I know all these guys and there's no point to that.") A Northeastern nighthawk, probably not on the Dean's List, misspelled the names of Don Chaney (Cheney), Cazzie Russell (Kazzie), and Mike Riordan (Reardon) after another game and, unedited, the words made the player/coach/writer look as if he didn't know how to spell. A reporter for the *Boston Record-American*, Pat Horne, upset with some nonanswers in the locker room after a Knicks game, complained that the coach "probably is saving his best material for his own column [in the *Globe*]."

These were the vagaries of the newspaper business. Welcome to the club. This was his column after the final win against the Knicks. . . .

BY BILL RUSSELL
Boston Celtics Coach
I gave the guys tomorrow off. We were going to have a meeting, but the earliest we can possibly play is next Wednesday.

O, yeah, there was a game last night and it was a very interesting little thing. I thought we were going to break it open because we went up 10 points and one time to 12, but New York wasn't going to let us run away. I think the Knicks played great.

For the first time in the series they got some real help from their bench. [Mike] Riordan played 16 minutes. They usually use him just for fouls, but he wound up getting 15 points, which hurt us badly since all of them were in the last quarter. He and [Bill] Bradley carried them in the last period.

But let's get to the winners.

Emmette Bryant was one of our key performers. This was probably one of his best games ever, especially under the conditions.

John [Havlicek] played his usual outstanding game. And, most important, Sam came back for us, which particularly pleases me. It was truly good to see him get a standing ovation because he has had a tough time the last couple of days.

Last night he went out and tore the place up.

I felt so sure he was going to have a pretty good game that we used different plays just so he would get the ball more. I went into the high pivot and tried to feed the guards coming off me.

The result was 13 big baskets from him. Plus he made the free throw that put the game out of reach.

As he was standing there at the free throw line after he missed the first one, he looked at me. I started to laugh but I thought I better not in this situation, even though he knew what I meant—I'm glad it's you and not me up there.

Another bright spot was Tom Sanders. He came in and made one of three clutch baskets with two guys all over him. [Dave] DeBusschere and Bradley were right on top of him and he still hit nothing but strings with his shot.

I'm so proud of this group. They really respond to any situation. For example, I took Sanders and Larry Siegfried out of the lineup. Larry came out because he got hurt.

But even though they're not starting, their attitude

has been fantastic. A coach couldn't ask for any more cooperation than I've been getting from these two guys.

I got great production out of my backcourt. And with John getting 28 I got good scoring punch out of my frontcourt.

I didn't score much last night, but there was a reason for it. Not that I'm a great offensive player, you understand. But when the ball was coming to me a lot I was eliminating the guards from the offense because they were giving the ball up and there wasn't much chance for them to get a shot.

So what I was trying to do was set picks and get motion and in that way I could go to the basket and the forwards could go to the basket. And that diversifies our offense.

[Willis] Reed had a really outstanding game for the Knicks, hitting 14 for 14, and you can't beat that.

Here's a guy who was really hurting. Yet he came out and gave his all. To me, that is the epitome of a professional. I put a premium on that word—professional. It means you go out there and give your best performance possible. Pain doesn't mean anything because to the professional, there's no excuse. You win or you lose. There's no valid reason for losing as far as the professional is concerned.

You do the very best you can and if you win—beautiful. If you lose—that's the way it goes. I think that Frazier showed last night that he completely fills that definition of professional.

The bright young man bumped along with the Celtics' unlikely play-off progression. There is no more enduring American sports story than the underdog coming off the canvas, shaking the cobwebs out of his scrambled head, pounding his gloves together to renew his focus, then doing the good things he wasn't supposed to be able to do in the first place. That is the plot of every sports movie ever made. That was the plot here, different because the underdog was a defending champion, historically the greatest team in the history of the game. The bright young man might have missed the glory years of the early and mid-sixties, but he was here in 1969 to watch them dusted off.

"It's bad, overall, for the fourth-place team in a six-team division to make the playoffs," said Sam Jones, perennial All-Star guard and perennial champion. He was talking about his personal Celtics embarrassment before the run started. "But the league needs the money and here we are. We are going to do the best we can. The thing for us to do now is try to win one game down here and then the advantage has shifted to our favor."

Everything went from there. Win one game. Another. Another. Just like that. The Sixers won a game in Boston, but the Celtics won the closeout at the Spectrum, easy, 93–90. Everything was a hoot.

"There's this big fat guy who sits by the side of the court," John Havlicek told the bright young man at the end, delivering a New Journalism scoop. "The guy always has a big shopping bag with him and I've always wondered what was in it.

"During the last game the ball rolled near him out of bounds. He told everyone not to touch it, to let the referee work. I decided to get the ball for the ref and also to get a peek into that shopping bag. You know what was in it? Peanuts. More peanuts than you can imagine. That guy must have his whole season's peanut supply in that one shopping bag."

Now it had to be next season's supply. The Sixers were headed to an extended vacation and the Celtics were headed to New York, where they would be underdogs again when they faced the Knicks. The New Yorkers had throttled the first-place Baltimore Bullets in four straight games with an average winning margin of 9.5 points. The Bullets were hampered by the loss of All-Star forward Gus Johnson with a knee injury, out for the season, but the Knicks were a team clearly on the rise.

This was the lineup—Reed, Bradley, DeBusschere, Frazier, and Barnett—that would be captured by Knicks fans in future years in word, song, and wistful remembrances by filmmaker Spike Lee. After a 5-11 start, management had shipped center Nate Bowman and guard Howard Komives to the Detroit Pistons for DeBusschere, the complementary piece they needed. Reed could move to center, his natural position. DeBusschere, at forward, was a steady, experienced hand.

The change was almost immediate. The team won seventeen of nineteen at one stretch and started to fill the splashy, futuristic version of Madison Square Garden, opened only a year earlier on Thirty-Third Street. A franchise that had totaled only six regular-season sellouts in its previous twenty-two-year history had fourteen during this season.

The Celtics, businesslike, professional, experienced, put a damper on the developing New York fun. They executed the Sam Jones win-early strategy, taking the first two games and the home-court advantage and went from there. In the fourth game, Havlicek stared down Frazier at the end, forced him to pass the ball to Reed, who missed a shot and the Celtics won, 97–96, to take a 3-1 lead at Boston Garden. In the fifth game at Madison Square Garden (sold-out Madison Square Garden), Frazier was the hero with 23 points in a 112–104 win that cut the lead to 3-2. He also pulled a groin muscle in the last moments of the game and despite a three-day break was slowed in Game Six, which the Celtics won, 106–105, to take the series.

The bright young man's best memory—New York on an expense account, terrific basketball—was a visit to Toots Shor's restaurant on Fifty-Second Street. He was accompanied by fifty-nine-year-old Jack Barry, a sweet man, another straight-from-high-school sportswriter at the *Globe* who had grown up with Congressman Tip O'Neill in Cambridge. An old-school writer, Barry now was being moved to the side from the morning basketball beat he had occupied since the Celtics began operation. The New York trip was the last trip he would take for the paper.

It was an awkward situation. The change, the demotion, had to bother him, but he never said anything about it. He was such a gentleman that in his early years at the *Globe,* when an important editor also was named Jack Barry, the younger Barry agreed to be called by his middle name, "Fred," to end all confusion. When the other Jack Barry left the paper to become a banker, Fred became Jack again. TBYM would drive him home sometimes to Cambridge, where Barry would ask to be left at the gate to Mount Auburn Cemetery so he could follow a shortcut home and "take two tablets before I go to bed."

At Toots Shor's, TBYM explained to the fifty-nine-year-old geezer that the restaurant was famous, a New York home to many celebrities, ranging from Jackie Gleason to Joe DiMaggio to Mickey Mantle. This was an attraction that had to be seen. Frank Sinatra came here. The Rat Pack. Joe Namath. Everybody.

The time was three in the afternoon, not many people in the place, but TBYM said that undoubtedly some celebrity would be in attendance. Sure enough. From a seat at the table, he spotted Jimmy Breslin at the bar. Did poor sweet Jack even know who Jimmy Breslin was? Forty years old, top of his newspaper game, Breslin was the columnist's columnist, a New Journalism saint, turning out assorted fact-stuffed tales for the *Herald Tribune* and now for the *New York Post*. He had a novel coming out, *The Gang That Couldn't Shoot Straight,* and was going to announce any day that he would run for city council president on an Independent ticket with novelist Norman Mailer, who would run for mayor. The bright young man was just about to detail all this information when Breslin ·looked up, looked straight at the table, smiled, and started coming across the room.

"Jack," he said in a loud voice.

Jack?

Breslin came close. Jack stood up. They not only shook hands, they embraced. Breslin, it turned out, had worked for a period at the *Globe* on the sports desk. The New York papers had gone on a 114-day strike in early 1963 and Breslin, with a young family, needed a job. He came to Boston and the *Globe* to edit copy and write headlines.

"It's great to see you, Jack," he said as he left the table after a five-minute conversation. "Be well."

"G-great to see you," said Jack, who stuttered a small bit.

That was the best scene of the New York series. TBYM was leveled. If Jack used the right language, which he didn't, he easily could have told his young associate to calm down, grow up, could have delivered a perfect comeback, a deserved slap on an inflated wrist, but he was so nice he never would. Beautiful. Hilarious.

There also was a worst scene of the New York series. The worst scene was much worse than the best was best.

The third game was on April 10, 1969, a night game at Madison Square Garden. The trip to New York involved flights on the Eastern Shuttle sandwiched around the game and a stay at the Paramount

Hotel, a shopworn establishment in Times Square that had earned Red Auerbach's loyalty during hard financial times. ("Wear your pointy-toed shoes when you stay at the Paramount," New York sportswriter Harold Rosenthal advised. "You can kill the cockroaches in the corners of your room.")

Not counting Bill Russell, the *Globe* had a three-man team for the game. The bright young man would handle the afternoon paper's coverage, Bob Sales would handle the morning. Clif Keane, primarily a baseball writer, but also with a history of covering the Celtics, was added to write a morning sidebar since the game would start late and deadlines would be tight. Trouble was built into this lineup. Sales and Keane hated each other. That was a well-known newsroom fact.

Sales was Jewish, younger, came from New York, where he had worked with Breslin for the now-departed *Herald Tribune,* a paper famous for the quality of its writing. He was a full participant in the turbulent social times, a civil rights activist, a voice for change, both in his life and in the stories he wrote. He had a beard and was one of the few white men at the *Globe* who often wore a dashiki to work. Keane was Irish, fifty-six, born and raised in Dorchester, the neighborhood where the *Globe* was located. He was a dull writer, but a noisy and somewhat dominating presence wherever he went. He had a sense of humor, made people laugh with zingers, comments that walked the same line of racial and ethnic stereotypes that comedian Don Rickles had used on a 1968 record album called *Hello Dummy!,* which reached number 54 on the Billboard 200 chart. The difference was that Keane's comments, especially on race, often missed the line. He did not wear a dashiki to work.

Sales had arrived in Boston three years earlier, thinking that he would be a columnist, a New Journalism wonder in a backward newspaper town. Things didn't happen the way he wanted. The institutional hierarchy was tough to change. He wound up on the Celtics beat, not a columnist, which was a disappointment. The warps of social change seemed to be woven without him. He sometimes would read a book during the middle of games instead of taking notes. He was covering basketball while the world was changing in a hurry. He was pissed.

Keane had joined the newspaper in 1929 as an office boy straight from the Dorchester High School for Boys. Never went to college, same as Herb Ralby, Jack Barry, not unusual for a newspaper job at the time. He eventually worked in the advertising department until World War II opened some spots in the sports department. Rejected for military service, he was available to become a sportswriter. He covered the Red Sox, sometimes the Celtics, a range of subjects, always with a mock cynicism in person, but not in print. He would loudly ask a visiting manager or coach, "What kind of garbage are you bringing in here this time?" as players who didn't know him would stare at this short, antic character who had invaded their territory. He called everyone "bush," as in "bush-league." *Sports Illustrated* did a humorous story on him.

The racism that sometimes flowed in his conversation was not reported in the *SI* story. He often referred to black players as "stove lids" or "shines" or would say a certain team "has a lot of coal on that roster." There were a bunch of words he used but never said to the black faces he might encounter. The bright young man once remarked to him that Chicago seemed like a great city. Keane said he would agree, "if they painted half the people white." He often referred to basketball, the sport, as "African handball." It was a term many of the older writers used.

Sales, of course, could not abide any piece of this conversation. He had a low voice, a Kris Kristofferson gargle with a New York accent, and he was not shy about talking about Keane. Keane, of course, could not stand Sales's activism, the idea of change, and made fun of that. I don't know if there had been any confrontations between the two men. I suspect there must have been. I only know what happened on April 10, 1969.

The bright young man sat between his two coworkers at courtside. Terrific seats. The game was no farther than the other side of a folding table, three feet from the out-of-bounds line, the players almost close enough to touch. TBYM knew about the friction, knew the two men did not talk to each other. It was an uncomfortable situation. He wanted to be friendly to both of them, a good *Globe* teammate or whatever he was supposed to be, but how did he do that? He wound up turning sometimes to his right to make a comment to Sales. Then he would repeat the comment to his left to Keane. Right, left, right, left. The night promised to be a string of repeated thoughts.

Then Keane started to yell.

"Look at those ******s sweat!" he boomed from our side of the folding table as players came back and forth on the other side, the game in progress.

What?

He said the word, the bad word, the worst, most racially divisive word in the English language. He not only said it, he said it loud. Very loud.

There was background noise from the sellout crowd, which meant this was not a quiet setting, but his voice was on the level of "Hey, get your peanuts." If someone was within close enough proximity, this was easy to hear.

"Look at those ******s sweat," Keane repeated.

The bad word. The bad word again. The bright young man could hear. Sales could hear. The players could surely hear if they weren't so busy.

What was Keane doing?

"Look at those ******s sweat," he said yet again.

Maybe he said the bad word those three times. Maybe he said it twice as many times. Maybe he said it more than that. Time froze in embarrassment and the bright young man froze with it. He didn't know what to do. The word clearly was used to infuriate Sales. Could the fans in back hear? The ushers? Other sportswriters? The bright young man wanted to sink out of sight, not be where he was. Jesus Christ. This was awful.

Sales finally stood up. Took his notebook and belongings and walked away. No words were exchanged. Nothing. He somehow found a seat at the far end of the floor. Keane stopped shouting.

There will be times in this book when the bright young man will make mistakes, will say or do things that can be written off to youth, inexperience, or stupidity, but this was a different level of failure. He froze and never unfroze. He sat at his seat and did nothing. He didn't get up and follow Sales. He didn't say anything to Keane. He didn't say anything to anyone. He sat in his seat and wrote down in his little notes "basket by Havlicek" or "foul by Bradley," and wished the other stuff would go away.

The sad outcome was that it did. The Knicks won the game, 101–91, to close the series to a 2-1 Celtics lead. Sales wrote a game story. Keane wrote a story about how Bill Bradley's aggressive defense held

Havlicek to 8 points on 3-for-13 shooting. The bright young man
also wrote about Bradley and Havlicek. It was the story of the game.
Everyone went back to a hotel room. Everyone flew back to Boston
the next day.

Life continued.

I have thought for all these years of the things I should have done.
I should have told Keane to shut up. Right away, I should have done
that. If he didn't shut up, I should have grabbed him, done something.
I at least should have left with Sales, found another seat, left Keane
alone and isolated. I should have reported all this to someone at the
Globe on our return. I should have decided never to talk to Keane
again. I should have done any of this stuff.

I did nothing.

I stayed friendly with Sales. When my son was born a couple of
years later, Bob and his wife, Naomi, gave me their old baby car-
riage. I stayed friendly enough with Keane. I laughed at a bunch of
his jokes. He left the *Globe* in 1975 but became a presence on local
sports talk radio. He had his own show. I was friendly enough with
him. I went to his wake in 2003 when he died at the age of ninety.

Sales went ahead to a diversified newspaper career. He covered
some more sports, covered some politics, wound up as the editor of
the *Boston Phoenix,* the local alternative weekly, and as the sports editor and then the managing editor of the *Boston Herald* before working
in the MIT public information department. He was eighty-six years
old when I had lunch with him not so long ago, still had the beard and
that low-register Kristofferson voice.

I never had talked to him about that night at Madison Square Garden. I talked now. He remembered the events as well as I did, Keane
shouting, the word that just hung out there as the players went down
the court. I told him I wanted to apologize, that I should have said
something, done something, but didn't and I was sorry. Sales said I
did fine.

"Keane wasn't looking for a reaction from you," he said. "That was
all for me. I was the one he wanted to react."

No good. I still am embarrassed. I am embarrassed typing these
words right now. The truth was Russell had reason to be bothered
about race in Boston.

Chapter 4

WILT

By Mal Florence
Los Angeles Times Staff Writer

Wilt Chamberlain is acknowledged as one of the greatest basketball players who ever lived. He commands a higher salary ($225,000) than any other member of his profession. He is the NBA's all-time leading scorer and possesses practically every significant record in the game.

No one will dispute his individual prowess. He stands, literally and figuratively, above the crowd.

Yet, he has had to endure a whispering campaign that charges he is not a winner.

This is brought into focus whenever Chamberlain is confronted by Bill Russell and the Boston Celtics.

The record book is a cold, dispassionate thing. It states clearly that the Celtics, under Russell, have won 10 NBA championships in the past 12 years. Chamberlain, now playing with his fourth franchise, has been a member of only one championship in his 10-year career.

Boston will be seeking an unprecedented 11th title against the Lakers (11-5 series favorites) tonight at the Forum in the opening game of the best-of-7 tournament.

Chamberlain is philosophical and knowledgeable about

this winning and losing business. He reasons that the thin line that separates genius from insanity often applies to victory and defeat.

"I don't feel any different about this series than any other one," said Chamberlain Tuesday. "When you get into the playoffs, any team is capable of beating another team. We could just as easily lost our first two games to Atlanta instead of winning them.

"The Celtics have won many, many, many games but they have usually had home court advantage up until now.

"They are a very, very talented team and a very, very lucky team. Remember, luck plays an important part in these games."

Luck, by Wilt's definition, means injuries, the imponderable bounce of the ball and, at times, a home court edge.

"Boston doesn't sweep all these playoff games it is in," continued Chamberlain. "A lot of things go right down to the final moments of the seventh game. I know because I've played in these games and they could have been turned around just as easily. When you lose or win by one or two points, there is a certain amount of luck involved."

The record supports the Lakers' center.

Chamberlain, as a member of the Philadelphia and San Francisco Warriors and 76ers, has confronted the Celtics in seven playoff series and has been on the losing side on six occasions.

But, in four series the outcome was not decided until the waning minutes or seconds of the seventh game. Boston prevailed in each instance, winning by one point, twice by two points and once by four points.

"Some of those games were unbelievable," recalled Wilt. "Take the series in 1960. [Bill] Sharman drove on me and I blocked his shot almost to midcourt. So what happens? Tommy Heinsohn just slaps at the ball and it goes in.

"Or, take last year's series [the Eastern finals]. Billy Cunningham was hurt against New York and we never got a full game out of him. Then, Luke Jackson pulled a muscle. There were a whole conglomeration of injuries, but we still managed to get a 3-1 lead before losing. It's very important to be healthy.

"If [Walt] Frazier doesn't get hurt in Boston's series with New York last week it might have come up the other way."

Chamberlain contends that he is not "bugged" by the fact that fate has decreed him a loser in most of his dealings with the Celtics.

"The intelligent fan knows how close the difference was," he said. "Except for this break or that, I would be a member of six or seven world championship teams."

Then Wilt paused and chose his words carefully:

"I may be selfish or prejudiced, but I have a great deal more respect for someone who keeps coming back after losing heartbreaker after heartbreaker than I do for the winner who has everything going for him. Basketball, as you know, is the game of variables."

As for the task at hand, Chamberlain indicated that his personal duel with Russell is not as complicated as the overall team problem posed by the Celtics.

"If you check," said Wilt, "you won't find Russell in double figures very much against me, I love to see him with the ball."

In regard to the defensive aspect, Wilt added:

"Russell will out-rebound me for a game, but not for a series."

Chamberlain has a career playoff average of 29.3 points and 26.6 rebounds. Russell is 16.9 and 15.2, respectively.

April 23, 1969

An interview nine years earlier took place at the front door of his mother's house in Northwest Philadelphia. This was the morning of March 25, 1960, after the final loss of his first playoff series against the Celtics and Bill Russell. As his mother and two of his sisters watched, Wilt Chamberlain confirmed his retirement from the

National Basketball Association. He had told *New York Post* sports editor Ike Gellis about his decision in the gloom of the Philadelphia Warriors locker room at night, and now he repeated it in the sunshine to a small knot of assembled sportswriters.

Twenty-three years old. He was done.

"If I continue [to play], it might be bad for me and my race," he said. "If I come back and score less than I did last year, I might have to punch eight or nine guys in the face. I might lose my poise and I don't want that. I want to keep my equilibrium. I have achieved everything a man can achieve in pro basketball."

His youth and his great ability made this a major story. Retire? He was the rookie of the year and the most valuable player, first time that ever happened. He had set eight NBA records, including scoring (37.6 points per game) and rebounds (27). There never had been anyone like him in the abbreviated history of the league. At seven feet one, 240 well-distributed pounds, with the coordination of someone a foot shorter, he broke through invisible barriers of height and space, defied the physics of the game. His reach extended to nine feet, six inches, most of the way to the ten-foot-tall basket. With a modest jump he added three feet to that. He seemed like some laboratory creation, the perfect offensive player, the most intimidating defender ever seen, perfect, perfect, perfect.

Except he wasn't perfect.

He was another human being.

"Is your decision irrevocable?" a reporter asked.

"I don't know what that word means," Wilt replied, "but I ain't going back."

He said he had thought about retirement during the middle of the season, but the playoffs had confirmed the idea. He had been attacked every night, treated differently by players and officials and fans. The punching and the shoving were too much. The referees called only a small portion of the fouls that were perpetrated on his long and substantial body. He didn't need the aggravation.

"It's all over," he repeated. "I didn't make this decision to change it. There's not enough money to get me back to play in the NBA."

He didn't seem to know—or didn't care—that his decision was public-relations suicide. In the casting call for professional sports, the assignment of roles for a lifetime, right or wrong, good or bad, he couldn't have made a worse choice without a gun, duct tape, and a ransom note. A seven-foot-one man was complaining about being pushed around? What about the rest of us, smaller, normal-sized nobodies, pushed around every day? Where was the stiff upper lip? He wasn't just a whiner. He was a giant whiner.

"Wilt has never grown up," an unnamed "close friend" declared. "For as long as he can remember, he's been 'Wilt the Stilt' and 'The Big Dipper' and everything's come pretty easy for him. It's hard to grow up when things are that easy. He sulks when things go wrong and he says things he doesn't really mean. Then he gets stubborn and sticks by them. He may have trouble getting out of this jam, but I bet he changes his mind and plays for Philadelphia next year. His pride will bring him back—that, and all that money."

He had shown tendencies to look for excuses when he left Kansas University a year early in 1958, selling his good-bye story to *Look* magazine for $10,000. He said the college game was not for him. Teams triple-teamed him. Teams held the ball to shorten the game, to keep him from dominating. The environments on the road were hostile. He didn't need this stuff. He was signing a $50,000 contract to play with the Harlem Globetrotters, those barnstorming comic ambassadors of basketball, before possibly going to the NBA. Good-bye, college. Good-bye, Kansas.

When he had signed with the school after a recruitment process that featured offers from over two hundred of the nation's leading educational institutions, official and unofficial representatives from all of them arriving with gifts and promises, salesman pyrotechnics unleashed in his family's living room, the idea was that he would play one year of freshman competition, then lead the Jayhawks to three straight national championships. He left with none. Only played in one final, the famous 54–53 loss in overtime to North Carolina, when he was triple-teamed and his teammates were distracted and the game was reduced to slow motion. Had to be talked out of quitting after that game.

"Chamberlain says he's being pushed around more than anyone else in the league," Celtics point guard Bob Cousy told Tom Carey of the *Worcester Gazette* when the latest retirement story landed. "The guy has averaged more than 36 points per game, broken the rebound record and had more foul shots than anyone else. How easy does he want it?

"He said he's accomplished everything in the first year. As an individual, that's true. He had a fantastic season. Wilt is between five and fifteen inches taller than the rest of us. He is adept at putting the ball in the basket directly above the rim. As a team man, Chamberlain has proved again that he never has played on a club which has won a title. Wilt is the biggest complainer ever to hit the NBA. Standing 6 feet one inch, it is difficult for me to feel sorry for a man seven feet tall."

The next step was the predicted one. Wilt came back for the next season. Of course he did. There was a little something extra in his paycheck—OK, a lot of something extra—and that was that. Or was it? The role he had chosen for himself stuck. He was the complainer, the sore loser, a Brobdingnagian character in a Lilliputian world, beset by mortals who could not understand the indignities faced by a tall man in his daily existence. Poor Wilt. Poor, poor Wilt.

Nine years later, the same things are being said about him. Poor Wilt. The giant still has to prove himself.

He is a Nixon man. Maybe that says more about him in his battles with Bill Russell than any other fact. If Russell is seen as the civil rights warrior, front and center in the march toward equality, Chamberlain is the odd, tall black man in a three-piece suit standing with the corporate Republican cats on the cover of *Esquire* magazine. He is on the Nixon celebrity list with Art Linkletter, Dr. Billy Graham, Lawrence Welk, Rudy Vallee, John Wayne, Hugh O'Brien, and Shirley Temple Black. He is one of them, a rich Republican from the Hollywood Hills, a business mover, a business shaker.

When Martin Luther King was murdered and his funeral was held in Atlanta, Russell was there, somewhere in the background. Chamberlain was also there, head stuck out of the crowd in pictures with Nixon, yes, that's Nixon, standing close. When the Republican convention came around in August in Miami, featuring none of that chaos the Democrats had in Chicago, he was there to shake delegates' hands. Two weeks later he was with Nixon at a conference of black capitalist leaders at a hotel in Mission Bay, California, posed next to a sign that promised "Bridges to Human Dignity."

The role was perfect. Black capitalist.

"I've never gotten involved in politics before," he said after Nixon won in November. "But you have to get off the fence and declare yourself sometime and this is the time for me. I've known Nixon and been impressed by him for ten years, and I decided to join him. It's intriguing to know that I might have some hand in shaping the future of this country."

Life is lived as a boast for Chamberlain. He is quick to talk about the apartment houses he owns, the women he has met, the seven-feet-square bed that he will have in his home in the clouds that is being built in the Bel Air hills, the lavender $22,500 Bentley he drives, the clothes he has designed and wears on his back, the president he helped install in the White House. He is an epicurean. He is "tied up" in six corporations. He owns racehorses. His conversation is punctuated by words he finds in a thesaurus then takes out for a walk with strangers. He is a proud bachelor, a confirmed hedonist, late to bed, late to rise.

Is there nothing he can't do? He is great in track and field. He is great in volleyball. He says he might decide to fight for the heavyweight title someday. Maybe tomorrow. Maybe next week. He could be a movie star. Then there's politics. What'd he say? He might have "some hand" in shaping the country?

When he left Philadelphia to come to Los Angeles, he said one of the factors was that he had been promised a piece of 76ers ownership, but that never had developed. (He could own a team!) He also said he had talked to Sixers owner Irv Kosloff about being the coach of the team, player/coach, same as Russell. (He could be the coach!)

"I wasn't demanding it," he said. "I think I'd make a good coach, but I wasn't dying for the job. All I said was that I would do it if they couldn't find the right man to handle the club's special problems."

"Are you one of the special problems?" he was asked.

"Of course. A superstar is always a special problem. A coach has to know how to use him to his advantage."

The contrasts with Russell—the personalities, the histories, the approaches to the game—are striking. The two men are friendly, maybe even friends, linked into a small, but tall fraternity. Neither can travel in public in anonymity, perpetually surrounded by gawks, stalks, questions about how the weather is up there. They have shared Thanksgiving dinner together, played cards, talked into the night. (Russell took out a Massachusetts gun permit from his wallet at the start of a gin rummy game. Said there could be repercussions if he lost.) They are still very different.

Russell was the sixteenth player on the junior varsity in his sophomore year at McClymonds High School in Oakland, forced to share the last available game jersey and alternate games with the fifteenth player. He was six feet five when he graduated, a starter only as a senior, offered a late, final scholarship to USF, the local school, after he played well in an all-star tournament. He grew five inches in college to become what he became, the thought that he still had things to prove running through his head during all of those fifty-five wins and those two NCAA championships.

Chamberlain, again, was touched by magic from the start. The son of a five-foot-eight handyman, one of nine kids in the family, he was six feet tall by the time he was ten years old. He was six feet eleven when he was a freshman at Overbrook High, already famous in the sport, a basketball commodity. Red Auerbach, who didn't see Russell play in person until after he had drafted him, a West Coast mystery, saw Chamberlain in that freshman year of high school. Coached him at Kutsher's Country Club and Resort in the Catskills Mountains. Tried to convince him to go to Harvard so he would be property of the Celtics under the territorial draft rule of the time.

Famous? He made so many trips to visit different colleges that one referee claimed he had worked four straight games where Chamberlain was in the crowd being wined, dined, and entertained. The FBI began investigating him in high school for illegal payoffs when he signed with Kansas. (He denied all, but would admit years later that there were some small amounts of money handed to him by boosters.) Famous? The Globetrotters wound up paying him an alleged $65,000 for his one season, including bonuses for increased attendance. This was much more than anyone who ever had played in the NBA had been paid. (Bob Cousy, the highest-paid player, made $25,000. Eddie Gottlieb, owner of the Philadelphia Warriors, who drafted Wilt, had paid $25,000 for the franchise seven years earlier.)

Russell had done a quick negotiating dance with the Globetrotters when he left USF, two years before Wilt left Kansas. The public-relations offer was $50,000. The actual offer was $17,500. Russell signed with the Celtics.

On the court, the differences were obvious from the beginning. Chamberlain was a basketball force of nature, a force of basketball nature, whatever you wanted to call it. He was overwhelming. The only way to stop him seemed to be to put sandbags at the front door, plywood on the windows, and say the prayers of your family's faith. He was a blot on the weather map, ready to do any damn thing he wanted to do. Russell was the earnest defender of the city, trying to keep the menace at bay. Sweat dripping from his goatee, he hurried to the spots where the most trouble could occur. He might be overwhelmed on occasion after occasion, but he kept at the task. He bumped, pushed, blocked shots when he could, accepted help from all quarters, persevered.

If Russell's team won, it was a triumph of the spirit, a mixture of cunning, planning, and hard work. If Chamberlain's team won, it was a show of force, talent, brute power. The theatrics, either way, were wonderful.

"The game was played at an exciting tempo, but was extremely ragged at times," an unnamed correspondent reported from the Garden for the *Philadelphia Inquirer* after the first meeting, a 115–106 Celtics victory before 13,909 fans at the Garden on November 7, 1960. "This was due in large degree to the presence of Chamberlain and Russell, who were disrupting the offensive patterns at both ends.

"Time after time, one team, then the other, was surrendering the ball without a serious challenge from the opposition. It was almost like the athletes were paying too much attention to either Chamberlain or Russell."

Both men played all forty-eight minutes. Wilt had 30 points, the lowest output in his four-game career. Russell had 22 points, but won the rebound battle, 35–28. Wilt, it was mentioned, missed six of his twelve free throws. Russell was 8-for-8.

Russell detailed his early thoughts on Chamberlain in *Go Up For Glory*, the book he wrote in 1965 with the help of Boston sportswriter Bill McSweeny. The introspective big man promised the pages were full of his real thoughts because "you paid good money for this book. Ergo, you should get the truth. . . ."

"Chamberlain came into the league in 1959–60 and from that moment Russell had a big challenge on his hands," he wrote. "The theory was that Chamberlain was going to ruin my style of defense. Few realize that we play an entirely different kind of game. Chamberlain's concept of the game is basically offensive—the style, that is. . . . [He] was supposed to put me into total eclipse. I think he has had the opposite effect. In a sense, I think he has magnified my importance to the team.

"It may be the so-called 'man-to-man clash' that the sportswriters like to refer to, but actually, when I play Chamberlain, I play a team," Russell added. "Wilt, conversely, plays his game and the others fall in his wake and are swept along. The theory of playing against Chamberlain is to keep the ball from him as much as possible.

"His physical power is awesome. Most certainly he can jump higher from a crouch than any man in the league. He is a fine shooter as well and shoots as finely as any pivotman in professional basketball, using that fallaway jumper. . . ."

By the time the 1969 championship series started, the two men had played ninety-four regular-season games against each other. Russell had won fifty-seven of them, Chamberlain thirty-seven. They had played forty-two playoff games against each other. Russell had won twenty-five of them, Chamberlain seventeen. They had played seven playoff series against each other, including the past five years in a row. Russell had won six of those seven series. Chamberlain had won one. Russell had won eight NBA titles in the nine previous years Chamberlain had been in the league. Chamberlain had won one.

In personal statistics, the results were lopsided in the other direction. Wilt was on top in virtually every category. He scored 100 points in that famous game against the Knicks in Hershey, Pennsylvania, on March 2, 1962. (Russell's high game was 37.) He had 55 rebounds in a game. He had an alleged quintuple double—53 points, 32 rebounds, 24 blocks, 14 assists, 11 steals versus the Lakers on March 18, 1968. He averaged 50.4 points in the 1962 season. He had more than 4,000 points in a season, more than 2,000 rebounds in the same season. He averaged 48.5 minutes per game—which is higher than a regulation forty-eight-minute game because he played in overtimes. He led the league with 8.6 assists per game in 1968, the only center to ever do that, did it just to do it, to go against the narrative that he was a selfish player.

The numbers were staggering. No one ever had done what he had done. (In 2020, he still held seventy-two NBA records. He scored 65 or more points fifteen times. Fifty or more points 118 times. He still was the career rebounding leader.) He dominated a small league filled with big talent. His talent was so overpowering that he seemingly had been able to do whatever he wanted. A cartoon lightbulb indicating a new thought seemed to ignite above his head and one night he would say, "I want to score" and he would pound the basket with dunks and his self-invented finger rolls. Or he would say, "I want to score from the outside" and he would hit a succession of fade-away jumpers. Or "I want to rebound." Or "I want to play shutdown defense."

The only thing he hadn't been able to say and complete is "I want to win a championship." He did it once, in 1967 with the 76ers, but every other time he had wound up in defeat.

"When I was a little boy I used to think of myself climbing a high wall," he says. "Some people were helping me up, but a lot of people were holding me down. Sometimes I wondered if I'd make it all the way. In 1967, I guess I did."

Could he do it again?

The best chance for another title was a major reason why he had talked his way out of Philadelphia. That was why he had landed in L.A. At least that was what he said.

"I've done as well as anyone ever did financially in sports," he says. "My parents live in a fine apartment building that I own and I've got everything I could want. I approached all my negotiations and major decisions like a poker game with high stakes. The stakes were my future and big money—and I won. I made a lot of big decisions and I was criticized for many of them. I chose Kansas. I chose to leave Kansas. I picked to go to the Globies and then the NBA. Now I've decided to come to Los Angeles. Considering all those decisions now, I think they were the right ones."

The drama continues.

—

The first time the bright young man saw the epic confrontation—Russell against Wilt—in person, he was sixteen years old. The date was March 19, 1960. The place was the Boston Garden. This was the playoff series that sent Wilt into that early retirement. He was the twenty-three-year-old rookie wonder for the Warriors, already named the MVP for setting the scoring and rebounding records. Russell, twenty-six, was trying to win his third NBA championship in four years. This was Game Three of the Eastern Division semifinals, the series tied at a game apiece.

The bright young man's $2.25 reserved seat was in the top rows of the third deck, a far-away, reduced-price section high above the action. Wilt was maybe an inch tall on the miniature version of the parquet floor seen from this view. Russell was a little less than an inch and everyone else was smaller than that. A cloud of cigar and cigarette smoke hung close to the rafters and made the 2 p.m. game seem as if it were being played in a black-and-white spy movie that started with the J. Arthur Rank gong. The predominant smell—mixed with the predominant sounds of horns and huzzahs and announcements and organ music—was beer. The smell of beer was everywhere. Fresh beer. Spilled beer. Beer stains from a previous decade or two. Beer. Beer. Beer. Everywhere.

This atmosphere, combined with a maximum-impact headache that could have been recorded on seismographs at the Massachusetts Institute of Technology, created a less than enjoyable experience for the bright young man. He had an unremitting urge to become sick at his seat, wipe his face, apologize to the people in his section, go home, and lie down. He was in the second day of his first alcoholic hangover.

Sixteen years old.

This was his first road trip.

There was a story.

In a string of upsets a week or so earlier, Notre Dame High School from West Haven, Connecticut, had qualified for the New England High School Basketball Championships, a three-day annual event held in Boston in March at the Garden. Two teams from Connecticut, two more from Massachusetts, and one each from the other four

New England states were involved. Teams from New Haven had done well in the tournament throughout the years, but this was the first (and ultimately only) appearance by Notre Dame of West Haven.

In the biggest upset of all, the bright young man, a junior at this institution of Catholic adolescent learning, had convinced his parents that he should be allowed to go to Boston with his friends for three unchaperoned days (and two nights). He used the "everyone else is going" card, paired it with the "this is history" card, and pulled out the "I have my own money" card for the victory.

His youthful group traveled to Boston on the New York, New Haven, and Hartford train on Thursday morning. Hijinks were mixed with grand anticipation. (Never had been on a train without parents. Not once.) Everybody sort of checked into the Statler-Hilton Hotel at noon. (One kid registered. Six others sneaked into the room and left their bags.) Everybody then departed for the matinee at the Casino, the last surviving burlesque house in the city.

The headliner was Miss Tempest Storm, who was dressed entirely in red. She took off her red clothes piece by red piece, slowly, slowly, even more slowly. She writhed on a bed with red sheets and a red spread. She seemed to be in either pain or great desire. An unseen orchestra played music in the background. High school students and resident degenerates applauded at the end.

The high school group next went to the Garden. Saw a bunch of basketball games. Saw ND, the Green Knights, pummel poor Springfield, Vermont, 70–47. Yes!!! The return to the hotel went through Scollay Square, the low-rent section of Boston where trouble could be encountered. Inspiration arrived instead. The afternoon sighting of the naked female form—BARE BREAST!!! Saw it!!!—followed by an historic basketball win by the school quintet could only be followed by, let's think . . . alcohol seemed to be a fine choice.

The group found a sailor. Paid him a couple of extra dollars to buy two QUARTS, not fifths, of whiskey. Took the QUARTS, not fifths, back to the hotel. Opened the first QUART.

"You drink it fast," one of the seven apprentice drinkers in the room suggested. "That's how they do it in the cowboy movies. They fill up a glass and chug it down."

"Yes, of course," the other apprentices agreed, each chugging two water glasses filled with whiskey.

Hijinks and sickness followed. Details have been redacted by time.

Friday became the longest day in the history of the world. Notre Dame was not scheduled to play Lewiston High School from Maine in the semifinals at the Garden until 9:30 that night. Seven characters in green woolen jackets, the Catholic school name embroidered across the back in gold script, wandered the streets. There might have been food somewhere. There might not.

The bright young man and his cohorts eventually made their sad ways to their seats for the 9:30 tap-off. This tap-off did not happen on time. During warm-ups, six-foot-eight Paul Fortin, a senior from Lewiston, five inches taller than anyone in the Notre Dame lineup, dunked the ball, perhaps to show the advantages of height, perhaps simply because he could. The entire glass backboard shattered, pieces landing everywhere on the fabled floor.

This had never happened at the Garden, not in the pros, colleges, or high schools. Not once. Forward Chuck Connors, now an actor, famous as the star of *The Rifleman* television series, shattered a backboard on November 5, 1946, during warm-ups for the first game in Celtics history, but that happened at the Boston Arena, not the Garden. The Arena, a smaller facility, seating maybe five thousand people for basketball, was in the South End. A worker had not tightened the rim enough to the backboard. Connors took a set shot that hit the rim at a weird angle and the backboard shattered. Celtics history started an hour late because a replacement backboard and basket had to be brought from the Garden. There was no replacement at the Arena.

Fourteen years later, the process had to be done in reverse. There was no replacement at the Garden. A backboard and basket had to be brought from the Arena. The game started at ten thirty at night. Maybe eleven. The plucky lads from Notre Dame took an eight-point lead in the first half, led by six in the second, but were smothered by a late 12–0 Lewiston run and lost, 76–67.

The bright young man, exhausted, sick as he ever had been, walked back to the hotel, the Statler, later to be named the Park Plaza, with the six other zombies. They went straight to the room, where they picked out their sleeping places on the floor. The time was well after midnight. There were no QUARTS of whiskey.

The hangovers persisted the next day when everybody went back to the Garden for the 2 p.m. Celtics game, as planned, a once-in-a-lifetime chance to see the matchup of all basketball matchups. The Celtics (featuring Russell) and the Warriors (featuring Chamberlain) had played Game Two on Friday night, a raucous affair at Convention Hall in Philadelphia, won by the Warriors, 115–110. The important news was that Wilt had hurt his hand in that game when he punched the Celts' Tommy Heinsohn in the head. Nothing was broken, not even Heinsohn's head, but three of Wilt's knuckles were swollen and sore. There was doubt that he could play in this game back in Boston, starting only fifteen hours later, a tough bit of NBA scheduling.

The result was the Celtics cruised to a 120–90 win to take a 2-1 lead in the series. Wilt did play, but hurt the hand again and was ineffective. Russell killed him with 26 points and 39 rebounds. Wilt finished with 12 and 15. An up-close report was provided in later years by Pat Elia, a point guard on the Notre Dame team, which had been given seats under one of the baskets. He confirmed what Chamberlain described in his retirement speech.

"I remember two things," Elia said. "One was how big everyone was. You never got that feeling from television, but these guys were huge. They were from some other world. The second was how much they hit each other. Chamberlain, there was this one guy from the Celtics. Jim Something . . ."

"Jim Loscutoff?"

"Jim Loscutoff. He just kept punching Wilt Chamberlain in the stomach. Every time the referee wasn't looking, he punched him. Punched him in the stomach. Punched him in the back. Punched him everywhere. I said, 'Whoa, this is a whole other game than I know.' I couldn't believe that Chamberlain didn't either fall down or just turn around and start hitting Loscutoff back. I don't care how big you are. That had to hurt."

The bright young man and his friends could see none of that from the third deck. They filed down the stairs at the end, walked from North Station to South Station, and took the train home to Connecticut. They skipped the New England final high school game that night at the Garden, won by Wilbur Cross High of New Haven with a 70–58 verdict over Lewiston. This was the twenty-fifth championship for a Connecticut team in the thirty-four years of the New England tournament. Notre Dame won a consolation third-place game, 76–69, over Westerly, Rhode Island.

"How was the trip?" the bright young man's mother asked when he returned home. "Have a lot of fun?"

He was an only child of two older parents. They lived on the third floor of a six-story, seventy-two-unit apartment house, 80 Howe Street, in New Haven. The apartments were small, four or five hundred square feet, everybody too close together for too much of the time. He sat in the small living room, his mother no more than five feet away, his father no more than ten, made the smallest of small talk, chewed gum to mask his still-alcoholic breath, and said he had to go to bed because the train trip was, you know, very tiring.

Surrounded in his room by the familiar books and possessions of his childhood, the F-86 Sabre jet and MiG-15 model airplanes locked in perpetual plastic combat, the Topps baseball cards in the Thom McAn shoebox, the Fats Domino, Elvis Presley, and Chuck Berry 45 rpm records in a tilted pile on top of the portable Decca three-speed record player, the *Sport* magazine pictures by Ozzie Sweet on the walls next to the Red Sox and Yale felt pennants, he had the feeling that something important had happened in Boston, that something was different and probably would stay different for a long, long time. That was his thought as he went to sleep.

Wilt and Russell were part of the biggest weekend in his life.

Chapter 5

ESTABLISHING POSITION

REGULAR-SEASON RESULTS

November 19, 1968—@*Los Angeles* 116, Boston 106
November 29, 1968—*Los Angeles* 93, @Boston 92
January 10, 1969—@*Boston* 88, Los Angeles 82
February 21, 1969—*Boston* 124, @Los Angeles 102
March 7, 1969—@*Los Angeles* 105, Boston 99 (OT)
March 16, 1969—*Los Angeles* 108, @Boston 73

The Celtics and Lakers had met six times during the regular season. The spacing on the eighty-two-game schedule was early, middle, and late, an easy way to check each team's progress toward the finals. Every game was played against the preseason predictions that the Lakers probably had the greatest NBA team ever assembled and the Celtics were slowly shedding their championship history, undressing from past levels of excellence as they moved toward the dull, mid-level existence they had consigned to everybody else for so long.

The Lakers were ascendant.

The Celtics were descendant.

That was the prevailing thought.

The Lakers' addition of Chamberlain in July dominated all discussions. The caveat was that in addition to adding Chamberlain's wonderful body in the deal from the Sixers that *Sports Illustrated* described "as if the Niblets people traded the Jolly Green Giant to Heinz for a soup recipe and two vats of pickles," they also had to take Chamberlain's scattered mind. How would he fit with resident superstars West and Baylor? How much would he alter the many good things they did? How much would they alter the many good things he did? Would there be enough mental or physical basketballs for everyone to share? The big man's moods, broods, and eccentricities would determine a lot.

Since he joined a team that requested its employees to shave facial hair, his beard was a first test. That turned out to be an easy choice. Beard? No problem, Big Fellow. Looks great. Next the Lakers had to consider the thornier facts: he didn't like to have a roommate, he often didn't like to travel with the team, he didn't like to go to practice and could be a disruptive figure when he did. A buzz accompanied Wilt wherever he went.

Second-year coach Butch van Breda Kolff, forty-six, noisy and opinionated, another strong personality, former coach of Princeton and Bill Bradley, had to handle that buzz. Or not.

"Bill van Breda Kolff of the Lakers is a very peculiar coach," the preseason forecast read in the *Sporting News*. "He likes to have all of his players at practice. If he can learn to live with the fact this rule has never completely applied to Wilt Chamberlain, their first year together may not only be harmonious, but extremely productive.

"There is a tendency to say that no one can beat LA in the West this year except the Lakers themselves. Chamberlain is the kind of person who continually needs a new challenge to be at peak efficiency and now he has one. He knows that with him LA is expected to win—and win big. And he also knows what everyone will say if it doesn't."

The Celtics—the preseason pundits decided—had an entirely different situation with their own famous center. While changes from Mr. Chamberlain were desired, an alteration of style to fit his new surroundings, changes were dreaded from Mr. Russell in Boston. How much had he slipped? How much had the aging cast around him slipped? The Celtics—it was noted—might have won two of the last three NBA championships in the playoffs, but they had not won the Eastern Division regular-season race once in that time frame. They were another year older now and hadn't found a solid backup for their coach/star, who had reported to training camp fifteen pounds heavier than when he finished the last season. A shopworn, tired look was seen with this team before the first games even were played. Everyone said so. Enough was enough. Some law about diminishing returns was going to be invoked.

"The Celtics, because 82 games are involved, may have more trouble winning a division championship than the playoffs," the *Sporting News* declared. "If one could be positive that Russell, who will be 35 before the season ends, will not fade from overwork, injuries or both, the Celtics would be the more solid pick in the East. But Tom Sanders' knees are no better than they were a year ago, there is no backup help for Russell, etc., etc., etc. . . ."

The *Sporting News* previews of both teams were written by forty-one-year-old Phil Elderkin, who was a Boston-area guy and worked full-time as sports editor of the *Christian Science Monitor*. The bright young man knew him, saw him at different events. One of the first pieces of advice TBYM received in Boston was to watch Elderkin when the check came due at local sports luncheons. The representative from the *Christian Science Monitor* suddenly would slide from the table, head toward the men's room or out a back door, again missing his chance to contribute to the bill. This happened so regularly it was a running joke.

Elderkin was a capable writer, never a stylist, an inside whisperer as a reporter, had a close connection to Red Auerbach because they both played tennis. He was a small guy, feisty, had a withered right hand that he often covered with a glove. He boasted that he had seen every home playoff game the Celtics ever had played. In group interviews, he had a tendency to be long-winded in his questions and dominate the conversation. This would drive TBYM to mumbled distraction.

"The guy writes for the *Christian Science Monitor*," he would say. "Who reads the *Christian Science Monitor*?"

(Actually, at that time, the *Monitor* had a daily circulation of 220,000 and was read worldwide in Christian Science reading rooms. Elderkin also wrote regularly for the *Sporting News* and *Baseball Digest* and assorted outside publications. He was prolific and solid and well-read. In the seventeenth round of the 1973 NBA draft, he was selected as a joke by Bill Fitch of the Cleveland Cavaliers "because Phil is the only guy I could find who didn't have an agent, will play for the 1960 minimum and will bring his own sneakers.")

I read the clippings from Elderkin with a much kinder eye now. He moved from Boston to Claremont, California, in 1975, died in January 2020 at the age of ninety. His obituary told how he interviewed Groucho Marx, played basketball against the Harlem Globetrotters and tennis against Bobby Riggs two nights before Riggs's 1973 match in Houston against Billie Jean King in "The Battle of the Sexes."

"By the time Bobby finished me off," Elderkin said, "even the tongues of my sneakers were hanging out."

For the 1968–69 regular season, his forecasts in the *Sporting News* proved to be solid. Especially for the Lakers and Celtics.

THE SEASON

November 19, 1968—@Los Angeles 116, Boston 106—The anticipated first matchup came at the end of a warm and foggy autumn day in Los Angeles. The temperature was seventy-five degrees, but the fog that came off the ocean closed the airport, then drifted inland, where it was so thick that a section of the Riverside Freeway was closed after "hundreds" of cars had been involved in crashes, turning the road into "a flaming junkyard" in the description of the *Los Angeles Times*.

The last time the teams had met at the Forum was the end of the previous season, on May 2, when the Celtics had won their tenth NBA title with a 124–109 thumping of the Lakers in Game Six. It was this result that started all the machinations to bring Mr. Chamberlain (age thirty-two) to the Pacific Coast.

Mr. Russell (age thirty-five) made a joke to the local press about the changes the Lakers had made. He said that in his role as Celtics coach he had talked with Lakers general manager Freddie Schaus about a trade that would involve Celtics guard Larry Siegfried in exchange for a backup center. Schaus said that the Lakers' Mel Counts certainly was not available.

"I said I didn't want Counts," Russell reported. "I wanted the other center he had, Whatshisname, the one you got from Philadelphia. He'd make a good back-up center."

Both teams led their divisions out of the gate, the Celts with an 11-3 record, the Lakers at 12-4. Russell said his team "easily" could be unbeaten, that it had given away the three games it lost. The Lakers stumbled at the start, losing three of the first four—bringing about the first recorded meeting between van Breda Kolff and owner Jack Kent Cooke about the status of Wilt in the lineup—but then knocked off eleven wins in their last twelve games, seven in a row.

"We knew it would take a while to adjust to the big fellow," van Breda Kolff said. (Hopefully.)

This first game between the Lakers and Celtics turned out to be a rout, exactly what the sellout crowd of 15,878 wanted and expected at the Forum. Chamberlain was solid in a 116–106 Lakers win. He matched Russell on the backboards while Baylor scored 30 points, West 29, and newcomers Johnny Egan and Billy Hewitt gave notable help to the cause. Havlicek scored 32 for the sluggish Celtics, who fell behind by seven at the end of the third quarter and never could come back.

"We were ready for this one," West said. "This game meant something."

The sports story of the week was the fallout from NBC's early departure on television from the New York Jets' game against the Oakland Raiders on Sunday. The network left to show the much-advertised movie *Heidi* as scheduled at 7 p.m. The Jets were leading, 32–29, with 1:01 remaining. The Raiders came back to win the game, 42–32. Three days after the fact, sports fans still were not happy.

November 29, 1968—Los Angeles 93, @Boston 92—Ten days later, the night after Thanksgiving, the two teams met again, this time in Boston. The temperature was in the thirties, almost forty degrees colder than Los Angeles had been, windy and gray. The feel of a New England winter had arrived.

The two teams were still both in first, but the Celtics now were tied in the East with the up-from-nowhere Baltimore Bullets. Rookie Wes Unseld of the Bullets, the second pick in the draft after the San

Diego Rockets took Elvin Hayes, had teamed with Earl (The Pearl) Monroe to revitalize the last-place finishers in the East from a year ago. This was a surprise. (Even to Phil Elderkin.)

The Lakers, despite a solid lead in the West, had sputtered on their first two stops on a three-game trip to the East. This was their third game in four nights, and not only had they lost the first two in New York and Philadelphia, but Jerry West had been sent home with the flu. The team held a talk-it-out meeting before the game.

"We decided that our superstars had to do better," Wilt Chamberlain reported. He did not describe the areas of needed improvement.

The first appearance of Wilt in a Lakers uniform in Boston was an attraction. The Garden was sold out for the first time in the season, a record crowd of 14,929 for a basketball game. Management reported that "over 1,500 people" were turned away at the gate.

The Celtics seemed enthused by the attention—the team would average crowds of 8,948, a lot of quiet nights to offset the noisy ones like this—and zipped to a 14-point lead at the half, 12 points at the end of three quarters. Then the home team fell apart. It scored 10 points in the final period.

"Ten points in a quarter?" Russell asked in statistical amazement. "That has to be a league record."

Nothing seemed to work. In the final nine minutes of the game, his team scored only one basket. The absence of shooter Sam Jones, missing with a pulled groin muscle, hurt the most. The Lakers made up lost ground, edged ahead, then hung on to win, 93–92, when Siegfried was called for traveling in the final seconds before he could lift a potential game-winning shot. Russell and Chamberlain were even with 22 rebounds apiece. The Lakers had six players in double figures, even with West at home. This was a Boston-esque kind of box score.

"This game might have been the turning point," Chamberlain said. "Certainly it's our most significant win so far. The great thing about it is there's no one you can single out."

An added piece of bad news for the Celtics was that the Bullets had won, 124–106, in Phoenix to edge into first place. Unseld, a blocky and diligent rebounder at six feet seven, 245 pounds, one of the many college stars to decline a spot on the 1968 U.S. Olympic team (he said he was "tired"), would wind up not only as the NBA rookie of the year but also the most valuable player. He joined Wilt as the only winners of both awards in the same year. The Bullets would win eleven of their next thirteen games, never relinquish first place for the rest of the season.

The sports story of the week—at least the Boston week—was unbeaten Harvard's grand comeback to tie unbeaten Yale, 29–29. The Los Angeles sports story was the three-way race to the NFL bottom between Philadelphia, Atlanta, and Buffalo to determine who would have the first draft pick and be able to pick University of Southern California running back O. J. Simpson, who had won the Heisman Trophy in the middle of the week.

January 10, 1969—@Boston 88, Los Angeles 82—A message was delivered from the Celtics' front office to the Lakers before the third game in the series, also in Boston. The speaker was general manager Red Auerbach, who sent a dark little cartoon balloon to float into the visitors' locker room among all those sweet expectations.

"I predicted that the Lakers would die a horrible death if they didn't get some guard who could pass the ball," Auerbach said the day before the game. "A horrible death."

The bright young man reported these words. In a week in which he also covered a Harvard hockey game against RPI and basketball games between Nebraska Wesleyan and Bentley and Boston College and UCal-Irvine, TBYM had made his season debut with the Celtics a night earlier for their 113–104 win over the Detroit Pistons.

The interview, no doubt, was in Red's office, a crowded affair with pictures, more pictures, even more pictures, memorabilia, a world-class collection of letter openers, file cabinets, and a black-and-white television that provided rerun excitement in the middle of the afternoon. (*Hawaii Five-0* would become a favorite in later years. "Don't disturb Red during *Hawaii Five-0*.")

Sitting on the visitor's side of Auerbach's overrun desk was like visiting some insurance agent who had been in business a very long time, some accountant who smoked his cigar and dropped ashes on your return while he talked about a world problem or an undeserved parking ticket just yesterday. He would give out advice ("Dress British, think Yiddish"), would ask questions ("Why don't sportswriters make any money? I've never met one of you guys who has any money."), would offer coffee and candy ("Want a Charleston Chew?"). He would laugh. He would get mad. He would seem to fall asleep sometimes.

An easy normalcy filled the room. He was a fifty-two-year-old guy who would tell you if your fly was open or if a piece of lunchtime salad had been caught in your teeth. There was no button-down artifice. Red was Red. If a person came into the little office and wanted to buy season tickets, yes, it was still true, Red would take him upstairs into the Garden and show him the different options for seats.

He certainly knew the value of a good quote. "A horrible death" was an example. He knew the Lakers would read what he said. A horrible death! Had he planned this far in advance, released the balloon at the perfect moment? Did the words simply slip into his mind at the moment, perfect for the occasion? This was a man who had been famous/infamous as a coach for lighting a victory cigar on the bench when he thought the game was out of reach for the other side. He knew how to tweak a prominent nose.

The Lakers said they had remedied their backcourt situation with the trade for point guard Johnny Egan, the former Providence College star, and by the purchase of former UCLA swing man Keith Erickson. Auerbach wasn't completely convinced. The Lakers were still in first in the weaker West by four and a half games over Atlanta—the Celtics had dropped to third in the East, three games behind Baltimore—but clearly weren't the super team that many people had feared.

"It's a fine ballclub, but it's going to have trouble," Auerbach said. "It's not going to race through the playoffs. The loss of Darrall Imhoff and Archie Clark [two of the three players the Lakers traded to Philadelphia, plus cash, for Chamberlain] has hurt."

The game that followed on a wintry night, temperatures in the low twenties, another sellout, another record with 14,933 customers in the stands, gave the general manager a first bit of empirical evidence. The circumstances were the same as the last meeting between the two teams—Jerry West back in Los Angeles again, this time with a pulled groin muscle, Sam Jones scheduled to sit out for the Celtics with his own balky groin—but a late change occurred. Russell ordered Sam to play.

"Get dressed," the coach said.

Jones was ready to watch again in street clothes. In the game against the Pistons two nights earlier, he had played two painful minutes in the first half before leaving the floor for the night. His groin muscle did not feel much better now, but orders were orders. Russell wanted him to play.

"I didn't say no more," Sam said.

He came into the game to start the second period, proceeded to miss his first three shots. Russell told him to keep firing. He wound up hitting 10-of-13 the rest of the way in the 88–82 win. Four of the hoops came down the stretch after the Lakers tied the score at 77–77 and threatened to repeat their comeback in the last game.

"See?" Auerbach could say.

The cartoon balloon. The season series was 2-1, L.A., but the Celtics were on the board.

The sports story of the week was Super Bowl III scheduled for the next day in Miami. The Baltimore Colts were favored by 18 points over the New York Jets and Joe Namath.

February 21, 1969—Boston 124, @ Los Angeles 102—Almost seven weeks later, this was a game the Celtics needed for peace of mind. They had developed their own substantial cartoon balloons of doubt. They were in fourth place now, behind Baltimore, Philadelphia, and New York. The worry was that they would wind up being passed by the Cincinnati Royals for the fourth and final playoff spot in the East if they didn't change their trajectory. They hadn't been in this position in the standings, fourth place, since Russell arrived in 1956.

The coach/player had become the important story. Looking tired, missing easy shots, he had gone down in a painful heap at the end of a 95–94 loss to the Knicks on February 2 at the Garden. The verdict, after a night in the hospital, was a sprained knee that kept him out of the lineup for the next four games. Auerbach returned as interim coach, an interesting situation, but the team was winless for him, too, as it stumbled to its first five-game losing streak since 1949. Russell returned to reestablish a small sense of order with a 122–117 overtime victory over the Sixers, but the preseason mumbles of doubt now were full-throated statements. The Celtics were hitting low points they never had hit.

On the other coast, the Lakers had continued their weird adjustment problems with Chamberlain. Van Breda Kolff now hated Wilt. Wilt hated van Breda Kolff. That situation was in the open. The stories about their twisted relationship did not stop. There was a report of a near fistfight in Seattle, a report of a cut-it-out meeting with Jack Kent Cooke. A continual grumpiness persisted. Van Breda Kolff wanted Wilt to spend time at the top of the key, the high post, to free up drives for West and Baylor. Chamberlain liked the low post, where he had always operated, always dominated. His moods, as advertised, dominated the situation. Van Breda Kolff privately referred to Chamberlain as "The Load," because he slowed down the offense so much.

A graph on a piece of paper could show the effects of this discord. The man who once scored 100 points in a game now had scored 2 in one game, 4 in another only a few weeks ago. He then had come back to score 60 at the end of January in a game against the Royals, then 66 only twelve nights ago against Philadelphia. What did this mean? He was comfortable, not comfortable, what?

"Wilt and I understand each other a lot better now," van Breda Kolff said hopefully after the 60-point night. "I'm definitely pleased with the attitude and spirit of the whole team the past month. I wish people would stop trying to beat a dead horse."

Alas, the beatable dead horse appeared in this fourth meeting with the Celtics. The weather was partly cloudy, sixty degrees, not a grand Southern California day at all. With Jerry West out again with a pulled hamstring muscle, missing his third of four games in the series, the visitors kept 17,018 Forum fans very quiet. The night became a track meet—the familiar Boston strategy for success— and the Lakers couldn't keep the pace. Havlicek scored 30 points, Sam Jones 27. Russell had only 5 points, but matched Wilt with 16 rebounds. He was happy to talk back to the critics.

"'They Said' and 'I Heard' are two of the biggest liars in the world," he said, talking about his personal rejuvenation. "I'm 35 . . . that's the prime of life. What difference does it make if I'm 50 as long as I play well out there."

The series was tied, 2-2. Both teams had won once on the road.

The sports news of the week was that Stan Musial and Roy Campanella had been elected to the Baseball Hall of Fame. The UPI story noted that Campanella, the former Brooklyn Dodgers catcher, "joined former teammate Jackie Robinson as the only two Negroes in the hall."

March 7, 1969—@Los Angeles 105, Boston 99 (OT)—High-Scoring Wilt was replaced by Killer-Rebounding Wilt in this one. He pulled down 42 rebounds to keep the Lakers afloat in a game they almost squandered in regulation, but put away easily in overtime, 105–99, before a Forum crowd of 16,887.

Forty-two rebounds was a stunning number. Forty-two rebounds?

"Have you ever had a better rebounding game against Bill Russell?" a sportswriter asked.

"Yes, I did," Chamberlain replied. "I got 55 rebounds once against the Celtics."

(This was, and still is, the NBA record. November 24, 1960. The Celtics won the game, 132–129 over the Philadelphia Warriors.)

The performance here was another Wilt statement. See? This is what I can do. He had found himself on the bench for longer and longer stretches in recent games, replaced by Mel Counts, the seven-foot backup the Lakers told Russell at the beginning of the year was "unavailable." Counts was able to do one thing Wilt couldn't do. He could run . . . and when he ran, the Lakers ran with him. They looked, for lack of another word, "better" when Counts was in the lineup.

A story in the morning *Los Angeles Times* titled "Chamberlain: A Laker Dilemma" pointed out the fact that the Lakers had beaten only one team of "considerable stature [the Knicks]" in eight weeks. Chamberlain had appeared disinterested at times and "has not hustled at both ends of the court." Writer Mal Florence wondered if Chamberlain was saving his strength for the impending playoffs, when "the REAL season begins."

"One thing is certain: the Lakers are in a box," Florence concluded. "They may not win the playoffs and they can't win it without him."

The 42 rebounds were Chamberlain's obvious answer.

This was a Lakers record for a single game (previously set by George Mikan seventeen years earlier as a Minneapolis Laker), a Forum record, and the biggest rebounding performance in the NBA season. With Russell on the bench for much of the third quarter with four fouls, Chamberlain seemed to be everywhere on the boards in a freewheeling offensive game by both sides.

Owner Jack Kent Cooke said he had never seen a center play a better game, but Chamberlain downplayed the performance. He said there are nights when the ball seems to land in your hands and nights when it seems to bounce in another direction. Effort can be constant, but results can vary.

"Why does Elgin Baylor go 15-for-24 one night, and then 4-for-23?" he asked. "Sometimes it appears that you're loafing when you're going all out. Forty-two rebounds is not something you can do every day, but that doesn't mean you're not trying."

This was the fourth loss in five games for the Celtics, caught in a downward stretch that cemented their fourth-place finish in the East. They hadn't scored over 100 points in any of the five games. Their 42-31 record was a record. They had never lost more than thirty games since Russell's arrival in Boston.

"It just may tell the story that the aging Celtics don't have it any more," Herb Ralby wrote in the *Boston Globe* (taking a few minutes off from his Bruins PR job, the bright young man no doubt would note). "Despite what Red Auerbach says and what coach Bill Russell says—'we'll be all right when we get everybody healthy'—they won't be pulling any miracles in the playoffs this year."

The sports news of the week (Boston version) was that Harvard would play Cornell for the ECAC hockey title the next night, a game Cornell would win, 4–2, behind senior goalie Ken Dryden. The sports news of the week (Los Angeles version) was UCLA's double-overtime win, 61–55, over USC at the Sports Arena. Senior Lew Alcindor had 14 points and 9 rebounds for the Bruins, whose record moved to 25-0. One night later, USC would come back to beat its rival, 46–44, in a slowdown affair (college had no shot clock) at Pauley Pavilion. This was Alcindor's second and final loss in an 88-2 college career that included three NCAA championships.

March 16, 1969—Los Angeles 108, @Boston 73—The final matchup was the ass kicking that had been predicted from the beginning. The stardust Lakers ran the decaying Celtics off the parquet floor. This wasn't just a 108–73 rout, it was a grand embarrassment for the home team. Jeers came down from the third deck, at least from the fans who had stayed to the end. The Celtics were a silent group of imposters as they walked to their locker room, not related at all to the champions of the past.

The Lakers clinched the West with the win. The afternoon game was on national television, ABC, and convinced the country that they had cleared out all cobwebs and inconsistencies and clearly would be the team to beat when the playoffs arrived in two weeks. The Bullets, winners in the East, would finish with the best record, but the Lakers had the most talent. That seemed obvious.

The idea that the Celtics and Lakers would be matched in the finals would have been considered laughable to any of the 14,171 spectators who watched any part of this game at the Garden. Russell kept the locker room door closed for forty-five minutes while he ran down the list of his team's problems. It hadn't hustled, hadn't shot very well, defended very well, done anything very well. The coach clearly was disgusted by the performance.

Laker coach van Breda Kolff had an obvious opposite perspective. He was delighted.

"The box score says Boston shot only 25.7 per cent from the floor, but we played good defense," he said, holding a mimeographed (look it up) statistics sheet. "If you have a low percentage, it means you are taking bad shots. And you take bad shots because of good defense."

Buried deep underneath the results of the day, not mentioned in any paper, were two votive lights of hope for the losers. The first was that the Celtics had played a night earlier in Baltimore, a grinding 99–98 loss to the Bullets that hadn't started until eight o'clock. There was a touch of NBA schedule warp here, the Lakers in bed in Boston after a Friday night win in Milwaukee, the Celtics scuffling to return home. This was a situation built for embarrassment. The second hopeful note was that this same result had been delivered on ABC, national television, Sunday afternoon from the Garden a year ago when the Lakers ran away with a 141–104 rout. They were ahead, 70–40, at halftime in that one. Russell scored only 4 points. Terrible. Two months later the Celtics had won their tenth title at the Forum.

"We'll rise or fall as a team," Russell said, his voice cracking from overuse in the team meeting. "I'm coughing to keep from crying."

The sports story of the week (Boston version) was Ted Williams's return to baseball as manager of the Washington Senators. A staff writer had been assigned to write a series of articles about the former Red Sox slugger from the Senators' training camp in Pompano Beach, Florida. Today's article was "Ted's Batting Tips Invaluable." The sports story of the week (Los Angeles version) was that unbeaten three-year-old Majestic Prince did *not* run in the San Felipe Stakes on Saturday. The favored Prince stayed in the barn while long-shot Elect the Ruler ($26.40, $9.40, $9.60) won the race. The plan was for Prince to run in the Santa Anita stakes in two weeks (a win) and then possibly in the Kentucky Derby (a win), Preakness (a win), and then in the Belmont (an injury-plagued second). Bill Hartack would be his rider.

The bright young man covered the final game, the blowout, as the start of his late-season immersion with the Celtics. He was fresh off assignments involving the undefeated Northeastern University's women's basketball team, headed to the National Invitational Intercollegiate Women's Basketball Tournament in West Chester, Pennsylvania (six women on a side, no scholarships, red-and-black school jumpers for uniforms), and the Tufts baseball team, headed to Mexico on a spring trip despite coach Herb Erickson's fear of flying (never had flown, not once) and a local woman fencer who was in love with her sport. The excitement of covering a big-time event, Sunday afternoon, day before St. Patrick's Day in Boston, Massachusetts, full house at the Garden, national television, was obvious for TBYM after these previous assignments, none of his stories stopping any presses, but here it was doubled, tripled, increased by some exponent—this was his first chance to write a column for the *Boston Globe*.

This was a moment.

Being a sports columnist was his goal. It was pretty much a universal goal in the business, to be featured in the left two columns of the front sports page, name in large type, perhaps accompanied by an earnest headshot. Unencumbered by the need to report the details of the action in front of him, the columnist was freed to give his opinion, set his own tone, concentrate on any damn thing he wanted, funny or sad, introspective or light. The columnist covered the biggest events, from the World Series to the Kentucky Derby to the recently invented Super Bowl. The columnist made the biggest money. (Or so it was said.) The columnist was the star.

The normal resident in this spot for the *Evening Globe* was Jerry Nason, the sports editor for both the morning and evening editions. He was sixty years old, an executive one-man band, tall and important. He looked a bit like Franklin Delano Roosevelt in history books, glasses and white hair and a patrician attitude about common events. He smoked Tiparillos, which left a sweet smell wherever he went. He never seemed ruffled about any detail, large or small, which probably was very good as an administrator, but maybe not ideal for a columnist. In addition to writing five columns a week, he coordinated the daily assignments for both sports staffs, handled the administrative duties of his position, and sometimes drew cartoons for the paper. He did all this on a strict Monday-to-Friday schedule, nine to five, banker's hours that sent him home for dinner each night and kept him from attending events. He weaved around this lack of watching actual games with chatty day-late finesse, but often would seem out of touch. He was a character from the journalistic past, TBYM decided, talented but hopelessly dated.

Since Nason did not work on Sundays, the column for the Monday evening paper usually was written by forty-two-year-old Ray Fitzgerald. A former first baseman at the University of Notre Dame, a feisty character with a flattened prizefighter's kind of nose, the father of four kids, two boys and two girls, Fitzgerald was the columnist in waiting. He was a wonderful writer, breezy and funny, different. ("What you do is you turn what you're looking at just a little bit," he advised TBYM about writing columns. "You don't have to turn it a lot. Just a little bit, so you're looking at it from a slightly different angle from everyone else. That's what makes you different.") When Nason retired or when morning columnist Harold Kaese, also age sixty, retired, Fitzgerald was more than ready to step into the job. He wrote columns now on Sundays and when either man was sick or on vacation.

TBYM was next behind Fitzgerald on the list of future columnists. Or at least that was what TBYM thought. This Celtics-Lakers assignment—Fitzgerald off for the day for some reason—was the first chance to prove what he could do. I don't remember the particulars, but I would bet TBYM was the most excited person in the large building. Certainly more excited than anyone in a Celtics uniform.

The following was his 610-word audition for the rest of his sportswriting life. Do note that he was intrigued once again at the idea of interviewing Russell in a whirlpool tub. Write what you see. That was the idea. Details, details, details.

Bill Russell sat in the small, stainless steel whirlpool bath.

His head and shoulders and both of his kneecaps were visible. The rest of his body was crammed into the tub, which was making noises like a washing machine chugging into its rinse cycle.

The setting was perfect for talking about a sinking ship. A decal, showing the Boston Celtics' cocky leprechaun mascot, even gave the boat a name.

"I talked," Bill Russell said. "I talked for quite a while."

A reporter asked what words had been used in the talk.

"You couldn't print them," Bill Russell said. "Not in a newspaper."

The talk had lasted for a half hour yesterday afternoon. It had been preceded by the worst basketball game the Boston Celtics have played in recent memory.

In front of 14,178 people at the Boston Garden, in living 21-inch color on the American Broadcasting Company's game of the week, the Celtics were demolished, 108–73, by the Los Angeles Lakers. It was terrible. A talk was necessary. Russell called it a "monologue."

"A basketball team is not a democracy," he said. "It is a dictatorship, an absolute dictatorship. On a day like today it cannot be a benevolent dictatorship."

There were two things missing, Bill Russell said. One was teamwork. The other was hustle.

". . . and that pretty much covers it, doesn't it?" he asked. "We were missing that something extra that if you don't give it, you get the hell kicked out of you.

"We don't have great one-on-one ballplayers. We have

to work together, to help everyone else take the best shot. If we don't work together, we're nothing.

"If we do, we're the best team in basketball."

Yesterday the Celtics were quite a distance from being the best team in basketball. "Nothing" was a good description. The Lakers gobbled up the easy shots. They had fast breaks and lay-ups and dunk shots, a lot of dunk shots. The Celtics took a lot of long jumpers. The jumpers missed and there were no rebounds.

"Basketball is such a large part mental," Lakers coach Bill van Breda Kolff said. "Bob Cousy, in his book, said when he retired he thought he could still play the game physically, but he just couldn't prepare himself mentally any more.

"I think there's a lot of truth in what he said."

Russell agreed.

"We have a bunch of sweet, lovely guys on this team," the coach said. "They have a tendency to relax and every now and then I have to bring them back to life, the hard, cold commercial society."

The coach took the quickest route to the cold, commercial society. He mentioned the word "money" and he mentioned the word "fines."

"Nothing will be done now," he said. "Now is not the right time. But there had better be a rapid change of attitude. If something happens like this Wednesday [against Chicago] it is likely to be very expensive."

A reporter asked if Russell, the player, was in danger of being fined by Russell, the coach. The head over the stainless steel shook positively.

"When I talk to the team, I'm not talking to 11 players," he said. "I'm talking to 12. The center has been fined this year as much as anyone."

The machine whirred and it was now almost an hour and a half after the basketball game had ended, an hour after the post-game talk.

"Did you throw any furniture?" the captain of the whirlpool ship was asked. The head bobbed negatively.

"No, I don't throw furniture around," Bill Russell said.
"That's not my style.

"I don't get ulcers. You see, I'm a carrier."

The bright young man read this column the next day on the printed
page, again and again. I am sure of that. He picked it apart, dismantled it as if it were some erector-set creation from his youth, some pre-
cursor to Legos. He moved the pieces around, wondered if they would
have fit better this way or that. Sometimes he was proud of himself.
Sometimes he was embarrassed. He was both at the same time. His
self-absorbed opinions flew back and forth. I am sure.

The game story that day was written by the previously mentioned
Herb Ralby. The bright young man took notebook and printed statis-
tic sheets and box score back to the *Globe* office, using the time in
the car, a 1968 forest-green Ford Mustang, to organize his thoughts.
Ralby pounded out his effort in his public relations office with the
Bruins. This was one of those magic days at the Garden. By the time
Ralby was finished—and he was a fast writer—the parquet basket-
ball floor had been removed in sections and the ice had been cleaned
and a new crowd filled the seats. The Bruins proceeded to wallop the
Toronto Maple Leafs, 11–3.

In the coming week, the Celtics did, indeed, follow Russell's admo-
nitions. They won their last four games of their season. There were no
fines as they outlasted the Chicago Bulls, 104–92, three nights later
at the Garden, then took care of Cincinnati, Baltimore, and the San
Diego Rockets. The bright young man was on the job at three of those
games, the final one the first neutral half of an NBA doubleheader at
the Spectrum in Philadelphia.

(Doubleheaders were a basic economic part of NBA life. The Celtics played in four doubleheaders on the road during the season, two in
New York and two in Philadelphia. They also played an earlier game
against San Diego in Houston and the final game against Cincinnati was played in Cleveland. All possibilities for increasing revenue
were explored by the league. The final game against San Diego in
the Philadelphia doubleheader was bolstered at the gate by the addition of a few daredevil acts and an eating contest between a diminu-

tive girl named "Little Audrey" and five potbellied men. Little Audrey devoured sixty-seven hot dogs to crush her opposition.)

The most interesting part of that game—a listless 111–107 win over the listless Rockets, who were headed home—was that backup center Jim (Bad News) Barnes, situated in the farthest rooms of Bill Russell's doghouse for much of the second half of the season, was called to make an appearance in the final half of the final quarter of the final game. Barnes had been involved in a strange incident in January, when he was swept into the air by the thrust of a jet engine while the Celtics changed planes at O'Hare Airport in Chicago. He was thrown across the tarmac, landed hard, and was hospitalized with "an outrageous headache," fuzzy hearing, and "a pain from my right shoulder down my arm to my right hand." Concussions didn't attract much attention at the time. He hadn't played well and hadn't played much since the injury.

He took the court now, ran up and down a couple of times, then put up a hand for a timeout. He asked to be removed from the action.

"What's the problem?" Russell asked.

"My jock broke," Barnes reported.

(Note to Generation Z, Generation X, and maybe the millennials: a "jock" was a jockstrap, which was a slingshot type of undergarment male athletes wore at that time for added protection of their nether regions. Ask your dad. Everyone wore them.)

Russell took off his warm-ups and put his weary self back into the last minutes of the last quarter of the last game of the season. He was not happy. He was really not happy. Jim Barnes returned to that doghouse. He would never play another second for the Boston Celtics, stuffed at the end of the bench, an option never to be considered. Russell basically would go into the playoffs without a backup.

No problem.

Chapter 6

TIME TO GO

LOS ANGELES—John Havlicek, seated on the rust-colored hotel-room couch, pointed at the window. It was eight feet away.

"You can be as far from Wilt Chamberlain as that window is from me," Havlicek said yesterday. "He can still block your shot."

Bailey Howell agreed.

"For John or me to block your shot we just about have to be standing on your feet," he said. "Wilt? Wilt can easily block a shot from that window."

It had finally happened. Jerry West would have loved to have seen it years ago. The Boston Celtics were in the finals of the National Basketball Association playoffs against the Los Angeles Lakers, and for once, finally, they had to worry about the Lakers' center.

The series begins tonight at 11 o'clock (EST) at the circular Forum and the Celtics will have to contend with Chamberlain. No more Darrall Imhoff. No more Gene Wiley.

This time, unlike the five other times the Celtics have beaten Los Angeles in the finals, the Lakers have a center.

"Match-ups are the thing," West, the LA all-star guard said yesterday referring to the man-to-man basketball games played in the middle of the one, big game. "In years past, we always had strong points, but we always knew the Celtics had strong points we didn't have."

Like center?

"That was the big one," West said. We just didn't have anyone who could match [Bill] Russell. Wilt can match Russell very well.

"This is the best basketball team I've ever been associated with."

It is a team that would seem to have everything. Wilt is there for the rebounds. West and Elgin Baylor, who suddenly recovered with a 29-point effort on Sunday (in the 104–96 win over the Atlanta Hawks to clinch the Western Conference title) after four bad games, are there for the scoring.

Johnny Egan, the little guy from Providence College, gave the team a ballhandler. Bill Hewitt, the Rindge Tech [of Cambridge, Massachusetts] rookie, who is the protégé of Russell and Bill Sharman and a lot of the Celtics, adds youthful aggressiveness.

"He is the best defensive forward in the NBA," West said. "He did a fine job on Rudy LaRusso."

Hewitt, who hadn't been starting, took the job against LaRusso in the third game of the Lakers' first-round playoff series against San Francisco. LaRusso had been scoring in double figures. San Francisco had won twice.

Hewitt stopped everything. LaRusso slumped to a total of 40 points in the next three games. The Lakers went along to rattle off eight wins in their next nine playoff games.

"Hewitt is a good defensive ballplayer," Havlicek, the man Hewitt will have to guard, said. "He's tall [six feet seven]. He can run and he can jump. He can really jump.

"Also, he can be as aggressive as he wants to be on defense. It reminds me of how I was when I was a rookie. Red Auerbach would tell me to just go in there and play good defense and run and run and run and make the man guarding me get tired.

"I figured any offense I contributed was a bonus because Bob Cousy and Tom Heinsohn and those other guys took care of most of the offense. Hewitt, with Chamberlain, Baylor and West, can do the same thing."

The Lakers also have a bench. Mel Counts and Tom Hawkins are scoring forwards. Fred Crawford and Keith Erickson both play at the guards.

"It is," Howell said, "the best team I think we've faced in the playoffs. This is going to be a really close series."

THE NOTEBOOK—Both teams practiced yesterday at the Forum . . . The Lakers scrimmaged only at one half of the court, with Wilt Chamberlain idly taking jump shots at the other end.

The Celtics' practice was closed . . . "We just worked on a few things we think we can do against LA that we couldn't do against New York," Havlicek said . . .

Tom Sanders missed the workout and is doubtful for tonight's game . . . He suffered a muscle spasm in his back on Monday, the same type of injury that caused him to miss the entire Lakers series last year.

The Lakers are four-point favorites for tonight's game, 9-5 for the series . . . "We have to get offense from Russell again," Howell said. "He has to be a threat against Wilt. He has to keep Wilt busy."

Hewitt said there were no special thoughts about playing Boston in the finals, even though his brother and grandmother still live in Cambridge . . . "I didn't care who won in the East," he said with a smile. "I was concerned over who won in the West."

Time to go.

Time to play the games.

—

Breaking News: Sirhan Sirhan has been sentenced to gas chamber for murdering Robert Kennedy.

Breaking News: French President Charles de Gaulle promises to resign if a referendum he favors is defeated in a country-wide vote on Sunday. His declaration has sent both the French franc and the British pound into a "tailspin."

Breaking News: Israel celebrates 21st birthday after day of hostilities.

Breaking News: Mama Cass Elliott (27) is awarded a divorce from James R. Hendricks (29). The lead singer for the Mamas and Papas claimed Hendricks "became jealous as I became more and more famous" and "used to yell and scream and throw tantrums." She waived alimony.

The Lettera 32? Check.

Stenographer notepads? Check.

Bic pens? Check.

Boston Weather: Cloudy and Cooler. Temperature in the 40s. Twenty percent chance of rain.

Los Angeles Weather: Drizzles this morning. Partly sunny this afternoon. High today: 64.

Lunch.

Kill time. Kill time. Kill time.

Time Magazine Cover: Artist rendering of statue of John Harvard holding a sign that says "Strike Harvard." Background collage of black-and-white photos of student demonstrations, riot police.

Rolling Stone Cover: Sun Ra. (Leader of the Sun Ra

Arkestra.) (Pioneer in electronic music.) (Teacher of a course in "The Black Man and the Cosmos.")

Field and Stream Cover: Drawing of fisherwoman paddling a canoe by artist Don Stivers. Articles include "How to Improve Your Deer Hunting," "Fish Fighting Myths Explored," and "Your Exclusive Tire Guide for Cars, Trucks and Trailers."

Wait in lobby.

Nervous. Nervous. Nervous.

Read anything.

DEAR ABBY: A very good friend of mine promised her husband she'd quit smoking, but now she chews tobacco, which I think is even worse. I feel she has the habit so bad she can't quit. Will you please ask your readers to pray for her? LUCY.

DEAR LUCY: The whole world could pray for her, but unless the Lord has her cooperation, she'll continue to chew.

Odds for series: Lakers, 9-to-5.

Point spread for Game One: Lakers by 4 points.

Today in Sports (Los Angeles): BASEBALL: Cincinnati at Los Angeles, KFL, KWKW, 8 pm; California vs. Chicago at Milwaukee, KPMC, 5:30 pm. BASKETBALL: Boston at Los Angeles, KNX, 8 pm. WRESTLING: Olympic Auditorium, Channel 5, 9 pm.

Today in Sports (Boston): BASEBALL: Washington at Boston, WHDH Radio, 1:25 pm. BASKETBALL: NBA Playoffs, Boston Celtics at Los Angeles, WHDH Radio, 10:55 pm.

—

Time to go.
  Best-of-seven. NBA finals.
  Game One.

Time to go . . .

Chapter 7

GAME ONE

GO WEST—AND LAKERS GO 1-UP, 120–118

BY LEIGH MONTVILLE
Staff Writer
LOS ANGELES—Jerry West said he took the family car and went for a drive yesterday.

He said he visited a few friends, drove back home and took a nap. He said he woke up, ate a meal and snapped at his wife a few times.

The rest of his day you probably already know, because after Jerry West left home the next time he went to the Forum and played a perfect basketball game.

He scored 53 points, 53 beautiful backcourt points, as the Los Angeles Lakers defeated the Boston Celtics, 120–118, to take a 1-0 lead in the finals of the National Basketball Assn. playoffs.

The job West did was almost out of a computer. He stepped on the court and looked at the man next to him for the opening tap. It was Emmette Bryant. The strategy was obvious.

Bryant at 6-feet-1 is two inches shorter than Jerry

West. West knew the routine. He would get the basketball a lot. He knew he would shoot a lot.

He was business-like. He was efficiently calm.

"The pressure really gets to me before a game like this," West later said softly in his now-muted West Virginia twang, every razor-cut hair in place, his slender, angular face California tanned.

"It gets to the point sometimes before a game that I can't really stand the pressure. I'm impossible to live with. I invariably scream at my wife a few times the day of the game.

"But then when the game comes, I just go out there. I just go out to play. I know I'll either play good, play poorly or play average and I don't worry about it anymore."

The first few shots he took last night were not good. They were good shots to take, but they did not finish with the basketball in the basket.

Then, with the Lakers leading, 12–8, and less than five minutes played in the game, life became nicer for Jerry West. Bryant slammed into Wilt Chamberlain. A foul was called. It was his third foul of the game. He put his hands up in frustration.

"Those fouls hurt," Bryant said. "They were some bad calls. And they put me in the hole. One more foul and I don't get to play much the rest of the game.

"I had to give West some room. I had to give him some shots. Some shots I wouldn't normally give him, because I couldn't get that fourth foul."

The first thing West did, the next time the Lakers had the ball, was drive toward the basket. Bryant couldn't touch him. Bill Russell tried, but was called for goaltending and a foul at the same time.

"When I scored on that drive, I started to go," West said. "I hit another one and then I started to get into the groove."

By the end of the period, West had scored 17 points.

By the half, he had scored 26 and Bryant now was guarding Johnny Egan, who is short.

Sam Jones had charge of West. It didn't matter.

The same things would happen every time the Lakers came down the floor. West would get the ball. Everybody else would move away and let him work.

"Every time down he'd get that ball," said Celtics rookie Don Chaney, who also tried a few minutes of defense against West. "Every time the ball would go in the basket."

One time, however, it didn't. The miss almost lost the ballgame, the best-played game of the (overall) playoffs, "the most exciting game in which I've ever played," said West.

The shot was a jumper from the top of the key, 18 feet from the basket. There were 33 seconds left, the Lakers leading, 115–114.

"The ball bounced off the rim and the backboard. Then it bounced off someone else and it came to me," said the 7-feet-1 Chamberlain.

The next step was predictable since Chamberlain was standing three feet from the basket. The ball was crammed, two-handed, through the hoop.

The Celtics came back, Russell scoring a layup and Chamberlain was called for goaltending with nine seconds left. But West was fouled by Howell with four seconds remaining and scored the two points. The Lakers had a three-point lead and the ballgame.

"I just had a good game," West said. "Who knows? Maybe I'll be terrible in the next game Friday night.

"Yes, I think the Celtics would make some changes defensively in the next game. I would think we'd see something different defensively."

The Celtics, however, may be thinking about trying the same things once again. Russell, as he dressed and talked to Jim Brown, the football player turned actor, said there would be no sweeping changes.

"If we lost the game by 18 points," Russell said, knotting a maroon striped tie, "there would be some changes. But we didn't lose by 18 points. We gave Jerry West 53 points and we lost by two."

THE NOTEBOOK—West said it was a nice feeling to win the first game of a playoff series against the Celtics . . . "It's the first time (in six)," he said. "It's a good feeling, but all it actually does is keep our home court advantage and move us one game closer . . ."

The game was unbelievably close . . . The Celtics had a seven-point lead in the second period, but the Lakers quickly scored six points in a row and from there the teams were never more than four points apart.

Each team took 100 shots. The Celtics had one more rebound, two more assists and one less turnover . . . "I was surprised at how well the Celtics shot," Chamberlain said. "This is the best I think I've seen them shoot."

Havlicek had a terrific night, hitting 14 of 26 shots from the floor, scoring 37 points and grabbing 12 rebounds . . . "We were running well in spurts," he said, "but then we'd die out."

Tom Sanders, bothered by a muscle spasm in his back, didn't play at all, even though he was dressed . . . If he does play Friday night at the Forum, it is conceivable Havlicek could move into the backcourt to play against West.

"But I don't think they'll do it," Lakers coach Bill (Butch) van Breda Kolff said. "They need Havlicek's scoring too much to wear him out on defense."

The game was a sellout, as is the game Friday night, which will be shown on closed-circuit television in two Los Angeles movie theatres and a hotel ballroom . . . Both teams will practice today . . . The Celtics workout again will be closed.

Boston Evening Globe
April 24, 1969

A regulation size 7 NBA leather basketball is nine and a half inches in diameter, 29.5 inches in circumference. A regulation NBA rim, orange, is a circle, eighteen inches wide in its inner diameter, 56.55 inches in circumference, formed by a 5/8-inch diameter steel rod. The rim—also called "the basket," "the hoop," and assorted bad names in times of stress—is mounted ten feet off the ground on a backboard that is six feet wide by three and a half feet high.

The object of the game is to lift the leather ball, inflated to a pressure between 7.5 and 8.5 psi, weighing no more than 22 ounces (1.375 pounds), and propel it through the opening in the steel hoop. The ball is 27 percent as large as the clear area opening, which makes the feat sound easy enough, but often can be quite hard. A perfect placement, dead center, will allow four and a half inches on all sides of the ball. Two balls may not be propelled through the rim/basket/hoop at the same time (a move sometimes mentioned in local folklore), but they can be stuffed next to each other, both wedged inside the rim at the same time.

There are nights, it must be noted, when the ball seems to be heavier than the designated 1.375 pounds, more like a ton, when it is some foreign object invented just to frustrate the common man. A bad meal, a bad night's sleep, a slow-healing injury, a few domestic problems, maybe simply the phase of the moon, will leave a human body tired and out of sync, fighting to propel that nine-inch-diameter ball through that eighteen-inch-diameter steel circle. The game of basketball will be a mystery, a chore, a fiendish puzzle devised by some cruel gym teacher in Springfield, Massachusetts, with spare time and a peach basket.

There are other nights, though, when the ball will be a feather with a steel tip at the end, a dart, flying off the hand with purpose and direction, control and beauty, nights of basketball magic and basketball wonder. This—April 23, 1969, Los Angeles, California—was a night of basketball magic and basketball wonder.

The Lakers' 120–118 win in this first game of the 1969 NBA finals could have been framed and preserved, hung in a gallery under a professionally lettered sign that read THIS IS HOW BASKETBALL SHOULD BE PLAYED. Players flew up and down the regulation court at the Forum, ninety-four hardwood feet long, fifty feet wide, made shots they were supposed to make, dunked on each other, blocked each other's easiest paths, played the game with high-fidelity grace and style.

The lead changed hands twenty-seven times. The game was tied fourteen times. The Lakers had an even 100 shots. The Celtics had 100 shots. Five players on each team scored in double figures. The Lakers were ahead by a point after the first quarter, the Celtics ahead by two at the half, a lead they maintained after three quarters. The Lakers won the game with 38 points in a dramatic fourth quarter, the Celts with 34.

Whew.

The losers still were clawing at the end as Sam Jones hit a bank-shot jumper to cut the margin to a point with a second left. On the inbounds pass, they then whacked Elgin Baylor, whose foul shot created the final score. This was a photo finish. The hometown team was ahead by a nose at the end. That was what the picture would show forever.

"We were fortunate to win a game like that," Jerry West said. "As a sports fan, I wish I could have been a spectator for that one."

On the way to the finals, both the Warriors and the Hawks had double-teamed West the entire way on defense, an attempt to keep him under control while forcing other Lakers to do more on offense than normal. The Celtics' approach was to play straight-up man-to-man, one-on-one, an attempt to shut everyone down, not just the best scorer. This gave West free air, room to maneuver. He went over and around Emmette Bryant, Larry Siegfried, and Don Chaney. Half his shots seemed to go through the steel rim with four and a half inches to spare on all sides.

"Was West the difference?" a reporter asked the Celtics' Russell at the end.

"When the man scored 53 points, you've got to be kidding," the player/coach replied.

"I've never seen West play better," the Celtics' Havlicek said. "Don't forget he had 10 assists. He accounted for 73 points tonight."

The Lakers star said the addition of Chamberlain made his life much easier. Time after time, the Lakers would isolate West one-on-one with whatever troubled soul was guarding him. Then they would watch him go to work. He would beat his man, slice to the basket for a layup, unimpeded by the familiar shot-blocking presence of Russell.

"Wilt freezes him," West said. "He can't contest me that much on drives because of Wilt. He can't afford to leave Wilt to come after me.

What I try to do is look for him first on a drive. If I don't see him, I just forget about him."

Russell did not seem too concerned about all of this. He dissected the mimeographed score sheet and the purple number that impressed him most was the closeness of the final score. The Celtics lost by two points in a close, well-played game. They scored 118 points, enough to win pretty much any NBA game except one where they surrendered 120 points. The adjustments would have to be made on defense.

"We gave up 38 points to the Lakers in the fourth quarter," he said. "That's too much, although we got 34 points ourselves."

West's assists bothered the coach as much as the 53 points.

"We have to cut down on those assists," he said. "If he got 53 points and only two or three assists, that's another 20 points or so they have to come up with."

The Lakers had never won the first game in a playoff series against the Celtics. (They also never had played a first playoff game against the Celtics at home.) This fact was an instant injection of confidence. Old patterns might be changed. The Celtics at the same time were happy that they were a far different team than the one that was blown out by the Lakers, 108–73, the last time the teams met at the Garden. They had given West his 53 points in this one, the most he ever scored in a playoff game, and lost by a basket. Was he going to score 53 points every night? Probably not. Definitely not. That brought confidence right there.

What was one loss in the first game of the playoffs?

"You're never out of a playoffs unless you've lost four games," Havlicek said.

What was one win?

"The way I look at, we got the breaks at the end," Wilt Chamberlain said. "Was this a psychological win? Let's say we're one up with three to play."

The winner really was everyone. In a golf match, there is always the debate about whether a person is playing against his opponent or against the course. In basketball, the game almost always is against the opponent, but tonight it was against the course. And the humans won.

"A game is a game is a game," Red Auerbach said in the Celtics locker room.

(Pause.)
"Didn't Gertrude Stein say that?"

One reminder from the night was that West still was the leading man in this production. Win or lose, the spotlight would shine first on him. That fact had been overlooked in the buildup to the clash between Russell and Chamberlain. The newness of that storyline—these two highest-paid pituitary wonders, these well-crafted basketball giants, meeting in a new circumstance—had created a science-fiction, monster-movie excitement. Forgotten was the baseline drama, the art-film tale of the local hero's eternal quest to yank Excalibur from that stone, to beat the Celtics in a seven-game series, fair and square.

West was the long-suffering local athletic heartthrob, thin and stylish and precise, good-looking, efficient, humble and proud, a Maserati of a man, perfect for star-conscious Los Angeles. Thirty years old, finishing his ninth season, first player drafted when the Lakers moved west from Minneapolis in 1960, he had become the face of the team. He had accumulated a bunch of Chick Hearn nicknames, which included "Zeke from Cabin Creek," a tribute to his West Virginia roots, and "Mr. Outside," to go along with Elgin Baylor's "Mr. Inside," but the one that stuck the most was "Mr. Clutch." He would take the tough shot. He would make the tough pass, grab the tough rebound, guard the tough scorer, win the tough game.

Except when he didn't.

The five losses in the finals to the Celtics were ink blots on his résumé, a scattering of failures that blemished his career. The losses weren't entirely his fault of course—he still was Mr. Clutch to all of Los Angeles—but they brought great sadness to everyone involved. Every season was wonderful until the end. Frustration had followed frustration to create a discouraging pile. No matter how good things ever became in the winter, eyes always searched the sky for trouble in the spring.

"The same old story, Boston," West would say about the finish a year earlier, the 1968 loss in six games, in *Mr. Clutch: The Jerry West Story*, his first autobiography, written with Bill Libby. "I had been in the league eight seasons. We had reached the finals and lost to Boston five times. We walked down to our dressing room, which was closed to the writers and outsiders for a while. We sat there sweaty and sore and sick of losing for a long time."

What would it take to win this thing? How good would it feel?

He could only guess.

"I sat there remembering twice in the game when the ball was on the floor and Siegfried dove for it," West would write. "He didn't just go for it hard—he dove for it. And they're all that way on the Celtics. You can't teach it. Everyone wants to win. It's more fun and pays better. But the willingness to do anything you have to do to win, the willingness to spill your guts, the willingness to sacrifice yourself—this you can't teach and you can't talk into a man."

He had acquired a West Coast sophistication, this shy character from Cheylan, West Virginia, a town whose post office was located in Cabin Creek. He had been a lonely little kid, youngest of six in a big family, a kid who shot baskets by himself, day after day, expecting nothing until, God almighty, he grew six inches between ninth and tenth grade and became a high school star. The rest had been a wonder. Four years at the state university, where he set all the records and was a letter-sweater god. Drafted by the Lakers at number two after the Cincinnati Royals picked Oscar Robertson first.

He was everything the good folk of Los Angeles wanted, a basketball version of Sandy Koufax, Cary Grant in sneakers, almost elegant in the way he played the game. His white skin didn't hurt his popularity, but wasn't the basis for it, either. His ability was undeniable. He was the point guard every kid wanted to be. He was quick and steady, able to make the proper decisions, shoot or pass, stop or drive, at pell-mell speed, surrounded by trouble. His jump shot came out of a textbook. He was, yes, Mr. Clutch.

"The first time you see Jerry West, you're tempted to ask him how things are in Gloccamorra," Jim Murray of the *Los Angeles Times* wrote, trying to describe the beauties of the local man. "The Lakers didn't draft him, they found him under a rainbow. Either that or they left a trail of bread crumbs in the forest and they snapped the cage when he showed up. . . .

"Inch for inch, he's the greatest player in the world. There is no more exciting sight than Jerry West dervish-ing down the court with a basketball, eyes and nostrils flaring, basketball thumping. His shots are a blur."

His disposition seemed as steady as his game. He was the easiest of interviews. Win or lose, he told reporters how he felt. He had an Eagle Scout sort of honesty, hard to find in any setting, particularly hard in a professional sports locker room filled with egos and agendas. Ask him a question, he would provide an answer that came straight from inside his thoughts. No filters were involved. He told you what he felt.

"Is this the best game you've ever played in the playoffs?" he was asked on this night. "It's the most points you've ever scored."

"Scoring's not that big of a thing," he said, staying in perfect character. "The big thing is that we won and I just happened to score a lot. I've had nights where I only scored 15 or 16 points and I've thought I played better all-around than this."

His crusade to win a championship had become an entire city's crusade. He was too good not to win one. Even the Celtics said they felt bad for him when they beat him yet again in the finals the previous spring. Havlicek came to the Lakers' locker room to commiserate. Russell came. Even Auerbach admitted he felt sad—a little bit sad—for Jerry West every time. Now the quest had begun again. Mr. Clutch was three games from making everyone happy. Even, in a weird way, his opponents.

"If we don't beat the Celtics this time," West said in his Eagle Scout honesty, "it will be a crime for the game of basketball."

At the end of the 1969 season, sometime during the coming summer, NBA commissioner Walter Kennedy would decide the league needed a new logo. The old logo was a plain basketball, dull and unimaginative, with the letters "NBA" printed on the front. Kennedy wanted something with more zip, modern, maybe with a touch of red-white-and-blue patriotism on the side. Something like the logo that Major League Baseball introduced at the start of the 1969 season for its one hundredth anniversary, the white silhouette of a batter ready to hit a baseball against a blue-and-red background.

Alan Siegel, a young designer in New York who had overseen the MLB project, had started his own company. Kennedy contacted him. Siegel went to the offices of *Sport* magazine, where he looked at a file of basketball photos. He picked out one of West that was taken by Lakers team photographer Wen Roberts. West was leaning to his right in the photo, but dribbling with his left hand. The photo had balance, symmetry, action. Siegel created a white silhouette of West's figure, added half a background of blue, top to bottom, on the left side, then red on the other half. He added "NBA" in white at the bottom.

"I did the project in twenty to forty minutes," he said.

Kennedy approved the design. There were no focus groups, no company meetings. (The NBA office still had six people, including the commissioner.) West would be the figure in the NBA logo for the start of the next season until . . . well, present day.

There never would be mention of when the picture was taken. (There never would be official recognition, either, that West was the inspiration for the floor-based dribbler in short pants, though everyone who knew basketball knew it was him.) The picture cited most often, though, a perfect match, shows him dribbling at the Forum, gold home uniform, everything the same as the silhouette.

The idea here is that it was taken on April 23, 1969.

Why not?

This was his logo-perfect night.

The crowd for the game was 17,554, a basketball record for the sixteen-month-old Forum. The bright young man was suitably impressed with the surroundings. Like the few bits of Southern California he had seen so far, the Forum seemed as if it had been built last Thursday, everything new and shiny and perfect. Even the people seemed new and shiny and perfect, dressed in variations of golf-course casual, everybody clean and manicured and out for an evening of show-business entertainment.

Simply approaching the building was an experience. Built to fulfill the $16 million vision of Jack Kent Cooke, the fifty-six-year-old chain-smoking, have-a-drink owner of the Lakers, the NHL Kings, and assorted businesses, it shimmered like a commercial mirage in the midst of an asphalt parking-lot desert next to Hollywood Park Race Track. Eighty Romanesque arches, sixty feet tall, dominated the outside of a perfect large white circle. The effect would have pleased George Jetson and Caligula at the same time, space-age modern, but based on the ancient, overstuffed glories of Rome.

"This is fabulous," Cooke said he told architect Charles Luckman when he first saw the design. "That's what we'll call it. The Fabulous Forum."

That was Story One about the derivation of the name.

"This place needs a special adjective, something more than 'The Forum,'" Cooke said at the start of Story Two. He had an audience of one.

"Why don't you call it 'The Fabulous Forum'?" Chick Hearn replied, no thought involved, easy as that.

Cooke immediately loved the name in this preferred version and told Hearn there would be "a little something extra" in his paycheck next week. The "little something extra" turned out to be a wallet-sized picture of the owner himself. This version had a better punch line to it than the first one.

The press entrance to the building strategically was shared with the entrance to the Forum Club, a swank and exclusive place for record and film executives, bankers and bullshitters, stars and character actors, ingénues and tap dancers to gather before and after the athletic dramatics. These people arrived, one by one, pulling up in a sequence of Ferraris and Lamborghinis, the odd Mercedes or two, maybe even a low-rent BMW. Keys were handed to uniformed valet parkers, cars whisked off to somewhere in the macadam desert, occupants left to glide to the next stop in their extraordinary lives. A canopy, leading to the door, showed that the moment was special.

Sportswriters, left at the same entrance by some taxi or minibus, carrying their Olivetti Lettera 32s, moved along with this glamour crowd under the canopy in $40 sports coats, khaki trousers, and Bass Weejun loafers in need of a shine. A certain acceptance of life's inequities was endured. The glamour crowd turned right en masse after entering the building. The writers, spit out like so many watermelon seeds, continued straight into the arena.

The inside was as spectacular as the outside. The seats were color-coded, orange on one side, yellow on the other. There were no balconies. The floor was sunken and the seats rose dramatically on each side of the inside oval, not as high on the ends. The colors of the seats were more muted the higher they went. The effect, first seen by new and unaccustomed eyes, was breathtaking.

"Perhaps two hundred years from now—or even two thousand—people will say that the Forum was one of the finest buildings erected during the twentieth century," Cooke said once between cigarettes and cocktails, or perhaps accompanied by cigarettes and cocktails.

The one disappointment for the bright young man—a major disappointment, at that—was the press seating. The press was located high, high, very high in the stands. In Boston and at most other arenas he had visited, TBYM had sat courtside. He could hear the plays being called, the bumps, the thumps, the exchanged pleasantries when the big men told each other to go fuck themselves. The first time he ever sat in the front row, next to the Detroit Pistons bench, he saw star guard Dave Bing take two steps out of a timeout huddle, turn, and ask coach Donnis Butcher what the Pistons were doing on defense.

"Take the man who takes you," Butcher said, the same defensive call for anyone who ever played pickup basketball of any dimension.

("That's the NBA?" the bright young man wondered. "Take the man who takes you?")

There would be no inside bits of information delivered from the Forum, no reports that Butch van Breda Kolff said, "Clear out and give the ball to Wilt, for Christ's sake." If there were, they would have to be brought to TBYM by a Sherpa guide. The show-biz Mr. Cooke had exiled the press to the cheapest, worst seats in his grand building.

The front rows were for celebrities and high rollers. Jack Nicholson, who would gain notice for *Easy Rider* in the summer of 1969, had not yet become famous enough to settle into his big-time seat next to the visiting bench (pretty much the same seat the bright young man occupied in Boston), but Tony Curtis, Peter Falk, Jerry Lewis, Walter Matthau, Doris Day, and Rhonda Fleming were regulars. The assembled recording and movie executives, the ingénues and bullshitters, would take time out, too, from their Forum Club excess to come down to the front row and watch a bit of basketball.

Cooke once showed a picture of a farm he had bought to *Los Angeles Herald Examiner* sports editor Bud Furillo. The farm looked beautiful, nestled in a valley in front of some very large mountains. Furillo pointed to the top of the largest mountain.

"I guess that's where you'll put the press," he said.

Without replay, without televisions, the game from these press seats was pretty much a mystery. The bright young man started calculating the amount of money his employers had spent to have him sit in the middle of nowhere, unable to see anything. He also calculated how soon he might be fired. Then again, everybody would be fired. The game was a mystery to every sportswriter in these stands.

(Cooke again was ahead of his time. Press seats have been moved farther and farther from the action in all sports. In many arenas, they are next to the championship banners on the ceiling. In many stadiums they are high in the end zone, or deep down the right field line.)

The press seating was why West, at the end, was a godsend. He was patient. He was reflective. There was no great rush to get the interviews done, a nuisance to be handled. This was part of the job. He was very good at all parts of his job.

Chapter 8

OFF DAY:
SPORTS ILLUSTRATED

By Leigh Montville
Staff Writer

LOS ANGELES—The bad omen appeared yesterday in the small drug store on the ground floor of the Airport Marina Hotel where the Boston Celtics are staying.

Bill Russell, in green-and-white basketball suit, stared from the magazine rack. There he was—on the cover of Sports Illustrated.

"Sure, it's a bad sign," Larry Siegfried said to John Havlicek and the rest of the team as it was taken by limousine to a practice at the Forum. "The team that has been on the cover for each of the past two years has lost out in the playoffs.

"Last year, Elgin (Baylor) and Jerry West were on the cover. Two years ago, there was a picture of John. Gunning from the hip."

And now it is Russell. And now, the Celtics are in some trouble already.

They play a game tonight at the Forum that they definitely need to win. Already they are behind the Los Angeles Lakers one game to none in the best-of-seven finals of the National Basketball Assn. playoffs.

A loss tonight would push the momentum in entirely the wrong direction. The Lakers would come into Boston for Sunday afternoon's third game and Tuesday's fourth game without pressure.

They could win one of the two games and have a perfect 3-1 cushion. At worst, they could lose both and still have home-court advantage.

It is a situation the Celtics avoided in their first two playoff series, taking a 3-0 lead on Philadelphia and getting a 2-0 jump on New York. It is a situation they would like to avoid again by winning here tonight.

They took steps in that direction yesterday. A few things were planned to try to stop Jerry West, who scored 53 points and picked up 10 assists in Wednesday's 120–118 Laker win.

"Fifty-three points in a high-scoring game like the one Wednesday are the same as the 35 points Walt Frazier scored when we beat the Knicks, 108–100," player-coach Russell said. "You just take the extra 20 points (in the opposing total) and give them to West.

"In that New York game, though, we shut out their forwards. We didn't do that Wednesday night."

Russell, as he dressed for the practice, did not have to mention that Emmette Bryant (first half) and Sam Jones (second half) did not have defensive success man-to-man against West in Wednesday's game. That was obvious.

"There may be some personnel changes," he said. "That's something we're going to have to talk about and think about.

"One thing I don't want to do, however, is put John Havlicek in the backcourt. He's too valuable to me at forward.

"It didn't get mentioned much, because we lost the game, but John scored 37 points Wednesday night at forward. I'd like to see him there again."

Russell didn't say any more, but he was left with two alternatives. He could put Siegfried, a defensive ballplayer, into a more prominent role. Or he could play the same and enlist more help for Bryant or Jones. Double-teaming West with the ball and leaving Egan, the other guard, open.

"Atlanta, in the semifinals, double-teamed West all the time," the Celtics' Tom Sanders said. "I would think we'll have to do it some also.

"The same thing holds true for Baylor. If he gets hot, no one man can handle him. You have to have help."

Sanders, as he talked, received a heat treatment on his injured back. A hot pack was placed directly in the center of the back.

"I can play," said Sanders, who didn't play at all Wednesday. "It's a question of how mobile I'll be."

Sanders, who has always had success guarding Baylor, is a key to Russell's last-ditch move of putting Havlicek into the backcourt. Sanders could move into the lineup for defense and Bailey Howell, who had shooting problems Wednesday, could shift to the easier side of the forecourt against rookie Bill Hewitt.

THE NOTEBOOK—The Lakers held a light shooting workout at the Forum before the Celtics arrived . . . Neither team is really anticipating the game Sunday, which will be time-lagged by the plane ride Saturday and the one-hour Daylight Savings Time switch to virtually a 10 am start.

"I'm ready to play in the backcourt if Russ calls me," Havlicek said. "The only way it could hurt my offense is if West guards me—and that is usually going to hurt your offense somewhat."

"The breaks just came our way," was Wilt Chamberlain's and just about everybody else's first game observation . . . Chamberlain sustained a slight cut on his hand in the game when he tried to block a Siegfried shot and blocked the rim instead.

Boston Evening Globe
April 25, 1969

—

The four-color cover of the newest edition of *Sports Illustrated* (April 28, 1969) shows Russell in a rare moment of offensive ambition as he prepares to drive toward the basket in the NBA East finals against the Knicks. There is a determination about him as he holds the ball high and starts to dribble and force his way from the foul line to the hoop. The explanatory words are "Boston's Old Guard, The Last Stand."

The title on the inside story on page 24 is ". . . And That Old Celtics Wheel Rolls Again." This is an extension of a dusty quote from Russell when he was at the University of San Francisco and teammate K. C. Jones was ruled ineligible for the 1956 NCAA tournament at the last minute. (Jones had played one game as a sophomore before losing the entire season after an attack of appendicitis. He was allowed to play an extra regular season, but then ruled ineligible for the tournament. A questionable judgment from the NCAA.)

"You change the spokes, but the wheel keeps rolling," Russell said when asked about his teammate's absence. He then led the USF Dons to a perfect 29-0 season and a second-straight NCAA championship.

The present situation somewhat reflects that past. Writer Frank Deford points out the missing player pieces from the previous Celtics championships, notes how they come back in street clothes as spectators to visit when the playoffs arrive, then notes how nothing changes. The Celtics keep winning, a lesson the New York Knicks, who had the audacity to think that the situation might have changed this year, discovered in the past round.

"The Celtics are a fourth-place team that did not even play .500 ball the whole last half of the season," Deford writes. "The regulars average over 31 years of age. That is about three years older than the world champion Detroit Tigers last year, six years older than the (Super Bowl champion) New York Jets. . . ."

Didn't matter.

"Some Celtics play alongside Russell, some sit on the bench, some retire and come back and shake hands," Deford adds. "The spokes change. Each supporting star leaves, as Sam Jones will now, and the soothsayers forecast doom. The wheel keeps rolling."

The jinx, the curse that Siegfried mentions, is a clunky byproduct of sports success. If being on the cover of the weekly magazine is an honor—and it is, an assortment of champions pictured in the publication's fifteen-year history—it also is an invitation to failure. People have dropped passes, lost games and championships, even died after their *SI* cover appearance.

A modest historical beginning came when Eddie Mathews, the Milwaukee Braves third baseman on the cover of the first magazine on August 16, 1954, soon suffered a broken hand and missed seven games. The Braves, who had won nine straight before the cover appeared, also saw that streak ended immediately. A more serious result came when U.S. skier Jill Kinmont crashed during a run at Alta, Utah, and was paralyzed from the waist down the same week her picture appeared on the January 31, 1955, cover. Then Indy 500 winner Bob Sweikert died in a sprint car crash three weeks after he was on the May 28, 1956, cover.

A November 18, 1957, college football cover shouted, "Why Oklahoma Is Unbeatable" and, of course, the Sooners lost that week to Notre Dame, 7–0, to end their record forty-seven-game winning streak. The entire U.S. figure skating team was wiped out in a plane crash in Brussels on the way to the world championships in Prague two days after teen sensation Laurie Owen was featured on the February 13, 1961, cover. Jack Nicklaus was on the June 17, 1963, cover before the U.S. Open, then proceeded to shoot 76 and 77 in the first two days and miss the cut. Golfer Doug Sanders and wife Joan were on the cover on January 22, 1962. Divorced in 1963.

Little attention was paid to the good things that happened after an appearance on the cover, the championships that were won, the records that were set. The bumps were what were important. Havlicek was on the cover two years ago, "gunning from the hip," and the Celtics lost. The Lakers were on the cover last year and they lost. In the preview to the past National Football League season, celebrated middle linebacker Ray Nitschke was on the July 15, 1968, cover and declared that the 1968 Green Bay Packers would be the best team they ever had. The Packers finished 6-7-1, their first losing season in eleven years.

The curse, the jinx, was foolish. Except if you were one of the possible fools.

—

The magazine is just now settling into a position at the front of the field in sports media importance in 1969, a position it will maintain for the next few decades before being pushed to the side, inch by inch, by television, especially ESPN, in the nineties and then by the Internet during the next century. This is the beginning of a thirty-year-plus golden age for *SI,* with its combination of sports, writing, photography, and glossy pages.

Forget the faraway venture-capital future when the magazine will be strip-mined from a weekly to a monthly, left in a lobotomized funk. *Sports Illustrated* is alive here. Exploding.

"It is a quality magazine with quality writers—the type of magazine you expect to find in waiting rooms," even broadcaster Howard Cosell proclaimed in a rare non-caustic moment.

Designed almost as a hobby by founder Henry Luce and Time Incorporated, *Sports Illustrated* didn't turn a profit for its first ten years. A snooty myopia that treated sailing and hunting and squash and bird watching and climbing the Matterhorn as important as fast-balls delivered at high speed under the chins of professional baseball hitters didn't work so well with the mass market. Three dogs, seven horses, a lion, a bull, a rainbow trout, a bowler, a hot-air balloon, and a skin diver appeared on the cover of the magazine in its first year. There were no professional basketball players. None.

The magazine still can show its patrician roots—this issue with Russell on the cover contains an eight-page story about learning how to play tennis with teaching pro Welby Van Horn and another about businessman Charles Engelhard, an owner of racehorses—but the turn toward the future has more than begun. In addition to the Celtics, there are stories about the NHL playoffs, the Indiana Pacers' success in the ABA playoffs, about a weird con man who impersonated skier Jean-Claude Killy, and a six-page spread on the influx of seven young third basemen into the major leagues. (Richie Hebner, Amos Otis, Bill Melton, Bobby Etheridge, Bill Sudakis, Coco Laboy, and Bobby Murcer.)

In this average-sized issue, ninety-six pages, there are thirty-nine full-page ads, eleven half-page ads, a total of fifty-six pages of ads. The companies represented include Sears, Chevrolet, Lincoln Continental. TWA, Magnavox, Zenith, Kodak, Avis, Canadian Club whisky.

The magazine that once lost $26 million for Time Inc. now is the third-largest American newsweekly behind *Time* and *Newsweek*. It is in the midst of a five-year surge to a 2,150,000 circulation and $51 million annual advertising revenue.

Improvements in color technology and printing have brought action shots—like Russell in this one—to the cover instead of that grand succession of dogs, horses, and rainbow trout. The rise of televised games, events, moments, combined with an influx of leisure time in more and more homes, has detonated a spectator sports boom that will grow much larger. The magazine has found its domestic niche, landing every week with the Thursday mail. There is no competition.

The writers—the familiar writers on the magazine—have acquired a status, a long-form excellence that places them above the pound-it-out newspapermen in the profession. George Plimpton, Dan Jenkins, Mark Kram, Ed Shrake, John Underwood, and Tex Maule are sports writing's literary stars. They are paid better, live better, travel everywhere on an unlimited expense account. They ONLY HAVE TO WRITE ONE STORY A WEEK. They are different. They talk different, act different, look different.

Frank Deford, the thirty-year-old writer of the Celtics story, is an up-and-coming example. His name is known. His work is known. The bright young man had spotted him at the New York series, both in New York and in Boston. He was hard to miss. Six feet four, gelled-up hair, dressed like a combination of Edwardian dandy and Wall Street money manager, he rolled through a locker room as if he were an eminence, a visitor from some important office in some important corner of the world. The older sportswriters with their soup-stain sports coats, the younger writers with their Anderson-Little, Robert Hall entry-level coatrack fashion, were only a background. Deford was another flower in that small garden of players and visiting celebrities and maybe a flamboyant few of the owners and maybe a television face or two. Everyone else was a weed.

"Hello, Frank," Bill Russell would say.

"Hello, Russ," Frank would say.

There would be a smile. Two smiles. The two men would talk on the side between each other. They were friendly, if not friends. Frank obviously was different from the members of the normal literary herd. He wasn't what he would become—the most celebrated long-form sportswriter of his time, a writer of eighteen books, nine of them novels, a regular on HBO and National Public Radio, a familiar voice, a familiar figure with a satin pocket handkerchief in a purple velour jacket—but there was little doubt he was on the way.

"The ice will soon be forming on Parry Sound, and within the month it will conquer the green waters that lap at the Thirty Thousand Islands and hold them tight until the thaw, late in April," he had written in an October 17, 1966, profile of Bobby Orr that was one of his first big stories for the magazine. "In this long winter the harbor will, as always, belong to the kids from town and their hockey games. They will play every day—against each other or against the Indian boys from Parry Island who come onto the ice with freshly cut saplings for sticks. The temperature there, 160 miles north of Toronto, falls to 40 below sometimes, and the ice can measure three feet deep. The games on the sound are hard. You don't get to play much unless you can grab the puck and keep it.

"Bobby Orr learned to grab the puck and keep it on Parry Sound. He is only 18 now, starting his rookie year with the Boston Bruins, but many people think that before long he will be controlling games in the National Hockey League as surely as he did against those Indian boys. . . ."

Magic.

The bright young man is jealous of Frank Deford. Can't help it. The jealousy oozes from his pores, would stain his clothes if it were perspiration. He not only wants to be Frank Deford, he has tried. When he graduated from the University of Connecticut in 1965 and decided it was time to conquer the literary world (sports division), TBYM decided that *Sports Illustrated* was the place that deserved his talents best. He didn't know how someone landed a job there, but he knew the magazine was based in New York City and he found a phone number, dialed, and was shuffled to a woman in human resources. We shall call her Ms. Gold.

"How do I get a job with *Sports Illustrated?*" he asked. "I was the editor of my college newspaper."

"First thing you have to do is have an interview with me," Ms. Gold said. "Bring your clippings. Whatever you have."

On the appointed day, the bright young man took a train from New Haven straight to Grand Central Station. He wore his little graduation/business suit. Haircut. Shoes shined. Carried his clippings from that stellar career on the school newspaper in the newly purchased briefcase at his side. He found the Time-Life Building at 1271 Avenue of the Americas, forty-five stories tall, directly across the street from the Radio City Music Hall. His head buzzed.

He found Ms. Gold's office. Was told to wait in one of those chairs over there. Ms. Gold would see him momentarily.

Two other guys also were waiting in the chairs. They were dressed in jeans and clean sweatshirts. They spoke Spanish to each other. Time stretched.

"You waiting for Ms. Gold?" one of the guys eventually asked in English.

"Yes, I am. You too?"

"Yes."

"I'm looking for a job as a sportswriter."

"We're looking to be custodians."

Sigh.

This was not the way to become a writer at *Sports Illustrated*. Was it? Ms. Gold didn't look at those clippings. Everything happened fast. She told the bright young man he should go out and get some experience. End of interview. Next?

He supposes he could tell that story now to Frank and they could get a good laugh, maybe become friends, but he doesn't. He doesn't speak to Frank. He is not afraid of Frank, not really, not overwhelmed. Just doesn't talk. Just watches everything Frank does. Jealousy runs wild. OK, maybe a little bit overwhelmed.

"Russ . . ."

"Frank . . ."

Different.

Even more different is George Plimpton. He not only is going to the games, he is kinda/sorta a member of the Celtics team. Known for his Walter Mitty exploits that included playing quarterback for the Detroit Lions, boxing against former champion Archie Moore, and pitching against a lineup of major leaguers, he had gone through training camp at the start of this season on an assignment for *SI* that probably would be expanded into another book. This could be classified as the ultimate inside knowledge. He was forty-two years old.

"Sam Jones used to get mad about him at training camp," Mal Graham said. "Russell had these layup drills, everybody had to make the layups or everybody would run laps. George would miss a layup and we'd have to run and Sam would be mad. Really mad."

"The last pass I made with the Celtics was to George Plimpton," Rick Weitzman said, a sign that he was going to be cut. "In an exhibition game against Atlanta."

Though he was tall enough at six feet four, slender enough at 180 pounds, Plimpton never had played much basketball on a privileged path that stretched through boarding schools and the private clubs at Harvard. The ball felt strange in his hands, too big to control.

He had worked out with Bill Bradley of Princeton and the Knicks at the New York Athletic Club in preparation for his tryout, dribbling around chairs, learning to stare at Bradley's belly button when attempting to play defense, but being on the floor with the defending NBA champions created a confused static in his head. The six basic plays were memorized, but memorization did not translate to the action on the floor.

"Each one had variations—backdoors, reverses and so on, and while I wrote them down in my notebook, and saw them in my mind's eye as I lay sleepless in my stark hotel room, they vanished utterly on the few occasions Russell sent me out on the floor in scrimmages," he would write. "I would see John Havlicek hold up two fingers as he came down the floor and then something would happen that wasn't in any of my clumsy diagrams. What I did then was start a kind of evasive action, mindlessly running helter-skelter through the pack, trying to 'get open,' hoping in the process to set up involuntary picks and cause chaos in the opposition. My teammates took very little notice of this. They went about their business rather calmly and they would score."

Plimpton fit well with the team when the practices were finished and the six plays didn't count. He had acquired a level of fame. The movie of his book *Paper Lion* was still in the theaters during camp, Alan Alda as the star. He was on talk shows, was on *Playboy After Dark* with Hugh Hefner. He sold Oldsmobiles in a commercial. Four months earlier, June 5, 1968, he was in the kitchen at the Ambassador Hotel in Los Angeles when his friend and presidential candidate Robert F. Kennedy was shot and killed by Sirhan Sirhan. He helped former New York Giants football lineman Rosey Grier wrestle Sirhan to the floor.

He also previously had dealt with the Celtics as a writer. Russell had been chosen as *SI*'s Sportsman of the Year winner for 1968, the last time he had been on the cover. Never a big believer in awards, Russell liked this one. He even appeared at a luncheon at the Harvard Club in Boston to accept the replica Greek amphora vase. Carl Yastrzemski of the Red Sox, the 1967 winner, was in attendance.

"This is the first trophy I will discuss with my children," Russell said. "I want to prepare my children to face the world and I'm working to make a world where they will succeed or fail on their own merits. But succeed or fail, I'll love them. I'm really excited about this award. More than anything I've ever received. It's my kind of thing."

Starting with Dr. Roger Bannister, the Englishman who ran the first mile under four minutes in 1954, names like Stan Musial, Rafer Johnson, Arnold Palmer, Pete Rozelle, and Sandy Koufax also on the list of recipients, the award had been given to "the athlete or team whose performance that year most embodies the spirit of sportsmanship and achievement." The social upheavals of 1968—the assassinations of Kennedy and Dr. Martin Luther King, the following riots in the ghetto streets of America—seemed to add significance. Russell was a perfect choice, both as a player and a coach.

"This award means to me, 'You've been a man. We respect you,'" Russell said. "I knew I was a great athlete a long time ago. A lot of people knew it. But not a lot of people know I am a man. Not a tall man, or a black man. Not a basketball player. Being a man. That's what this is all about. . . .

"I tried to count my trophies once. I got bored. They tend to lose their significance. But this trophy really means something. It is about people."

Plimpton wrote the story for the December 23, 1968, issue. He spent a day at Russell's house, noted the posters of Allen Ginsberg and Marlon Brando on the rec room wall, the grand piano in the living room, the filled bookcase stretching from floor to ceiling, the

African artifacts on the wall, the four thousand phonograph records, mostly jazz, the seven or eight birdhouses, and the swimming pool in the backyard. Oh, and his wife and three kids and the Lamborghini in the garage.

Part of the story, too, were quotes from different Celtics about their coach and star player. Different quotes.

"He's nicely hooked on clothes," Tom Sanders said in the best one. "Last year it was Nehru jackets and love beads—his kick as an overgrown love child. This year it's Africa—caftans and sandals. We shake our heads when we consider what he might turn up in next year."

Plimpton obviously is another character the bright young man would like to meet, but doesn't know what to say. He watches him move easily around the team in the Airport Marina lobby. Jeez, the guy just came back with Auerbach from playing doubles tennis with Pancho Segura and actor Ray Danton somewhere in Beverly Hills. (Pancho Segura!) (Beverly Hills!) (Tennis!) How does somebody get into that level of familiarity?

There is a moment, the bright young man in conversation in the lobby with Havlicek, when Plimpton approaches. No introductions are made.

"John," Plimpton says on this off day, "do you know Candice Bergen?"

"No," Havlicek replies.

"Well, she's an actress out here. I'm going to a party at her house tonight. Do you want to come?"

Havlicek declines.

There is a moment here when the bright young man could say, "I know who Candice Bergen is. And sure, I would love to go to a party at her house," but it disappears quickly. Plimpton is off to somewhere else.

Oh well.

There will be a pleasant enough end to this story. The bright young man will wind up at *Sports Illustrated*. Almost twenty-five years after he was sent back to New Haven by the efficient but diabolical Ms.

Gold, he will get a call from *SI* editor Mark Mulvoy that is as surprising as reading the proper sequence of numbers on a lottery ticket. Out of nowhere, just like that, TBYM is on the staff.

He will write ONE STORY PER WEEK. Doors will open easier. He will stay in great hotels, will send hearty expense accounts home. A photographer with him will rent twelve camels for the basketball team from Cameroon at the pyramids in Egypt, then will send the expense account home. He will live the *SI* life. Yes, he will deal with that *SI* jinx that is under consideration in the little drugstore at the Airport Marina Hotel. He will deal with it up close.

On one occasion, he will be assigned to write a long profile—a back-of-the-magazine "bonus piece"—on relief pitcher Lee Smith of the St. Louis Cardinals. He will travel to St. Louis, meet the future Hall of Fame flamethrower at his locker to set up a time for the interview. Turns out, there will be no time. There will be no interview.

"I don't want any story," Lee Smith will say. "Because of the *Sports Illustrated* jinx."

"There is no such thing as the jinx," the bright young (he is not as young now) man will counter quickly. "That's a myth. . . ."

"No."

The editors back at 1271 Avenue of the Americas, directly across from Radio City Music Hall, will not believe this exchange took place when the bright young man calls. They will send him back to ask again.

"Lee . . ."

"No . . ."

"We won't put the story on the cover."

"No . . ."

This will go on for three days. The bright young man will return home. No story.

On another occasion, he will be assigned at the Barcelona Olympics in 1992 to write a story on swimmer Jenny Thompson for the cover. Nineteen years old, she was supposed to win as many as five gold medals at the Games. The first one would be the important one for *SI*. She was swimming the 100-meter freestyle in the first weekend. She already was the world record holder from the trials in Indianapolis. This was perfect timing. She could be wearing that red-white-and-blue swimsuit on the cover as the Games progressed for the next two weeks.

The bright young man planned in advance. He met up with her family before the final, grabbed a bunch of background notes, went with everybody to the swimming pool to watch the race. One of her brothers had a video camera to record the moment. He decided he was too shaky to hold the camera. Would the writer for *SI* do it? No problem.

The focus was narrow. The writer from *SI* could see only one lane, Jenny's lane. He was at the close end. The race would be two lengths of the pool, out and back, starting and finishing in front of him.

"Bang."

Jenny was swimming, churning up that froth. Her family was cheering.

"Go, Jenny. Go, Jenny. Jenny, go . . ."

Jenny kept churning up that froth.

"Go, Jenny . . . go . . . Jenny . . . go . . ."

Jenny kept churning, but the family cheering slowed somewhere before the end, then simply died. There was cheering from the rest of the stands a half beat, maybe a full beat before Jenny touched the finish line. Second. Silver. The winner was Zhuang Yong from China.

The bright young man handed the camera back to Jenny's brother, no words exchanged. He slipped off to the side and wandered to the pressroom. A kid from Princeton named Nelson Diebel, not a favorite, captured the men's breaststroke a little later in the night. Nelson became the story. Nelson became the cover. Jenny was jinxed before she ever had the picture taken. She did win two gold medals in Barcelona, both on relays, but finished fifth in the 50-meter freestyle and did not qualify for the final in the 200.

The bright young man would work for *SI* for eleven years. He was hired in the summer of 1989 when the sportswriting business was in a grand upheaval. Frank Deford had left the magazine to become the editor in chief of *The National*, a daily national sports newspaper that would make its debut in January 1990. The bright young man didn't think about the fact for a while, but one day he put the happenings together and figured out that, yes, he had been hired to replace Frank Deford. How about that?

Then he realized that Rich Hoffer, formerly of the *Los Angeles Times,* had been hired at the same time. This was sort of a package deal. Rich Hoffer and the bright young man together were hired to replace Deford. How about that? The bright young man had been hired to replace half of Frank Deford.

That somehow felt just right.

Chapter 9

GAME TWO

Celts Bow to Lakers Again, 118–112

By George Sullivan
Boston Herald-Traveler Staff Writer
INGLEWOOD, Calif.—The Celtics led in every period last night, but were stopped 118–112 by the Los Angeles Lakers whose captain, Elgin Baylor, converted six free throws in the final minute at the Forum.

As a result, the series heads back to Boston for tomorrow afternoon's third game at the Garden with the Lakers ahead, 2-0, in the best-of-seven series to determine the National Basketball Association champion.

This was a frustrating occasion for the Celtics. They were in front, 26–16, in the first quarter and 81–71 in the third and were riding on a 108–104 advantage into the final four minutes.

Baskets by Johnny Egan on a sneakaway and Baylor from in close created a deadlock. The Celtics had several attempts at a floor goal yet could not connect.

Baylor broke the tie with 2:32 to go. Bill Russell tied it again for Boston, after which Baylor and John Havlicek traded hoops.

With the score tied at 112–112, Tom Sanders was guilty of a pushing foul on Baylor. Elgin converted both with 42 seconds to go. Baylor hit on two more with nine seconds left and added another pair with one second remaining.

Baylor made 18 of his 32 points in the frenzied fourth quarter. He made the last 12 for his side.

Jerry West was high scorer for the Lakers again, netting 41 points. Individual laurels, however, went to Havlicek, whose point total was 43.

In the battle between the big centers, Russell had 21 rebounds and nine points against 19 rebounds and four points for Wilt Chamberlain.

The Celts, winner of the NBA crown in 10 of the past 12 seasons, have never trailed by as much as 2-0 in 29 playoff series in their championship era.

The Lakers went to the free throw line 20 more times than the Celtics. The Lakers converted 38 of 48 foul tries, the Celtics settled for 20 of 28.

Tom Sanders reported his aching back improved before the game. But, Siegfried's pulled hamstring muscle, suffered earlier in the playoffs, is giving him trouble again . . . Both teams enplaned for Boston this morning and are scheduled to arrive in the early evening . . . Both tomorrow's and Tuesday's games at the Garden are sold out.

Last night's sellout here was closed circuit televised into three local outlets. Wednesday's closed-circuit attracted 2200 total at two locations . . . Wilt Chamberlain and Mel Counts are the only two Lakers to have played on an NBA champion—Chamberlain once with the 76ers (1967), Counts twice with the Celtics (1965 and 1966) . . . Only four Celtics have not been on an NBA titlist—Em Bryant, Jim Barnes, Don Chaney and Rich Johnson—all first-year Celtics.

Red Auerbach is exploiting the mid-70s temperatures here to prime his tennis game with actor Ray Danton his latest opponent. Arnold won't say who won the match . . .

Celts ballboys, Skip Welsh and Jimmy Jackson, both of
Chelsea, are on the trip . . . So is Rev. John Creed of St.
Margaret's Church in Saugus, who has been part of the
Celtics family since he was a South Shore schoolboy and
George Plimpton, who is doing a sequel to his "Paper
Lion" bestseller with the Celts . . . Going into last night's
game, Celtic statistical leaders for 12 playoff games were
John Havlicek with a 25.1 scoring average and Bill Russell
with a 20.8 rebound average . . . In the Lakers' 12 playoff
games, West is averaging 28.8 points, Chamberlain 24.3
rebounds.

Russell conducted post-game interviews mostly in one-
word answers, but would not don the crepe. Asked if he
was concerned being down 0-2 in the series, the Celtics
player-coach answered, "Not really." . . . Congratulated
on his 43-point performance, Havlicek said: "Don't talk
about me when we lose. It means nothing." . . . "I'm not
discouraged because both games could have gone either
way. What we've got to do is sustain our momentum when
we get an 8 or 9 point lead. Other than that, what can I
say?" . . . Havlicek had nothing but praise for West, Baylor
and Egan. "Johnny hit some big shots—some from way
out, too, the ones you want him to take. I guess we'll have
to cover him closer."

West labeled the game "just fantastic." The Laker
ace added: "The pressure is on them now. They can't
afford to lose another. We were fortunate to win both.
With the bounce of the ball they could have gone either
way . . ." Asked about the pressure now on the Celtics,
Chamberlain responded: "But they respond to pressure
pretty good."

Egan quoted on his 26 point performance: "It was a
great thrill, but my biggest won't come until we win the
fourth game." Asked what the difference has been for
the Lakers, the former Providence star answered: "We're
coming through with the clutch hoops." Asked what he
thought of the Lakers' 2-0 advantage, Cambridge's Billy
Hewitt said, "We're in beautiful shape."

Van Breda Kolff refused to make any predictions
on the series. The Lakers coach branded the game
"amazing," adding, "in fact, it's been two terrific games."
VBK has no fear playing in Boston tomorrow. "We always
play well in Boston, though we may get wiped out this
time. Who knows? But I don't mind playing there. In
fact, I don't care where we play. We've got to get better
rebounding defensively. They shouldn't be getting as
many second shots as they have been." On Egan: "He's a
good little boy and has made some key buckets."

Many Celtics were unhappy about the differential in
free throws between the teams . . . Nelson was knocked
woozy when Chamberlain's chin caught him on the top
of his head while Don was scoring from underneath with
8:36 remaining. He received six stitches afterwards . . .
The Lakers also had a casualty in Hewitt . . . The rookie
from Rindge Tech received a five-stitch cut on his chin in
the first half . . .

April 26, 1969

Elgin Baylor was writing a diary from the Lakers' point of view. The
finished product wouldn't be shown to the public until the July issue
of *Sport* magazine, but he was writing down his thoughts (or probably
telling them to a ghost writer) after each game. He had been duly satisfied with the result of the first game, but admitted he was nervous
about this one.

Losing the second game would be like losing serve. The first game
win would mean nothing. The Celtics, at 1-1, would have an infusion
of spunk that would make them peskier than ever. The mathematics
now would be on their side.

"On our day off, I realized how important this second game was
going to be," Baylor wrote. "The Celtics' objective in the first two
games is to get a split. If they managed to do it, that meant we'd be
going to Boston for two games and if they turned out to be as tough
at home as they usually are, our loss of this second game might give
them a chance to make it 3-1 before we got back to LA again. You
can't let that happen."

That was why he was a happy man when the Lakers won, 118–112, and kept the percentages friendly. The Celtics now were in the weird spot, 0-2, rosary beads and worry, the specter of failure running through their heads with heavy shoes. They had to be perfect in two straight games simply to be even in the series.

"The Celtics are great competitors, but I was thinking afterward that we were real discouraged after losing two close games in Boston at the start of the playoffs [in other years], and maybe they're in the same position now," Baylor wrote. "The thought occurred to me that the Celtics probably can't play any better than they've played in the first two games. But then again, we probably can't play any better, either."

This game was Baylor's personal triumph, his name superimposed on the result. He broke it open at the end, scored the final 12 straight points—six of them on foul shots—to close out the account. He had 32 points, with 10 rebounds and 5 assists in thirty-three minutes on the floor.

For Lakers fans, this was an extra delivery of good news. Baylor had been a worry for most of the season. The national idea that the addition of Wilt Chamberlain gave the team three bona fide superstars was a stretch to the day-to-day followers of the team. They knew Baylor wasn't the player he once had been. He was thirty-four years old, only seven months younger than Bill Russell. This was his eleventh year in the league, and while he was still a solid, serviceable player, the spectacular parts of his game had been removed by injuries and team doctor Robert Kerlan's scalpel.

His career was discussed in Before and After terms. In the Before, he arguably was the best player who ever had dribbled a basketball. He was almost an extraterrestrial wonder, seen only in comic books or that movie about Mary Poppins, the first player who could fly. He would lift into the air, guarded by two defenders, everyone leaving the floor at the same time. The two defenders then would come back down, same as the apple from the tree in Isaac Newton's backyard. Baylor would hang for an extra moment, seemed like an eternity, finish his business with the basketball, then descend.

Jeremiah Tax described this revolutionary style of offensive work in detail in "Bunyan Strides Again," an article in the April 6, 1959, edition of *Sports Illustrated,* the last month of Baylor's debut season. The description was a primer on how the game would be played in forty, fifty, sixty years.

"For spectators, probably the most pleasure-yielding move this graceful young man makes comes when he brings the ball upcourt alone and, unable to spot a free teammate, decides to work his way toward paydirt without help," Tax wrote. "He turns his back to his defensive man and begins a series of rhythmic dribbling feints from side to side, all the while sliding steps closer to the basket, protecting the ball with elbows and shoulders. If another opposing player moves in to double-team him, Baylor leaps high and hits his teammate with marvelous accuracy. If the defensive man gets no help, Baylor nearly always drives him, with continuous feints, to distraction and an error, and slips by for a twisting lay-up. In the climactic move, he hangs in mid-air seemingly for long seconds while he makes up his mind whether to shoot or pass off, so that to the very end the defense is mystified. It is the kind of man-to-man situation that brings out the best in Baylor and epitomizes even for the casual onlooker the superlative display of skills possessed by this great athlete."

Wouldn't this be a perfect description of Michael Jordan at work? Of LeBron James? Of the latest best kid on the neighborhood high school team, the kid who is filling up his desk drawer with letters from famous colleges? The hidebound patterns diagrammed by coaches did not have to control the game. That was the lesson from Elgin Baylor. There was room for individual innovation, athleticism. Give the ball to Elgin. That was a great play right there. Get out of the way. Let him go to work.

"I don't figure out in advance what I'm going to do," he said. "I react to what the defense does."

He was six feet five, not big at all in basketball terms for a forward, but his jumping ability and strength at 225 pounds made him a strong rebounder. From the outside, he had helped popularize the jump shot, the most revolutionary change in the game. He wasn't the first player in the NBA to jump when he took a one-handed shot, but he was one of the first, and when he jumped there weren't many people who could stop him. Play back and he would hit the jumper. Play close and say good-bye. Again, he was a look into the future.

"The biggest problem guarding him was the second shot," the Celtics' Don Nelson, one of Baylor's assigned defenders, said. "He would take a shot, miss, and just charge past you to the basket. Get his own rebound. Make the layup. He would do that all the time."

Drafted out of the University of Seattle at the end of his junior year with the first pick in 1958, signed for $20,000 (a big contract), he was the last hope of Minneapolis Lakers owner Bob Short to keep his team in his home city. The Lakers had finished last in the previous season, a 19-53 record, lost a lot of money. The arrival of Baylor was celebrated with a parade to opening night with the players in National Guard jeeps, coach John Kundla in a tank, and the Lakerettes, a dance team ready to perform during timeouts.

The new man did not disappoint on the floor. The team finished 33-39, upset the St. Louis Hawks in the West to have the right to lose to the Celtics in four straight in the finals. He was second in the league in scoring, third in rebounds, rookie of the year. The Lakers would, indeed, leave for Los Angeles after his second year, but he was on his way.

He scored 71 points in a game against the Knicks in his third year, a record at the time for points in a game. He scored 61 in the fifth game of the finals against the Celtics in his fourth year, a finals record that still stands. He averaged 19.8 rebounds per game in the '60–61 season, a remarkable figure for someone six feet five. He averaged 38.3 points per game in '61–62, a remarkable figure for anyone of any size.

"Pound for pound, no one was ever as great as Elgin Baylor," Tom Hawkins, teammate for six seasons, opponent for four, would tell the *San Francisco Examiner* in the distant future. "Elgin certainly didn't jump as high as Michael Jordan. But he had the greatest variety of shots as anyone. He would take it in and hang and shoot from all these angles. Put spin on the ball. Elgin had incredible strength. He could post up Bill Russell. He could pass like Magic and dribble with the best guards in the league."

"Who do I think was the greatest?" Oscar Robertson, the Hall of Fame guard, would say in that same distant future. "This may shock you: Elgin Baylor. He did so many great things. Nobody could guard him, playing in the forward spot. I'd love to see some of today's greats playing against Elgin. They couldn't guard him. Nobody could."

This was the Before.

The After began to arrive during the '63–64 season, when pain in both of his knees started to restrain the moves he could make, temper the explosions. The pain grew worse in '64–65, but still was manageable until the top third separated from the rest of his left kneecap in the first game of the playoffs against the Baltimore Bullets. This sent him to surgery, followed by self-doubt. He was not the player he was. Never would be.

His numbers edged down. The man who once upon a time averaged 19 rebounds per game now averaged 10. His 38 points per game became 24. He was a good player, yes, but he was not the best player ever to play the game. The '68–69 season, third year after the operation, was part of this. His explosive game was not resurrected by the arrival of Wilt. If anything, it was restricted when Wilt set up his store underneath the hoop and blocked Baylor's path to the basket.

In a nod to the great days, the Lakers held an Elgin Baylor Night on March 21, 1969, before the next-to-last game of the season, the same way the Celtics held a Sam Jones Night two weeks earlier in Boston. Baylor's wife, Ruby, and his two children, Alan (nine) and Allison (five) were in attendance as were his parents, who flew into L.A. from Washington, D.C. The gift was a car and there were ovations and speeches, the usual stuff, and everything about his career seemed to hover on the verge of past tense.

"He's the most inspirational person I've ever seen play basketball," Jerry West said. "And more than that, he's quite a man."

"At the time I thought the operation would enable Elg to become a part-time player . . . stretch out his career a bit longer," Dr. Kerlan said. "The fact that he's playing full-time and so effectively amazes me."

The Lakers went into the playoffs, escaped embarrassment in six games with the Golden State Warriors, then dispatched the Atlanta Hawks in five games, and in that fifth game, an intriguing thing happened: Elgin Baylor was great again.

"Do you believe in ghosts?" *Los Angeles Times* columnist Jim Murray asked after the home team whipped the Hawks, 104–96. "Do you believe the dead can walk? Do you believe they can run? Hang in the air with a jump shot? . . . Well, it's time somebody got a wooden pike and a prayer book and got down to the Inglewood Forum. People swear they saw the late Elgin Baylor haunting the place in broad daylight the other day."

Baylor was 14-of-18 from the floor in that game against Atlanta, scored 29 points, had 11 rebounds, 12 assists, yes, a triple double. He was his old, wonderful self, the superstar who had arrived in a gift box from Minnesota when pro basketball hit the West Coast.

"Yes, I've been sort of hesitant lately," he said, reminded that he had averaged only 12.2 points per game in these playoffs. "You know I haven't been taking too many shots and a lot of shots I normally would take, I passed up . . . Yes, you might say it was a lack of confidence.

"But I was getting pretty good shots (tonight) and I was pretty sure they eventually would go in."

The one good night had led to another and now another. In a Best Supporting Actor role behind West's 53-point extravaganza in the first game of the Celtics series, he had scored 24 points, grabbed 8 rebounds, added 5 assists. Played forty minutes. Now, two nights later, he scored 32 points, added 10 more rebounds, 5 more assists, shot 11-for-15 in thirty-three minutes.

The Lakers had gone ahead two games to none for the first time in their playoff history against the Celtics, and one of their best players had returned from the half-light and moved back to the center of the stage. Things looked very good indeed.

"We've got those two now," Baylor wrote in his diary of the first two games, "and their job is going to be all the harder."

The Celtics would need the rosary beads this time.

The report at the beginning of this chapter from George Sullivan of the *Boston Herald-Traveler* only hints at the performance of Baylor and the details of the game. Written for the morning paper on the tightest of deadlines, the action finished after 1 a.m. EST, the story starts with the score and some quick facts, then merges into some pregame notes, sent earlier. Then at the end, the notes turn back to the game. Sullivan has been able to visit the locker rooms, return to a pay phone, and dictate some added quotes, probably straight off his notebook and into the final edition.

If a reader sees only a morning paper, this is the mishmash that will have to sustain him. He will have to fill in the details from friends who have listened to Johnny Most, other friends who have talked to other friends, etc., second- and thirdhand reports.

Working for a morning paper was hard. Time and circumstance were perpetual enemies. The bright young man would wish for all his newspaper days that some editor would insert in agate type above all stories like this: "The writer had only fifteen minutes to compile this report. While he (or she) was writing, a reporter to the left of him (or her) in the press box spilled a diet Coca-Cola over his (or her) scant notes and a reporter to the right hummed an incoherent tune while he (or she) typed and someone with a broom from a cleaning crew asked him (or her) to please raise their feet. Shakespeare himself would have had problems in this situation."

Sullivan is the bright young man's main competition. Eddie Gillooly from the tabloid *Record-American*, the third paper in Boston, always is typing a story. The *Record* has multiple editions, one after another, so this story will replace the last story, which replaced the story before that. Gillooly always is too busy to search for new detail. Sullivan has more time. He uses that time to talk to more people, hunt more angles, gather more bits of information.

A Boston University graduate, a former Marine, a family man, he has a doggedness that is impressive. He is the slowest of writers, still scratches out his words by hand on a yellow legal pad, then copies them on a typewriter. Nobody else does this. Nobody. His game stories, especially from a situation with tough deadlines, are restricted by this extra step through the legal pad. He always is slow. Thorough, but slow.

His strength is in his notes columns. Nobody in Boston writes better notes columns than George Sullivan. They are mosaics of facts, opinions, rumors, a couple of laughs, and breaking news that can be small, medium, or sometimes extra large. He brings that same yellow legal pad with him everywhere, writes down everything he hears or sees.

Growing up in Cambridge, he spent at least one season as a water boy for the Harvard football team and became friendly with a running back reserve named Robert Kennedy. Later, he was a batboy for the visiting teams at Fenway Park and became friendly with a left fielder for the Red Sox named Ted Williams. He sometimes would get rides home from the games by Williams, who would shout out "Thanks, George, for that tip about choking up on the bat. Helped a lot," just loud enough for the neighborhood kids on the corner to hear.

Sullivan's sense of local history and local importance is a daily background discomfort to the bright young man, who had neither. The *Herald-Traveler* writer would see things, know things the bright young man would miss. Red Auerbach is playing tennis with Ray Danton? The Celtics ball boys are here? Father John Creed? The mosaic was a constant problem.

What would George do next?

(His long notes column for the next day would have a headline that read "Celts' Bailey Howell Mulls Retiring." Howell? Retiring? The bright young man had no idea about any mulling taking place. Another note would say Jack McMahon, coach of the San Diego Rockets, predicts the Celtics still will win the series, despite trailing, 2-0. "It's spelled R-u-s-s-e-l-l," McMahon declares. "The big guy obviously wants this one and I've never seen him denied anything he's wanted. Have you?" Jack McMahon? He was at the first game? Where was he? What does he look like?)

An important part of the day on the road will be calling home to find out what George wrote, what Eddie wrote, what Bob Sales wrote. George is the biggest worry. A nuclear bomb—OK, a big Boston basketball story—might have exploded. The bright young man would be an obvious casualty.

There was limited time for the bright young man to explore the local landscape during the California days—no Hollywood, no Rodeo Drive, no UCLA, no Dodger Stadium—but he did spend an afternoon at Venice Beach. How did he get there? Who was he with? Lost details. The beauty of Venice Beach was that it wasn't far from the Airport Marina. Maybe he simply took a cab.

The beach was honky-tonk wonderful. Roller skaters came past in bikinis. Surfer dudes drove around with their boards on top of their wood-sided station wagons. T-shirts and perfume and cheap shit were for sale everywhere, toys that would break as soon as you got them home. There was a bookstore. There were places to buy beer. Counterculture drifters stumbled along, searching for whatever they were searching for. Sports, games, were everywhere. There was outdoor weightlifting. (Outdoor weightlifting!) There was some weird tennis-like game played with paddles that everyone seemed to know how to play. Handball. Beach volleyball. A guy juggled an orange, a baseball, and a bowling ball. He was not as good as the guy who juggled the three chain saws, all running. Or the guy who ate fire.

This was California to an East Coast mind. Perfect. The map of the United States had been tilted every now and then throughout history and all the free spirits rolled across the country and landed here in the sunshine and incipient fog. This was the picture, the dream. Famous people shot movies here. Perfect.

Eighteen years later the bright young man would be asked to write about all this for *Sports Illustrated*. "Surf's Up" would be the headline on the cover with a picture of a surfer, hanging ten or whatever surfers did. Sport in California was the subject. TBYM had some experience in the state by now, knew some different places to go, but still headed straight for Venice Beach to interview those weightlifters, those paddle tennis players, maybe the chain-saw juggler. This was the perfect start.

He walked and jogged up and down Ocean Front Walk, all the way to Santa Monica and back. There was a special lane for skaters, delineated in public-works paint. He thought up a couple of lines for his story. *Southern California is not a banquet, it is an outdoor barbecue. Every day is like a day off. Darkness turns to light.* There was a theme.

Taking a break from his labors, he sat on the bleachers next to one of the side-by-side Venice Beach regulation basketball courts, half looking at his notes, half looking at the Pacific Ocean, maybe just daydreaming. A young guy came over and asked if the bright young man wanted to play basketball. They had nine players of various ages, ethnicities, and heights. They could use one more.

Sure.

Maybe this could be part of the story.

The bright young man—now transformed into a middle-aged worker, father of two, owner of a mortgaged home in the Boston suburbs—checked out the competition. Everyone seemed playground normal, except for one tall African American guy, maybe six feet seven, maybe taller than that. His age was hard to figure. Dissipation muted the clues. He could have been anywhere from late twenties to early fifties. He had dreadlocks that were filled with sand and dirt, as if he had been sleeping outside. He had ragged shorts, ragged sneakers. He was thin. There was little doubt that a Rose Bowl parade of chemicals had passed through his body for a number of years, little doubt that the parade was far from finished. He was drinking some weird concoction from a glass jar.

"This guy could be really good," middle-aged TBYM said to himself, thinking about a story of some Division I All-American who had hit hard times, but still could play some decent ball when he tried.

"This guy could also be really bad," middle-aged TBYM added, thinking that the chemical parade had just overwhelmed the big man.

The short answer, soon determined, was: terrible.

Passes bounced off the big man's hands. He couldn't or wouldn't jump. His shots didn't come close to the hoop. He was a jingle-jangly mess, even though he was at least half a foot taller than everyone else. Never was a factor until he finally grabbed a rebound and shouted. The score was 5–2 or something like that in an eleven-basket game.

Shouted?

"STOP," he shouted, maybe screamed.

"STOP," he repeated for the hard of hearing.

Everybody stopped. Everybody stared. The big man clearly was bothered. No, he was angry. Pissed. More than pissed.

"The next person who touches my ass is going to have to FUCK ME," he said.

What was that?

"The next person who touches my ass is going to have to FUCK ME," he repeated.

Yes.

Everybody stared. Everybody looked at everybody else. Everybody stared some more. This was not typical basketball dialogue. Nobody moved. Silence. Silence. Silence.

"Who touched your ass?" one of the other players finally said.

The big man replied in an angry hurry.

"HE KNOW WHO HE BE," the big man said.

Everybody stared. Everybody looked at everybody else.

The game was resumed in more silence. He knew who he be? Who? The big man set up shop near the basket, big man territory, and no one came close to him. It was as if he was radioactive. Eleven baskets were scored by one of the teams. (Probably the big man's.) The game was finished. Everybody faded from the court. There was no next. The big man disappeared.

The middle-aged version of TBYM picked up his notebook from the metal bleachers, went back to his wanderings. He wanted to put the story in his story, but couldn't find a way. The swear word would never pass the many *SI* editors. This was a shame. The big man with the dirt-filled dreadlocks, with the weird concoction in the glass jar, was a perfect representative of Venice Beach.

This was California to an East Coast mind.

Chapter 10

OFF DAY: BOSTON GARDEN

Thousands of persons from all parts of New England are expected to attend the dedication tonight of the Boston Garden, superimposed on the new North Station, where the Crosscup-Pishon Post, American Legion, will stage its fourth annual boxing tournament. The Boston and Maine Railroad has made special arrangements to handle crowds which are expected to come to the arena by train.

The lighting and ventilating arrangements in the arena are perfect, so that smoking can and will be permitted during the show. The ring will be found erected upon the middle of the floor, surrounded by choice floor seats, while the remainder of the audience will be in the fixed seats in the banks surrounding the floor, affording a clear, unobstructed view of the ring for all.

The seating capacity is sufficient for 17,500 persons. The entrance and exits are commodious and all sufficient for a speedy and safe filling of the arena. There are no stairs to climb, only long gradually inclined ramps to walk over and leave the arena.

The entire structure is fireproof. Monster electric signs on the roof of the building are visible from miles around on all sides, so the building will be easy to find.

A police detail of approximately 75 men, many of them World War veterans, who are giving of their services so that the Crosscup-Pishon benefit fund may be larger, will be on duty tonight to handle the crowd expected at the opening.

Ordinarily, police detailed to handle the crowd at a private function are paid for their extra work. In view of the fact that the affair tonight is for charity, Supt. Michael H. Crowley offered to ex-service men the chance of working on the detail without pay, believing that many of them would be glad of the opportunity to assist in the raising of the fund for their former comrades. Many of the veterans volunteered and the rest of the detail was made up of other men.

Unknown,
Boston Globe
Nov. 17, 1928

The Garden—the Boston Garden to the rest of the world to keep it separate from New York's Madison Square Garden—had become a character in all the Celtics' success. Especially against the Lakers. This was where Boston championships were won. This was where the Lakers' thoughts of championships had ended.

Point of view was everything.

The building was forty-one years old now. Hard years. In a cramped and shopworn corner of the city, one flight up from the train station, surrounded by elevated subway tracks and an elevated highway that kept sunshine and clean air at a distance, the place was sports' version of an Edward Hopper painting. Any ideas of luxury—"the lighting and ventilating arrangements in the arena are perfect"—had been replaced by a sad acceptance. This was the place where the games were played, the events were held. Take it or leave it.

The Lakers had played in five NBA finals here without success. Three of the series had ended right on this parquet floor, followed by a cross-country trip to figure out what went wrong. No good things ever had happened for the Lakers here. None that the Lakers could remember.

Now they were back again. This was pretty much the most un-California place in the world. The Sports Arena, the rental home the Lakers had left to move to the Forum, was only ten years old. How sick was that? After the Forum, visiting this place was like going to Paul Revere's house or some other ancient Boston stop on the red-brick Freedom Trail.

"The first time I went to the Boston Garden, I went with Chick Hearn and a couple of people," Steven Bisheff of the *Los Angeles Herald Examiner* said. "I kept thinking they were playing a joke on me as we were walking. They said the Boston Garden was on top of a train station. The Boston Garden is on top of a train station? I didn't believe them. They were just laughing at me."

Built in 1928 for $10 million by New York investors, the arena was pretty much a replica of Madison Square Garden. The plan was to build Art Deco replicas of MSG in six cities around the country, pieces of New York for everyone, but the Great Depression intervened and the plan went no further. The replica now had outlived the original, because the old Madison Square Garden on Eighth Avenue had been replaced in 1968 by the new Madison Square Garden on Thirty-Third Street in New York.

Calvin Coolidge, Franklin Roosevelt, Winston Churchill, and John F. Kennedy all had spoken here. Aimee Semple McPherson had led prayers here. Judy Garland, Rudy Vallee, and Perry Como had sung here. James Brown had put on a memorable show a year ago, televised live as a special on local PBS station WGBH the night after Martin Luther King was assassinated, a show that kept the city calm when riots broke out across the country. Sonja Henie skated here. Emmett Kelly clowned. Gene Autry did Gene Autry cowboy stuff.

If the Fabulous Forum was time travel into a Tomorrowland kind of Disney future, the Garden was a walk down the stairs into the cluttered carnival past. Or up the stairs. Up a bunch of stairs. Or up a ramp.

John Havlicek always liked to describe his first views of his new home. He arrived in Boston at eleven o'clock at night from the 1962 College All-Star game in Kansas City as the Celtics' number-one draft choice out of Ohio State, accompanied by Jack (The Shot) Foley, the second-round choice from Holy Cross. They took a cab from the airport through the tunnel into the city. Dark. They checked into the

Hotel Manger, next to the Garden. Dark. Foley went to bed. Havlicek decided he was hungry.

The Hayes-Bickford cafeteria across the street was the only place open. Dark. A couple of sad-looking patrons were sitting by themselves drinking coffee. Another sad-looking patron had his head down on a table and was sleeping. The counterman was wearing a soiled apron, the stains of the day accumulated on the front. Havlicek ordered a couple of eggs. He stared at the eggs before he ate. Dark. Rain outside. Cholesterol.

"What have I gotten myself into?" he asked himself.

The next day he went to a playoff game. The Celtics versus the Philadelphia Warriors. Russell versus Wilt. He was brought into the Celtics locker room to meet the players, who mostly were too busy with their own thoughts to meet him back. He couldn't believe what he saw.

"I was devastated," he said. "It was this little room tucked underneath a stairway. There were no lockers, just nails hammered into these furring strips around the room. The steps cascaded down, so one end of the room had a normal 15-foot ceiling, but the other end was as low as six feet. The shorter guys dressed at that end. The nails for the clothes, it seemed, were based on seniority. If you were a rookie, you were a one-nail guy. I had just finished my four years at Ohio State, which had the best facilities, and to come to this. . . ."

What had he gotten himself into? The game was as suspicious as the locker room. Sam Jones picked up a wooden stool and threatened to hit Wilt over the head. Jim Loscutoff chased Guy Rodgers into the stands, right out the door. The crowd howled, a beery mob in the middle of the afternoon. This was the Garden. This was different.

Quiet complaints about the building had been made by other teams early in the Celtics' success, but ten championships down the line the complaints had become much louder. The Celtics' old locker room, which had only one shower stall and one bathroom stall, had been abandoned for a better situation with wooden lockers, two toilets, and six showerheads, but was still substandard to most of the league. The visiting locker room was still primitive, players squashed together, forced to shower in shifts.

Temperature always was a problem. The visiting locker room—the entire building—could become a sweatbox on hot days, no air conditioning to be found. Cold was a big locker room problem throughout the winter, visitors complaining that their teeth chattered while they dressed, no hot air arriving into the room. (Havlicek once studied the situation. He said a twelve-inch pipe supplied warm air to both the home and visiting locker rooms. The closer you were to the source, the better heat you received. The Celtics were twenty-five feet closer to the source.) Showers in the visiting locker room sometimes seemed to dispense only cold water.

The arena itself was a three-tiered box, unlike the modern buildings that sloped gently toward the sky. Spectators hung over the action, seemed to watch everything from directly above or behind the players' shoulders. This encouraged an easy exchange of viewpoints from the paying customers. Games were raucous events. If the Fabulous Forum was a country club dining room, the Garden was a neighborhood tavern.

And then there was the floor. The Celtics had made their parquet floor famous to a nation that previously had no idea what the word "parquet" meant. The checkerboard pattern had become one of the most distinctive landmarks in televised sports. Black-and-white, color, didn't matter. The checkerboard meant Boston and basketball success.

Visiting players saw the floor as another part of the Celtics' conspiracy. The floor that looked so nice on television was a beat-up disaster in person. ("When do they put down the real floor?" a Detroit Pistons rookie once asked. "Isn't this the practice floor?")

The 264 pieces of the puzzle, each five feet by five feet, had been picked up and put down thousands of times since the floor was built in 1946. The oak boards, cut across the grain for strength, were leftovers from the construction of army barracks during World War II. Normal boards for normal basketball floors were eight feet long, put together for four-by-eight panels. The shorter five-feet boards allowed the panels to be built in squares. At some unrecorded point some unrecorded someone with an artistic temperament had decided to alternate the squares in horizontals and verticals. The parquet floor was born.

The problem that visiting players saw—after dressing in their cold locker room and before their cold showers—was the number of dead spots in the twenty-three-year-old floor. A player would be dribbling along, total control, ball on a string, when suddenly the ball would not return to his hand in the same rhythm. The air would disappear. He would have to reach down to adjust. The Celtics knew these secret dead spots and would be ready to pounce. Of course they did.

K. C. Jones, the retired Celtic defensive specialist, always had been happy to talk about this advantage. ("All the time your machine is ticking upstairs," he said. "You're thinking the guy is getting closer to a dead spot.") Bob Cousy, the retired Celtics star, said it all was non-sense. ("You're telling me that in a game as fast as basketball I could have the presence of mind to push someone over to the fifth board from the right because that's supposed to be a dead spot?" he said.) The important thing was that visiting teams thought about it. That was the advantage right there.

The bright young man, contrary to the common opinion, especially the one held by visitors from Los Angeles, loved the Garden. The place wore no makeup. It was just there every day, utilitarian, steady. The more city planners screamed for it to be replaced, to build some-thing grand to add to the city's image, the more TBYM wanted it to stay around. Boston wasn't a Chamber of Commerce kind of place. Take it or leave it. That was Boston. That was the Garden. Take it or leave it.

"The first time Wilt came here, I brought one of those containers filled with water to the bench along with a bunch of little paper cups," Brian Wallace, who was a twelve-year-old ball boy at the time, says. "Wilt said, 'You see the size of those cups? How many of those cups do you think I'd use during a game? Go to the concession stand. Get me a beer cup.' I went to the concession stand and asked for a beer cup for Wilt Chamberlain to drink water. The guy said, 'Sure. And do you want a hot dog for Bill Russell?'

"I got the beer cup, though, and after the game Wilt gave me $20. Every game after that, I'd get him a beer cup and he'd give me $20."

There were Garden corridors that led to nowhere. There were Garden characters, ushers who had worked in the building since the day it opened, members of the bull gang, hangers-on who were hang-ing out, curious people who could be found every day around every corner. Kids put themselves in danger by trying to sneak into the building from fire escapes near the roof. Cracks in the concrete floor had appeared underneath the ice, which was underneath the parquet court. They had been made by the rumble of the trains, which were underneath everything. Rats as big as rabbits could be spotted, bold as paying customers. The smell of the circus would linger for a good month. Tom Sanders said he once was doing rehab on his own, the team out of town, and was running some laps around the mezzanine level when two German shepherd guard dogs arrived to stop his workout in a fast heartbeat. He thought he was a dead man. He froze. ("Nobody knew I was here," he said. "They heard the barking. Someone finally came and took the dogs away.")

Look down and the parquet floor meant basketball was going to be played. Look up at the championship banners and it meant the Celtics were involved.

"What do you use to clean those banners?" the bright young man asked Walter Randall, a Garden character, Celtics equipment man, as he put one year after another into a washing machine on a workday afternoon.

"Tide," he replied.

Perfect.

The only Laker who could bring back championship thoughts when he crammed himself into the overheated or frozen-over visitors' locker room or dribbled across the dead-spot floor was point guard Johnny Egan. The five-foot-eleven ballhandler from Providence College, whose main job was to deliver crisp and inventive passes to Jerry West, had added 26 points on 10-for-19 shooting on Friday night and made Bill Russell notice. ("Russ Says LA's Egan Surprised, Hurt Celts" was the headline on the player/coach/writer's column today in the *Globe*.) Egan knew the Garden well.

He had found magic here back in 1957.

Remember that New England high school championship basketball tournament that featured water glasses full of whiskey, a burlesque show, and a side trip to see Russell versus Wilt? Three years before all that happened, Johnny Egan owned that tournament and owned Boston Garden. He was a Hartford Weaver High School Beaver from Hartford, Connecticut, a senior, the captain, the only white starter on a racially mixed team, an eighteen-year-old version of the famous Bob Cousy. He was a high school hero.

"In an almost unbelievable finish, during which 36-point man John Egan scored 12 of his team's fantastic total of 21 points in a thrilling three-minute overtime period, Weaver of Hartford defeated Lawrence Central, 85 to 73, to win the battle of unbeaten teams at the New England tournament before 11,071 screaming fans at the Garden last night," the *Globe* reported. "It was victory number 24 and first New England crown for Weaver and first loss in 28 starts for Central, which was looking to become the first Catholic school to win the tourney. . . ."

(The story was written by Ernie Dalton, an old-timer who parted his hair in the middle and still was at the *Globe* when the bright young man arrived. Ernie, other old-timers said, once wrote that a baseball player hit "an inside-the-park triple." Think about it.)

Thirty-six points! Double overtime! The Weaver Beavers!

So here he is now, thirty years old, married to former Weaver cheerleader Joan Grimaldi, two kids, eighth year in the league. He has been traded and traded and traded again, never close to that high school moment, not once, but he is the starter on the same team with Wilt, Jerry, and Elgin and they are ahead, two games to none, for the NBA title. Echoes can be heard.

Can't they?

"This was a good team for me to come to," the five-foot-eleven guard says. "It sort of shows, I think, there is room for the little man in this game."

He hasn't been a starter long, moved into the lineup only when the Lakers fell behind 0-2 to the Warriors in the first round of the play-offs, but since he has had the job the team is 10-1. He played forty-two minutes in Game Two. He was the X-factor reason the Lakers won.

"It was a desperation move, putting me in, but he [Butch van Breda Kolff] wanted to get some more speed in the lineup," Egan says. "It's worked out pretty well. If we come down and set up, we're a lousy club. We've got to get it out and run. Elgin and Jerry love to run, as do I."

Everything that happens on the floor starts with West. If the Celtics play him one-on-one, he will score. If they double-team, mostly with Egan's man, Emmette Bryant, that leaves Egan open. If Egan is left open, then he has to hit the shot.

"Egan is the key for the Lakers in this series," Celtics forward Bailey Howell says. "He can bring the ball up the floor. Without him, we can throw an effective press all over the court."

Howell's idea is to make Egan a liability on defense. Do the things that tall men always do to little men. Back him down for a close-in jumper. Not too close, because Wilt will be lurking, but close enough for an easier shot. Egan thinks that will not work.

"They always talk about bringing you into the pivot, but how many guards are tall enough or work well enough to do it?" he says. "There are a few, like Oscar Robertson and Sam Jones, but Emmette Bryant can't do it."

The bright young man is a quiet Egan fan. He does not say this to any of the other Boston writers, not to anyone, really, but when he was thirteen years old he probably wanted to be Johnny Egan more than anyone else in the world. In New Haven, Egan's Boston Garden heroics as a kid from Hartford were well reported. They were the stuff of adolescent dreams.

Wanting to be Mickey Mantle or Rocky Marciano or Rocket Richard or Chuck Berry or Elvis or John Wayne or Sugar Ray Robinson, somebody BIG already was out of the question, same as wanting to walk on the moon or become president of the United States. Wanting to be Johnny Egan? Maybe if I grow a little taller. Work a little harder. It was still impossible, as everybody could see already in seventh or eighth grade, but it still seemed more believable. This star was closer to home. This was another kid. A short kid. Probably had trouble with algebra, too.

"What's it like to be Johnny Egan?" the bright young man wants to ask, even now, but of course he doesn't. Unprofessional.

He did do a small sidebar about Egan before the series began. Nothing grand. He mostly wanted to hear Egan's voice, see what he looked like up close. The Lakers guard, one of the keys to the series, seemed personable, pleasant. He talked about how he had big hands for a small man, which helped him control the ball. He had a special shot that he used when he was driving to the hoop. He would palm the ball, then sort of flick it toward the basket. The only way a big man could block the shot was if he hit the top of Egan's hand. That would be a foul.

"See?" Egan said, flicking an imaginary basketball toward an imaginary basket.

Cool.

Want to bring a big crowd to its feet in that big old building over a train station when you're eighteen years old? Start by letting your hands grow large. Then your feet. Go from there.

Good to know.

There's a reason we're all not stars.

Chapter 11

GAME THREE

CELTS RUN, LEAVE LAKERS FLAT, 111–105

BY LEIGH MONTVILLE
Staff Writer

BOSTON—Jerry West turned to the Los Angeles Lakers bench late yesterday afternoon at the Boston Garden. He wanted to be taken out of the basketball game.

"After we caught up," West said later, "I asked to come out. I was tired. I hoped a few minutes' rest would help."

Bill van Breda Kolff, the Lakers coach, fulfilled the request. He put West on the bench for the last three minutes and one second of the third period.

It didn't work.

"As soon as I came back, I knew it," West said. "I was still tired."

The feeling was a common one. The rest of West's team also was tired and the Boston Celtics did something they could not do twice last week in Los Angeles—they won a basketball game in the fourth quarter.

The score for the period was 33–27 and the score for the game was 111–105. The win brought the Celtics back into contention in the finals of the National Basketball

Assn. playoffs, a position where they are now trailing two games to one in the best-of-seven series.

It was, on the surface, a game for the NBA cynic.

The cynic is the guy who watches the pro basketball only in the fourth quarter. He says the rest is meaningless, a 36-minute warm-up, for the fourth-quarter finale.

On the surface he was right yesterday. In reality he was wrong because the Celtics won the game in the first half.

They came out running—"the best we've run in this series," said John Havlicek—and took a 25–16 lead in the first quarter. By the half, the lead had ballooned to 17 points, 57–40.

The running had taken Wilt Chamberlain out of the ballgame, at least as much as it is possible to take a seven-foot, one-inch, nine-year All Everything out of a ballgame. The fast break had worked and the Celtics played their offensive basketball while Wilt was still coming down the court.

Celtics player-coach Bill Russell, who has done it often in other years of the Wilt-Russell match-up, continually was the first center down the court. He even finished two of his breaks with stuff shots.

The Lakers, after all of this, needed a comeback. They got it.

"I just told the guys to go out, play our game, take our shots," van Breda Kolff said, describing the halftime locker room scene. "Nothing special."

The Lakers stormed back. West, the dominant factor in the first two games, scored nine points in the third period. Elgin Baylor, who wound up with only 11 points, had his only spurt of the day and scored seven.

Mel Counts added eight, the Lakers hit 13 of 23 shots from the floor and as the quarter ended, the game was tied, 78–78. West, however, was on the bench and the Lakers were tired.

"After we caught up, we just died," said West. "The last quarter was very passive."

Havlicek and Siegfried—Ohio State East—dominated the period. Havlicek, who always can beat one man in a game of attrition basketball, scored 13 points. Siegfried scored 11.

Havlicek's last point, with 23 seconds left, was a foul shot after his left eye had received one of Keith Erickson's fingers. The injury was not serious—though Havlicek couldn't focus the eye while shooting the fouls—and he will be able to practice today and play in Tuesday's fourth game at the Garden.

Siegfried, who scored 28 points, hit the long shots. He fired quick jump shots from the key and long, set one-handers from the corners.

"You have to give it to him," Johnny Egan, the little Lakers guard, said. "None of those shots he hit were very easy."

The Celtics grabbed control early in the fourth period, 84–82, and never gave up the lead again. They moved ahead, 102–90, and held off a late personal charge by Egan, the last lively Laker, who scored seven straight points, 14 of 16 at one stretch.

The Celtics won because the other team was tired. They won because the other team spent too much time digging out of a hole that had been made too large.

Egan, surrounded by writers from Hartford, CT, and Providence, RI, where he has played basketball, wrapped it in a neat little package.

"When the fourth period came, we were flat."

THE NOTEBOOK—"The time in Los Angeles when I got up this morning was 4:30," said Wilt Chamberlain, talking about the time differential. "It certainly didn't help, but it shouldn't have affected one team more than another . . ."

"Just take a look at the stat sheet, you'll see the places where we lost the game," van Breda Kolff said . . . The sheet told this story—Siegfried scored the 28 points and Havlicek scored 34. Baylor slumped to 11, West to 24 and the Lakers hit only 27 of 40 foul shots. . . .

The Lakers' Egan was asked to rate Siegfried on an
aggressiveness scale for NBA guards . . . Egan paused.
"Eh, well," he said. "With him, defense is like trying
to rope a wild steer. That's the way he has to play. He's
small, like me."

Siegfried described his pulled hamstring muscle as
dull, "like a tooth ache . . . I'd rather have this than
a groin pull, though," he said. "A groin pull, like Walt
Frazier (of the Knicks) had is the worst . . ."

Keith Erickson, who has been a guard since he started
playing pro basketball, was switched to forward by van
Breda Kolff yesterday and may have won a job there . . .
"I liked the job he did," the coach said. "I wanted to see
how Keith did defensively against Havlicek. He did pretty
well."

Boston Evening Globe
April 28, 1969

The Celtics had returned from Los Angeles on Saturday, the day after
the second loss at the Forum. The flight landed late in the afternoon,
cusp of the evening, as morning flights did from the West Coast,
close to the time for a good family dinner. The players did not go
home. Russell called a practice at Melrose High School.

The Garden was busy on this Saturday night with big-time wrestling. (For the record, Professor Toru Tanaka won, The Fabulous
Moolah lost, Haystacks Calhoun beat Bulldog Brower by hitting him
over the head with a horseshoe, and WWF champion Bruno Sam-
martino's feature match with local favorite Killer Kowalski was ruled
a draw when Bruno threw a chair at Killer that missed Killer but
knocked out the referee. Both wrestlers were disqualified. Bruno kept
his title.) Melrose High in suburban Melrose, Massachusetts, was
available.

There were things to discuss.

"Here's the problem facing the coach: we've allowed an average of
119 points a game, and we can't allow to give up that many points
every game," Russell had said in his *Globe* column. "It doesn't matter

who gets points for a team. If we can hold them down, it's anybody's ballgame."

Russell, the coach, listed Russell, the player, as one of the top underachievers even though the numbers did not look uneven in his WWF-style spotlight battle with Chamberlain. He was outrebounding the younger, taller man 48–42, outscoring him 25–19, and had ten more assists in the two games. The performance was what felt uneven to Russell. He wasn't wearing Wilt down the way he wanted, wasn't controlling him.

"After Game Two, Russell had a locker room meeting," Siegfried told the *Celtic Nation* blog years later. "He admitted that he hadn't played up to his standard, and he wasn't ready to compete in that game. He asked us to forgive him, and told us that we were going to prevail in the series. That we'd figure a way to get it done."

The Melrose practice was part of the figuring, not a sweat-it-out, physical practice. The Sunday game, a 2 p.m. start at the Garden, the parquet floor reassembled overnight after the wrestlers departed, was less than twenty hours away. This was a time to talk about things, to tinker with a few changes, restructure a defense to double-team Jerry West as much as possible, double anyone trying to drive, leave other people—notably Johnny Egan, the other Lakers guard—freedom to shoot. Take away West. Leave Egan open. Jumpers instead of layups. Shuffle the deck.

The one-word thought, as always, was "run." Run on offense. Run back on defense. Run. Running always was the answer, the special elixir. Any time any Celtics team ever had faltered, the observation, top to bottom, always was "we didn't run." Any time good things happened, the explanation was "we were able to get out and run."

Running faster, better, harder, LONGER than anyone else had been the founding principle of Red Auerbach's offense. His training camps, which usually opened earlier than the other training camps in the league, were famous for their basic training brutality. Auerbach often wouldn't let his players touch a basketball for the first three days. All they would do was run sprints, run drills, run punishment laps, run and run.

The reactions of new arrivals to this process were legendary. George Plimpton described the sight of Princeton free agent John

Hummer hurrying to an open window to throw up. Willie Naulls, a veteran forward new to the operation, passed out and threw up at the same time. The oft-mentioned memory was that Willie had been dragged off the court through his own vomit. Bailey Howell said he never had seen anything like this in seven years in the NBA. No wonder the Celtics won all the time. They were in better condition than anyone else.

After a week or so of running, running, running, interspersed with some hard scrimmages, everyone pressing full court all the time, Auerbach not only would take his show on the road, he would choose a hard and bumpy route. The Celtics would play twenty-one or more exhibition games in twenty-one or more nights, mostly in the factory cities and towns of New England. Need a fundraiser for the local fire department or the Daughters of the American Revolution chapter? Schedule the Celtics for late September or early October. Have the NBA in the old hometown for a night.

When the regular season arrived, the goal was to use all this training to shoot out in front, gain control before the slow movers on the other team had time to tie their shoes or adjust their athletic supporters. The goal for the season was the same: shoot to the top of the standings before other teams could "play their way in shape." End the race before it even began.

The greatness of Russell was that he made this approach work at a high level. His concentration on defense, his mobility and timing, allowed his teammates to be more aggressive, to play closer to the men they were guarding. If their men broke free, well, Russell was waiting to erase baskets before they could be recorded in any scorebook. His blocked shots, usually directed at a teammate, started fast breaks. He followed along, beating the other center to the basket at the other end of the floor. Teamwork. Running.

The practice at Melrose High wasn't so much a practice as an affirmation of a long-held faith. Russell, as a coach, had followed most of Auerbach's guidebook. Remember those practices at the Tobin Gym in Roxbury? Remember the bumpy road? The players' union, the NBPA, had worked to shorten the exhibition season, and the league's beginnings of popularity had made the exhibition schedule more marketable, but the Celtics still had played twelve games before the season began in far-flung hotspots like Wilkes-Barre, Pennsylvania;

Kalamazoo, Michigan; Muncie, Indiana; Columbus, Ohio; Waterloo, Iowa; Burlington, Vermont; and Bangor, Maine.

This third game in the NBA finals was the time to draw upon the last reserves of all that work. Twelve exhibition games. Eighty-two regular-season games. Thirteen playoff games. Let's run the Lakers to death.

The plan obviously was a success for at least one night. Or so it seemed. Maybe the claustrophobic Garden was a factor with its heat and angry background noise and the dead spots on the floor. Maybe the afternoon start time, mixed with the three-hour time difference, was another factor for a team from Los Angeles. Maybe, then again, the old running approach worked by itself against a team whose coach called his center "The Load."

The Lakers were gassed. As the bright young man described in his story (B-plus. Hit most of the important bases, but needed more details, more oomph.) about the 111–105 Celtics win, the visitors fell behind early, staged a gallant comeback, but were tired, flat at the finish. It was a classic autopsy of a Celtics victim. Death by oxygen deficit.

"I just collapsed physically near the end," Lakers star West said with his no-frills candor. "Maybe it was the pace of the game. I was very tired. They talk about the Celtics being old, well, we've got some old guys, too."

"How many buckets did I get in the last quarter?" he added. "One of nine? I didn't have much left."

The most-noticed variable in the game was the scuffling performance by Larry Siegfried. The twenty-nine-year-old backup guard came off the Celtics bench to play the strongest defense of anyone yet on the tired West and added a surprising 28 points. He played thirty-three of the forty-eight minutes despite an assortment of physical woes, his body held together by Band-Aids, Ace bandages, and a good dose of fortitude. He looked like someone in search of Florence Nightingale and the first-aid tent in the Crimean War when he came onto the floor with three minutes left in the first quarter. He then pretty much played the rest of the game.

It was quite a show.

"When I saw him get off the plane yesterday, I didn't think he'd be able to play," Dr. Thomas Silva, the team doctor, said. "But thanks to a lot of therapy and Larry's great motivation, he was able to make it."

His list of injuries included two bad elbows, two scraped knees, a bruised left hip, a pulled hamstring muscle in his right leg, and a calcified finger. Lack of sleep also was a problem. The hip had been injured and the hamstring reaggravated on Friday night in Los Angeles. The two injuries effectively ended his sleeping. If he turned one way in bed, the hamstring would hurt. If he turned the other way, the hip would hurt. While he stayed awake and fretted about staying awake, he mostly sat in a hot tub.

Arriving at the Garden four hours before tip-off, "walking like a duck" he said, he spent more time in the whirlpool, then kept a hot and wet pad from a hydrocollator machine on his hamstring. He had to remove the pad when he was called into the game.

"It was fairly obvious where the Celtics got more than before from Siegfried," Lakers coach van Breda Kolff said.

"He did so many good things," West said. "And let me tell you, he wasn't scoring cheap baskets. He was shooting from downtown. And when he does that, he's tough to stop."

At six feet three, only an inch shorter than West, Siegfried was able to handle the one-on-one situations against the Lakers star much better than Emmette Bryant did in the first game. He brought an aggression to his approach that was rare. He slapped, whacked, bumped, bothered, dove for loose balls. Lakers fans called him a "hatchet man." He was an uncomfortable presence at all times, one of those guys who played basketball with a yappy belligerence.

The Celtics were a quiet team. Maybe there had been some noisy characters in the past, Heinsohn and Loscutoff at the top of the list, Auerbach a one-man filibuster, but business was done these days with the efficiency and decorum of a well-run bank. Siegfried was the anomaly, the noisy voice in the lobby. He would want to speak to the manager. Right now.

"Siggy is in his shirt!" Johnny Most would declare most often when Siegfried was guarding someone close.

"Playing against him," Johnny Egan said, "is like trying to wrestle a steer."

Now in his sixth season with the Celtics, he still felt a need to prove his worth. He was one of the low-budget discards Auerbach found again and again to fill out the roster. A starter at Ohio State on the 1960 national championship with Havlicek and All-American Jerry Lucas (and also on the 1961 Ohio State team that had its unbeaten season ended in overtime by the University of Cincinnati in the NCAA title game), he had made stops in Cleveland in the American Basketball League and then St. Louis in the NBA. He was a benchwarmer in Cleveland, cut in Atlanta when he joined the Hawks after the ABL went out of business.

Back in Shelby, Ohio, Siegfried was thinking about teaching school when Auerbach called. Havlicek had recommended him, first for friendship, second because of his defense, third because of his shooting. The Ohio State offense was designed around Lucas first and then Havlicek, everyone else's scoring almost incidental, but Siegfried had been a high-volume shooter and scorer in high school. Auerbach was surprised when he saw him shoot. He was a perfect fit for a team that was looking for an aggressive backup guard.

In the six years, he had expanded on his situation, become a starter at times, averaged between 12 and 15 points per game. He and Havlicek often were mentioned as a tandem, the Ohio State guys, especially on nights like this when they combined for 62 of the Celtics' 111 points. They knew how to find each other. They knew how to run. They had grown up together. Their places on that Ohio State team— with a kid named Bobby Knight as the sixth man—had put them in a special category of basketball success.

"That team set one record that never will be broken," Havlicek always declared in later years. "Everybody graduated. Seven guys got masters. Two became PhDs. Two became medical doctors. And all but one came from Ohio. You'll NEVER see something like that again."

Siegfried had made one dubious move into the Celtics record books in the run-up to the present season. He had become the first player in club history to be a holdout. Not only that, he was the first player to bring an agent with him to negotiate with Auerbach.

The defunct ABL and the present American Basketball Association, now finishing its second season, had brought some player movement and a general increase in basketball salaries, but Red still worked on a feudal system. A player should come to the office by himself, engage in some casual banter about the plusses and minuses of his previous season, then accept the contract that Red and management had decided was appropriate.

Siegfried truthfully was not too concerned with money. He was concerned about remaining with the team. Stories had been printed that Auerbach was looking to trade his overachieving Ohio State graduate to the Hawks for thirty-year-old Lenny Wilkens, who was not happy in Atlanta. Wilkens always had been an Auerbach favorite. The deal made sense. Hal Greer of Philadelphia also was mentioned as a trade possibility. Siegfried, dismayed by all this speculation, fought back.

He wanted to remain a Celtic. That was foremost. He felt that he fit into the Celtics' style. He was comfortable with the team, the city, with winning a championship just about every year. If that did not happen, if he was going to be traded, he wanted money. A lot of money.

To pursue negotiations, he brought Boston attorney Bob Woolf into the game. Forty years old, a onetime end-of-the-bench basketball player at Boston College, Woolf was one of the first modern sports agents. He was a self-promotional whizbang, name always in the papers with charismatic clients like Ken (The Hawk) Harrelson of the Red Sox and Derek Sanderson of the Bruins. ("Always stand in the middle for newspaper photographers, that way they can't crop you out of the picture" was a rule he always followed.) He had signed a number of Celtics for outside business, trying to find them endorsements, but Siegfried was his first contract dance with Red.

It was a weird negotiation, since Siegfried wanted love more than money.

"I assume Larry is technically a holdout as of now, but I'm working with Red on a technicality in the contract, which is not necessarily a financial one," Woolf said from his office above a Riley's Roast Beef franchise on Brighton Avenue. "I am of the opinion that we can work things out satisfactorily."

Siegfried worked out daily on his own at the Cambridge Y while the team ran and vomited through the first days of preseason workouts at the Tobin Gym in Roxbury. At a luncheon at the Hotel Lenox on September 23, 1968, to announce that Russell had signed a two-year contract "in the neighborhood of $200,000 per year (with a lawyer on his side for advice, but without an acknowledged agent), Auerbach delivered his point of view.

"I'd be remiss if I didn't mention something about Larry," Auerbach said, describing the holdout for love, not money, an assurance that there would be no trade. "He was given a substantial raise by me. He says, 'I'll see you.' I say, 'I'll see you.' That's it. A thing like that never has happened to me."

Three days later, Siegfried signed.

"Red was most amicable and we got along fine," Woolf said. "Larry received what he wanted and Red knows more than ever that Larry wants to be a Celtic and remain a Celtic and will give his usual 100 percent."

Two weeks later, Lenny Wilkens was traded from Atlanta to Seattle. Everybody was happy.

Siegfried's name also was mentioned in a trade discussion during the 1968–69 NBA All-Star Game in Baltimore on January 14, 1969, the biggest event the bright young man had covered before these playoffs. Siegfried was not in the game—Havlicek and Russell were starters, the East beat the West, 123–112—but became the subject of conversation in the suite of a famous NBA owner.

The owner, who will not be named, was the host of a small party the night before the game, open bar and conversation. Eddie Gillooly knew about it and took the bright young man with him. This was very interesting. The bright young man never had been in this kind of social setting.

I remember he talked to Dick Motta, who was the rookie coach of the Chicago Bulls, straight out of Weber State. TBYM, never a fan of Wilt Chamberlain, asked Motta if he would take Wilt and all his baggage if he had a chance. Wouldn't Wilt drive everyone else to daily distraction? TBYM thought so. Motta said he would take Wilt in a second.

"I could work with him," Motta said. "I'd figure it out."

Hot Rod Hundley, the former Laker, Chick Hearn's color man, was in the room. He was very funny. Jack Waldron, president of the Celtics, was there. A bunch of people the bright young man did not know were there. The center of everything was the famous owner, which figured, because this was his room. Somebody mentioned on the side that the owner was a renowned ladies' man, had not only bedded over a thousand women but had pictures of them in scrapbooks. This was an interesting fact. The bright young man had never heard of anything like this.

A conversation developed about potential trades. The famous owner was in the middle of it. Eddie Gillooly suggested Siegfried as a possible trade for someone on the famous owner's roster. The famous owner was interested.

"I'll trade black for white any time," he said.

What?

He said that.

Someone mentioned the possibility of a trade for another player, who was black.

"He sweats seawater," the famous owner said in declining the deal.

Jesus.

The bright young man never had heard anything like this from anyone, much less anyone in a position of power. The conversation bounced along from there. Was this one owner talking? Were there a lot of owners who felt this way? Were a few cocktails making this owner talk this way? TBYM wondered.

He never wrote a story about this. He never, in all his years in the sportswriting business, would hear anything like this again. (Never would be in this kind of situation again, either.) I can't remember whether he talked with Eddie about it. I know he talked about the famous owner with Celtics people. A story came back from public relations director Howie McHugh.

The famous owner was the host one year for the NBA All-Star Game. Everybody agreed that he was a wonderful host. The event was much smaller than the three-day mega-promotion blast it would become, but still had a social component. The famous owner threw a terrific party for all the visiting teams and owners. Memorable. The Celtics management wanted to do a little something to repay his generosity when he came to Boston with his team. The problem was that he was richer than rich and pretty much owned everything a man could want. What gift do you give a man who has everything?

"Well, he really does like women," someone said.

Yes.

The Celtics management decided they would provide a woman of the evening for the visiting famous owner. Someone found a perfect subject. She was briefed on the plan. The subject would be brought to the Iron Horse, the bar on the ground floor of the Garden, then left alone on some pretense. She would initiate a conversation, be charmed by whatever he said, and let nature take its devious course. She would never mention the fact she had been paid.

On the scheduled night, the woman arrived a little early. She spotted a single man in a suit at the bar who she thought was her prospective client. He was actually a Boston sportswriter who also will not be named. The woman approached the sportswriter who also will not be named. She initiated a conversation. He bought her a drink. She was suitably charmed. He was charmed in return. There might have been time for another round of drinks, maybe not, and devious nature took its course. The sportswriter and the woman stood up, started to leave the bar.

It was at this point that the Celtics party arrived with the famous owner. They spotted what was happening.

"No, no," someone, maybe public relations director McHugh, shouted to the woman. "Not that guy, this guy."

There were no further reports on what happened next.

It was a different time in the early years of the NBA.

Chapter 12

OFF DAY:
THE COLUMNISTS

By Jerry Nason
Boston Globe Sports Editor

Red Auerbach views the basketball playoffs these days from center stadium, box seat, on the Causeway Street flank of the Garden, and everybody says, "Lookee Ol' Red over there, with his fat cigar . . . really enjoying himself."

Enjoying himself, my eye! Enjoying himself like a guppy outside the fish bowl, like a rodeo cowboy with one leg in a cast; like Ted Williams with one arm in a sling while the fish are biting.

The truth is, 20 years at courtside, down where the action is, make of Red Auerbach, the one-time resident genius of the Celtics' bench, the worst of stadium-seats fans.

He squirms, he fidgets. His cigar fumes, and so does he. Auerbach is the silenced Voice of the Celtics when removed from both the bench and the broadcast booth.

You ask the Celtics' general manager, "Having a good time over there pretending you are a fan?" and he replies with candor, "No, I like to sit at floor level. Close to the game. I like to know what's going on."

But Red, ol' boy, that doesn't coincide with the weekly Saturday gripe of the football coach, which reads, "Don't ask me what happened. I have the worst seat in the house. Wait until I view the game film."

Auerbach nodded. "That may be so with the football," he said, "they have a field 300 feet long. Now you take a basketball court . . ."

Red said what he missed most of all were "the sounds of the game" when he was up there in a six-dollar seat.

Sounds? "Yeh, the guys talking it up out there," he said. "You can't hear any of that up in the stands. Like when some of the 'quarterbacking' is going on.

"When you're down there on the bench and a player yells 'Switch!' you know who the player is and who is to blame for not carrying out the switch."

But Red Auerbach among the section 31 clients at a basketball game feels completely defrocked and vulnerable.

"I guess I'm a creature of habit," he confessed. "Down at the side of the court I have a feel for the game that I don't have at all in the stands.

"Some of you people might have a valid point in saying you can watch a play develop better from up above the court, but this isn't true for me. I like it better close to the action, where you can study the contact and hear the sounds of the game."

The guy, alas, just isn't cut out to be a basketball fan. He has to be piped into the scorer's table, the game officials, and wire-tap the player huddles to have himself a real good time.

The final series with the Lakers, the way he figures it, can still be a Celtics property, despite the LA edge of 2-1 in games.

"The two games in Los Angeles could have gone either way," he said. "They went to the Lakers, but we could have won either one of them.

"Now we come to Sunday, here. That was a game we had to bust open twice. Ordinarily, a team will bust a game once. We had to do it twice and did. That tells you something.

"That tells you our guys didn't panic; they kept their poise when they lost the 17-point lead. Their attitude is good. They feel they should win it, and they can, too."

Nobody in the vicinity of Red Auerbach, fan, has detected him in the act of blistering his palms in applause for Wilton Chamberlain or chummying up with Mister Massive in post-mortem.

"I don't talk to him," Red said. "Haven't for years."

This celebrated cordial and mutual dislike for each other on the parts of Red and Wilt, contemporary giants of the NBA in their respective ways, has no foundation in feud.

"Actually, we used to be quite good friends. Summers at Kutsher's, up in the Catskills," Red said. "This goes way back.

"Then one of his coaches got Wilt all revved up about not talking friendly with anybody. All of a sudden, one day, I said 'Hello, Wilt,' and he told me 'Go poison yourself.'

"Well, you know me. I haven't spoken to the guy since."

Well, if they are going to live in that Hall of Fame peacefully together they'd better kiss and make up pretty soon.

Boston Evening Globe
April 29, 1969

Three columns on the Celtics appeared in the *Globe* the day of the fourth game. The first was by sports editor Jerry Nason, the sixty-year-old sports editor, columnist, and sometimes cartoonist, the newspaper's answer to the multi-employed Bill Russell. It was one of his typical efforts—a phone call to Red Auerbach, an old associate.

The bright young man no doubt hated it. I would admit now—easily—that the column reads fine. Red is as entertaining as ever. The light and breezy of long ago still is light and breezy today. There are valid comments on the series, what would be a solid blog post on any website today, but at the time TBYM could only see it as dull and outdated. Home by five for dinner.

The second column by Arthur (Bud) Collins was the exact opposite. The words came off the printed page in a happy conga line, shouted and danced. Topical? Charles de Gaulle had resigned as president of France while the Celtics were carving out that first win against the Lakers. Why shouldn't he be in the column? Why shouldn't Nestor and Agamemnon be in there, too, along with (assistant general manager) Jeff Cohen and Harold Furash, season ticket holder, and Larry Siegfried's iron lung. Larry Siegfried's iron lung?

The thirty-nine-year-old Collins was an ascending star. Everybody knew it. Any day he was in the office was a better day, a hoot. It was a rare quality that he had. He answered phones in a phony British accent, *"Globe Sporting,"* and entertained with everything he did. He wore bow ties. He wore wild printed pants. He complimented everyone on whatever stories everyone had worked in recent days. He was a happy tornado.

His second career as a tennis announcer, soon to be a first career that would make him famous, already had begun. He had broadcast the first U.S. Open from Forest Hills on CBS in 1968 with Jack Kramer, the newest member of the International Tennis Hall of Fame. The sport was transformed under Collins's approach. Tennis was boxing! He described forehands and backhands as if they were punches, vicious jabs and grand uppercuts, the stronger player looking for the knockout, the weaker player on his last legs. Every player suddenly had a catchy nickname. Matches were filled with Slams and Bams, action. You looked for blood and an ambulance at the end.

Collins knew the game. He was a good country club player and in his earlier life had been the tennis coach at Brandeis University. One of his players was Abbie Hoffman, who became famous as the noisy activist head of the Yippie Party and as a member of the Chicago 7 at the 1968 Democratic Convention.

"What was Abbie Hoffman like?" the bright young man asked.

"The big thing I remember is that he had a better car than I did," Collins replied. "He drove a Corvette."

The bright young man was fascinated by everything about Collins, by his knowledge, his personality, his pants. Everything. Collins had traveled on one of those Eastern Shuttle trips to New York for the

Eastern finals. TBYM heard Russell say to him, "What are you doing here? You should be doing bigger things than this."

Bud was Bud. He already was bigger than this, and this seemed to be pretty big.

By Bud Collins
Boston Globe Columnist

Now that Charles de Gaulle has gone the way of the New York Knickerbockers, the last of the world's aged leaders is Bill Russell.

Does he feel alone with de Gaulle gone? Is he worried that their kind of tall, imperious boss is fading? Does he sense that even his own world could crumble?

"Nope," said Russell as he girded himself for tonight's fourth installment of the unending hoop opera, "Playoff Place." In fact, prior to yesterday's practice, Russell suggested that he might bring in de Gaulle for backcourt protection. "He's 6-4, and a very hard man to push around."

And he's not as old as Sam Jones, who is also disappearing from the scene. Can't you see Jones and de Gaulle bringing the ball down, Charles screaming "Allez, monsieur Sam—Allez!" It would be the noblest bit of combative antiquity since Nestor and Agamemnon tried to fast break the Trojans. Throw in the bandaged juvenile, Larry Siegfried, and it'll look like the Spirit of '76 in short pants.

Jeff Cohen, a Celtics press attaché, told Russell he objected to picking up de Gaulle "because Charlie can only go to his right."

That's the way things were with the Celtics when they shuffled into the Garden—loose. Good and loose. They've been through the playoffs more times than Judy Garland listened to "On the Street Where You Live." The playoffs is where they live and no one can convince them they're going out with de Gaulle, even though they're 1-2 down to the group from Los Angeles.

"If," said Russell, "you have to worry about a guy getting up for the playoffs, then forget it. If he's not up now, he never will be."

But what about the fans? Players arrive and depart: fans go through this for ages. Shouldn't they be jaded and hard to arouse to screaming pitch by this time?

"You'd think so," says Harold Furash, 49-year-old veteran fan and insurance peddler, who was buying his tickets. He's been watching and fretting with the Celtics for two decades, paying his way in—and with no chance for a piece of the $7000 winner's share.

"You say to yourself—let's just win this one more time this year, and the hell with the future. That," smiles Furash, "is what I say every year. It's hard to keep watching intently when the season drags on like this, but I could watch Wilt Chamberlain vs Bill Russell every day of the year and not get bored. I'm always up for that . . ."

How would you steam yourself up for repeated playoff ordeals if you were a fan, Mr. Russell?

"Drink!" the elder replied.

Russell thought he might be ready for a stiff one Sunday night when the phone rang at his house.

"Hello, this is Beth Havlicek," said the pretty voice.

"O, good," said Russell, extremely concerned about her husband and his captain, John Havlicek. Havlicek left the Garden after the Celtics' victory looking like the Hathaway shirt man, his eye bandaged after being accidentally thumbed by Keith Erickson. "How's John, Beth?"

"John? Oh, he's OK, just a cut eye. I want to talk to your wife, not you, Bill."

"So I give the phone to Rose," Russell said, "and she and Beth are arranging a tennis date. That's the big game on their mind."

At least Beth didn't say, "John who?"

"I guess Havlicek's all right," Russell said.

He is. John came to the Garden pushing Larry

Siegfried's iron lung, and said Larry was allowed to get
out long enough to practice and, of course, play tonight.

If anybody was genuinely worried it was Sam Jones.
He's got a problem regarding the final disposition of his
elastic combat underwear when he hangs it up. Channel
2 wants it for the annual auction, and the Smithsonian
would like to hang it beside one of the corsets of his
contemporary, Mae West. Sam says he's promised to give
it to his high school coach for display in the Laurinburg
Institute trophy case.

With problems like this, who can worry about de
Gaulle or the Lakers?

Boston Globe
April 29, 1969

The third column was by Milton Gross. He was a columnist for the
New York Post, but was syndicated in as many as 140 papers around
the country by the North American News Alliance. The *Evening
Globe* used him quite often.

Gross was an older New York chipmunk, fifty-seven, but still part
of that New Journalism movement, strong on detail and information, a digger. Home by five was not a consideration. He was at the
games, the practices, in the middle of the action. The bright young
man didn't know him, never had spoken to him, but was an admirer.
This was the way to work.

Gross was a master of field position in all interview situations. The
star of the game, the goat of the game, the player who was the big
story, would reach his locker and be surrounded by men with note-
books. The one directly next to him always would be Milt Gross, who
somehow would edge his way to the front. He then would establish a
personal, close relationship in a group setting. His approach was brilliant. He would whisper.

"I heard you had a colostomy in the off-season," Gross would say in
the softest voice possible.

A law of physics would be involved. Or perhaps a regard for social
discourse. How does the normal person respond when asked a question in a whisper?

"Yes, I had the operation in July . . . ," the athlete would respond in the softest voice possible.

The other sportswriters in the circle would lean forward as far as possible. What'd he say? What was the question? What was the answer? The process was an art form.

By MILTON GROSS
North American News Alliance
John Havlicek couldn't see out of his left eye, abrased below and closing fast, but half a Havlicek is better than none at all. A whole Havlicek is spelled havoc, shiner notwithstanding.

With Bill Russell the Celtics won 10 NBA championships in 12 seasons. With Havlicek they won five in six years. If Boston should survive its one to two deficit against the Lakers and go on to gain another title, could anyone convincingly argue that their center would be more responsible than the raw-boned ramming forward.

One is the coach, the other the captain. One is the heart of the Celtics, the other their motor. "I can't do anything if Russell doesn't get the ball," says Havlicek. That's like saying a bulldozer can't do anything until somebody kicks over its starter. Try building a home without clearing the land. You need a foundation, but it's only a hole in the ground until the carpenters erect the framework and the craftsmen finish the interior.

Havlicek is the bulldozer as well as the cabinet maker. He's the co-ordinator as well as the artisan. Havlicek runs and the Celtics follow. He is their Pied Piper. Havlicek rebounds and the Celtics win. Havlicek defends and spreads frustration. Havlicek scores and is a scourge. John is a joy to behold. He's made the old men young and no matter what happens tonight at Boston as the championship resumes with the fourth game of this series, Havlicek has escaped the shadow of Russell's beard. He has super star status on his own. There is no better all-around basketball player in the world. What Hondo cannot do has not yet been done, not even by John Wayne.

There is a suggestion of Clark Kent in Havlicek off the court in his horn-rimmed glasses, diffident manner and soft-spoken way, which leads Russell occasionally to address him as "Country Boy." There is an injection of Krypton in John as he hurtles toward the basket with the ball or goes up to rebound. He doesn't have the fluid grace of Oscar Robertson or the speed of Jerry West or the water bug maneuverability of Walt Frazier or the pile-driving strength of Rudy LaRusso, but there is no other in pro basketball who can play front of backcourt with such an admirable blend of brute force, bouncy fancy and unrelieved stamina.

There was one point in the Celtics' Sunday victory over Los Angeles when Havlicek dribbled toward the lane and was picked up by seven-foot Mel Counts as he went up for his shot at the top of the key.

With Counts' long arms looming above him, Havlicek gave a perfect imitation of the Big O. His body moved from its vertical position like an upside-down pendulum into a 45-degree angle away from the defender, but the ball went unerringly for the hoop and bonged like Big Ben striking the hour.

At another juncture, Russell went to a high post to pick for Havlicek, but didn't reach his screening point swiftly enough to cut off 6-7 Bill Hewitt. The 6-5 Celtic twisted tight, lunged toward the basket, was fouled on his shot and completed a three-pointer.

At the end, there was Havlicek grabbing the rebound which locked up the game and put the Celtics back in the series and nothing could have punctuated the scene more than John moving the sight of his left eye as Keith Erickson's left hand flailed and ripped the skin. Havlicek made two foul shots and afterward looked at the world with one eye open and one eye closed. The rest of us look at him wide-eyed because there has been nobody who has played the three games of this title series in such focus and with such fervor at both ends of the court, 114 points, 37 rebounds, 17 assists.

Never say no to Havlicek. He never played tennis before, tried it in Phys Ed at Ohio State and won the round-robin tournament. He never had fenced, picked up a foil and hasn't been beaten yet. He once estimated he could throw a football 80 yards and, standing on the 20, threw it deep into the far end zone. In the coach country from which he sprung, there isn't much swimming. At college, his coach said he could develop into Olympic caliber. He could have been a big-league shortstop or an NFL quarterback.

Recently he took up golf, which his wife has been playing long and well. "I thought Beth was really going to beat me," says John. "I've never shot better than an 87. I had to shoot that to edge her out. I couldn't let her whip me. I almost panicked."

Note, please, that Havlicek said, "almost." When John panics, the Celtics, if not the world, will be in one helluva mess.

Boston Evening Globe
April 29, 1969

One more column probably should be added. The journalistic highlight of the first trip to California for the bright young man was meeting *Los Angeles Times* columnist Jim Murray. TBYM was hard in his judgments about many other sports columnists—sixty-four-year-old Red Smith, the favored typist everywhere in the business, the industry's highest standard, was "OK, but writes too much about horse racing and other unimportant stuff"—but he gushed about the forty-nine-year-old Murray. If he could write like anyone in the English-speaking world, living, dead or yet to be born, he would write like Murray.

The man was the king of the simile, the master of the metaphor, an amazing stylist. He was an everyday Charles Dickens on the sports page, a voice for the time. Plus he had started in New Haven, same as the bright young man.

This fact was an opener, a first sentence of introduction before one of the L.A. games. Two men. Same city. Same paper. Really? Yes. Is So-and-So still there? Yes, yes he is. A good guy. How about So-and-So? Yes, still there. The conversation went easily. TBYM's nerves stayed quiet. He talked with his idol as if his idol was a real person. That was an accomplishment.

"I came out here with the idea that I'd work here for two or three years and then move to a big city like Philadelphia," Murray said. "Then, you know what, I found this IS a big city."

The bright young man said that the *New Haven Journal-Courier* had run Murray's syndicated column every day for a long time. Did he know that? No. It was the best thing in the paper. Then one day it disappeared. Never ran again. Did he know that?

"Disappeared?" Murray said.

The publisher of the paper was Lionel Jackson, part of the Jackson family that had owned both New Haven papers since the turn of the century. He was a Yale man, of course, in a family of Yale men. He seldom tinkered in the editorial department, almost never in sports.

Then the Yale basketball team went to Los Angeles to play in a Christmas tournament. Then Jim Murray wrote a column about the appearance.

"I remember that," Murray said.

"Lionel Jackson decreed that you would never be in the paper again," the bright young man said. "And you never were."

This was a taste of the column from December 26, 1963.

There are certain things you don't expect to see in your lifetime. A guy in white tie and tails driving a truck. An Englishman making noise eating soup. Oscar Levant doing calisthenics. An honest wrestling match or a crooked church raffle.

And you don't expect to see Yale in a West Coast basketball tournament.

Honest, I couldn't have been more shocked if I caught

them using somebody else's toothbrush. But here they are: Yale men spending Christmas in, ugh! LOS ANGELES!

Heck, they should be out on Long Island or Bucks County or frostbite sailing on Oyster Bay. They should be making egg nogs or helping the chauffeur deliver plum pudding to the poor. And whatever will the glee club think? Or the tables down at Mory's. These are poor little sheep who have lost their way, all right.

Wait until they find out these kids out here don't even have their own yachts and get their allowances from grants-in-aid instead of mater and pater. The Christmas trees are all phonies and some people don't even dress for dinner.

Half the kids don't take Latin and wait'll the Yale boys shake hands before the tipoff and ask politely, "What year did you go to Choate?" and the other guys say "Where?" with a puzzled look.

I expect a terrible mistake has been made somewhere. When Yale got invited to the Los Angeles Classic, which starts today at the Sports Arena, they must have thought it was polo. I'm sure they dashed right down to Abercrombie and Fitch and said, "I say, old sport, what does one wear in the tropics around Los Angeles this time of year? Fix me up like a good fellow and send the bill round to Mama."

I just know they'll show up in Bermuda shorts and button-downs and not with, good grief, pre-tied ties. They play UCLA in the opening game at 1:15 this afternoon and I expect by 1:30 UCLA will be working on its second 100 points. You just know that Yale is missing the whole point when they have one guy exactly five-feet, no-inches tall in the lineup and two other guys just barely six feet. UCLA will die of embarrassment.

And just wait till old Eli finds out what has happened to Dr. Naismith's nice little "non-contact" sport in the rest of the country. They'll think the game is being played on the Hollywood Freeway.

I didn't think Yale would travel 3000 miles for anything

short of the unearthing of the Dead Sea Scrolls or a new translation of Ovid. The football team hasn't crossed the Hudson River in years or ever since Chicago dropped football and Yale found out the Big 10 needed shoulder pads to play the kind of game THEY played.

The boys will probably show up in pith helmets and elephant guns and ask if the Indians are friendly. Everywhere they look, they'll see those vulgar freeways and when they sit down to dinner they'll get only one fork and there won't even be one butler. It'll be worse than cook's night out back home.

There'll be some guys with padded shoulders and others who won't even take their hats off in the elevators. They won't even know all the words to "Boola, Boola . . ."

Dec. 26, 1963

There would be many more columns about many more names and situations to come in Murray's Pulitzer Prize–winning career, but this would always be the bright young man's favorite. Banned in the old hometown. What could be better than that? Unstuffing shirts should be a columnist's prime job.

Meanwhile, back at the playoffs . . .

Chapter 13

GAME FOUR

OFF WRONG FOOT—THE RIGHT SHOT
CELTICS WIN, 89–88

BY LEIGH MONTVILLE
Staff Writer
The basketball was in the air.

"I didn't think it would reach the front of the rim," said Sam Jones, who had shot the ball from 20 feet away.

Marvin Kratter, the fat man who used to own the Boston Celtics, rubbed a piece of black, polished coral, his lucky stone. Johnny Most, the radio announcer, told the world in an excited, shattered voice what was going on.

Emmette Bryant prayed.

"I saw the ball hit the rim," said Bryant. "I said, 'Hail Mary, full of grace . . .'"

"I was surprised . . . ," said Jones. The ball spun up—there wasn't one member of the Boston Celtics close enough to take down a rebound—it hit the back of the rim and came down. Through the middle of the basket.

"Around the rim and in, around the rim and in," Most cackled five times rapid-fire into the microphone. Marvin

Kratter, stone in hand, leaped and yelled. And 15,128 other people at the Boston Garden joined him last night.

Game time. Sam Jones' shot, going through the hoop with one second left in the game, gave the Boston Celtics an 89–88 win over the Los Angeles Lakers. The best-of-seven final in the National Basketball Association playoffs was tied, two games to two games.

The Celtics-Lakers game in Los Angeles tomorrow night will be carried on Channel 38 starting approximately at 11 pm.

The Celtics, once again on a last-minute, off-balance, off-the-wall spectacular shot were very much alive. They play in Los Angeles Thursday night, here Saturday night and back in LA on Monday if needed.

The best-of-seven had shrunk to best-of-three.

"Never in doubt," were the first three words out of Bill Russell's mouth when reporters entered the Celtics locker room. Then, the player-coach laughed.

He had to.

In doubt? Fourteen seconds before Sam Jones' wobbling, spinning shot bounced twice and slowly nestled through the basket, people were putting on coats. Searching for parking lot receipts, getting ready for the ride home.

The Lakers had the ball. The Lakers had the lead, 88–87. The Celtics did not have any more fouls to waste.

The Lakers needed only a few Johnny Egan dribbles, a couple of passes and a television interview to complete the win.

They didn't get any of them.

Elgin Baylor passed the ball in-bounds to Egan, the 5-foot-11 ballhandler from Providence College. Egan tried to move right. He couldn't. Bailey Howell was standing there.

Then . . .

"Egan turned toward me," Bryant said. "He came around with the ball and I slapped it up, out of his hands. For once I got the ball without a foul being called."

Bryant, at 6-foot-1, thought he might shoot. Wilt Chamberlain, at 7-foot-1, also thought Bryant might shoot. Bryant passed the ball to Jones, at the key, the same place Jones would be standing a few seconds later.

Jones shot. The ball hit the backboard, hit Chamberlain, then hit out of bounds—at least that is what referee Joe Gushue and the Celtics thought. Elgin Baylor, who made a good try at saving the play, thought otherwise.

It didn't matter. The Celtics called timeout.

"We had set up a play in the timeout preceding this one," Russell said. "We weren't sure we were going to get a chance to call another timeout."

It was a new play. There was no name for it, just "three guys set up a screen for Sam." Russell removed himself, putting Don Nelson, a better foul shooter, into the lineup.

"It's a play we worked at Ohio State," John Havlicek said. "Larry (Siegfried) and I both won games on it . . . we beat Indiana, 96–95, with it once and we won a game in the NCAA quarterfinals with it.

"Now it was Sam's turn."

Havlicek had introduced the play during the Philadelphia series in this year's playoffs. The Celtics had practiced it against the big Garden clock, deciding the play was good to run when there were 12 seconds to operate.

They had never used it in a game.

"That's why we used it tonight," Russell said. "The Lakers didn't know about it."

The huddle broke. Bryant passed the ball in-bounds to Havlicek, then broke to form the screen with Howell and Nelson. Jones came around the screen. He slipped and took the pass from Havlicek at the same time.

There were bodies everywhere ("Wilt was really pushing to get through," Nelson said.) but Jones didn't see any of them. Off balance, off the wrong foot, Sam took his shot.

"Of course I didn't feel graceful," one of the most

graceful shooters ever to play basketball said. "I was off balance. If I had that shot in a regular game, I wouldn't have taken it."

Marvin Kratter rubbed the stone. Johnny Most cackled. The ball went in as Chamberlain and Jerry West and all the Lakers had that stunned, auto-wreck look.

Boston Evening Globe

April 30, 1969

The earth had shifted in this little Boston–Los Angeles confrontation. Not a small shift, either. One funky, end-of-the-game, wrong-footed, off-balance, double-bounce jump shot and North became South and East became West and Up certainly became Down and All Bets Were Off. Amazing. Amazing. Amazing. Just like that.

This was the type of finish that made a night at the arena different from a night at the theater. There was no script. Anything could happen.

"When the Good Lord wants you to win, that's how you win," Jerry West said with resignation in that Eagle Scout way after the Celtics' 89–88 end-of-the-game escape victory.

The flip in emotions was total. On the flight from Los Angeles four days earlier, Lakers owner Jack Kent Cooke had said, "We're beating the Celtics the way they used to beat us." His words were part declaration, part hope, and until Sam Jones's prayer-laden jumper bounced once off the front of the rim and once off the back of the rim and wandered through the net where it landed in the hands of a disgruntled Wilt Chamberlain, they would have been true. Not now.

The one shot shrinked, shrank, shrunk the series to best-of-three from best-of-seven. Talent still was important in this situation, but not as important as it had been. Variables could defeat talent. The Celtics always had been very good with variables. This was the latest exhibit.

The game was a sloppy mess that somehow dissolved into high, then higher drama at the end. The Lakers had the ball and an 88–87 lead with fifteen seconds left. All they had to do was pass it inbounds to a good free-throw shooter, have him hold on to it, wait for the inevitable free throws to arrive, make them both, listen for the final whistle, and depart with a smile on Jack Kent Cooke's weathered face.

History had favored the Celtics in everything they did. Led by the combination of coach Red Auerbach and center Bill Russell (above, after another successful night at the Boston Garden), they had won ten NBA titles in the past twelve years. They never had lost a playoff series to the Los Angeles version of the Lakers, beating them five times in the finals. The championship-clinching celebration had become a basketball constant of every Boston playoff spring. Note the locker room elegance. (*Dick Raphael,* above | *Bettmann/Getty Images,* below)

Resident superstars Elgin Baylor (left) and Jerry West, pictured with former coach Fred Schaus, had been waiting for the arrival of a dominant big man to combat the Celtics' Russell. (*Bettmann/Getty Images*)

The Lakers became instant favorites for the 1968–69 NBA title on July 9, 1968, when they traded three players plus an undisclosed amount of cash to Philadelphia for the services of seven-foot-one Wilton Norman Chamberlain. He arrived two days later for a press conference happily hosted by Lakers owner Jack Kent Cooke. (*Associated Press*)

Below: The ringmaster for this instant basketball show now was forty-six-year-old coach Bill (Butch) van Breda Kolff, an outspoken character who had arrived a year earlier straight from Princeton University. (*Bettmann/Getty Images*)

The rivalry between Chamberlain and Russell or Russell and Chamberlain, depending on the billing, had stretched across eight years before Chamberlain moved to Los Angeles. Russell was two and a half years older, three inches shorter, and sixty pounds lighter, but his teams had won NBA titles in seven of those eight years. The seven-foot-one, 275-pound Chamberlain's Philadelphia 76ers team had caused the only interruption in the streak in 1967. (*Bettmann/Getty Images*)

The big games for both teams could draw fat sellout crowds—fans heading into the Boston Garden here on April 1, 1969, for Game Four of the Celtics' opening playoff series against the Philadelphia 76ers—but overall both NBA teams had to fight for attention. The biggest problem in each city came from competing young stars with the local Bruins franchises . . . (*Boston Globe/Getty Images*)

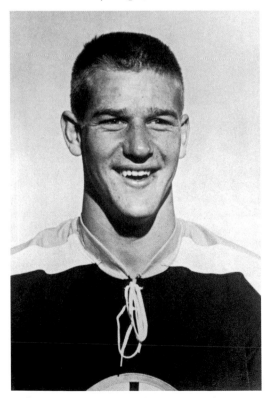

The Boston Bruins had become Stanley Cup contenders with twenty-year-old defenseman Bobby Orr. (*Bettmann/Getty Images*)

The UCLA Bruins were on their way to a third consecutive NCAA title with twenty-one-year-old senior star Lew Alcindor, who would later change his name to Kareem Abdul-Jabbar. (*Associated Press*)

The game, a perfect display of West's abilities, may have been preserved for NBA history. Designer Alan Siegel used a picture of West—maybe from this game—when he created the league's logo for the 1969–70 season. The logo has not been changed in fifty-two years.

The Celtics' idea in Game One was to guard Jerry West man-to-man, same as if he were not a matinee-idol star. This did not work very well. Emmette Bryant, given the task, picked up three quick fouls. West scored 53 points in a 120–118 win. (*Associated Press*)

West was the leading man in the production, but all attention was on the finals debut of Chamberlain. (*Bettmann/ Getty Images*)

Sports Illustrated had blossomed from a slow start in 1954 (the debut issue read at a New York newsstand) to become the preeminent sports magazine in the country. Along with its success had come the worry of the now-famous *SI* curse, bad fates falling to players pictured on the cover. (*Susan Wood/Archive Photos/Getty Images*)

Frank Deford was in the first years of an *SI* career that would establish him as the master of the long-form feature story. (*National Sports Media Association*)

George Plimpton, the all-time participant sport, had gone through training camp with Russell and the Celtics. He never would write a book about the experience, but stayed close to the team. (*Dick Raphael*)

The Lakers won the second game for a 2-0 series lead. Russell and Chamberlain seemed to balance out each other's production. Referee Joe Gushue seemed to be signaling for a waiter in the opulent Forum. (*Bettmann/Getty Images*)

The Boston Garden, built in 1928 on top of a train station, was a look at the NBA's creaky past. The building was filled with quirks and inconveniences, plus fans who drank beer and said bad things. (*Steve Lipofsky*)

The Forum—OK, the Fabulous Forum—was a year and a half old, the creation of Lakers owner Jack Kent Cooke. It was the look toward the NBA future with color-coded seats and show-business celebrities. (*Associated Press*)

The series settled into a physical grind. The Lakers complained about Larry Siegfried's scrambling, pesky defense against West. (*Associated Press*)

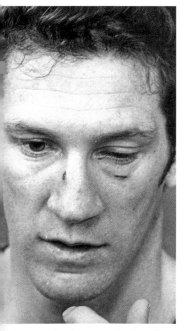

John Havlicek was poked in the eye by Keith Erickson in Game Three, but still scored 34 points in a 111–105 Celtics win. (*Boston Globe/Getty Images*)

Chamberlain was poked in the eye in Game Five by Emmette Bryant. This caused the big man to practice foul shooting in sunglasses for Game Six. The sunglasses had no effect on his foul shooting. (*Boston Globe/Getty Images*)

The Celtics tie the series at two games apiece on Sam Jones's last-second shot for an 89–88 win. Chamberlain collects the ball as it comes through the basket and Emmette Bryant cheers in the background. TBYM is one of the sportswriters at the table in the background. (*Bettmann/Getty Images*)

Larry Siegfried (far left) and John Havlicek (far right) suggested a play from their Ohio State time as 1960 NCAA champions. The result was Sam Jones's winning shot. Other Ohio State players are Mel Nowell, Joe Roberts, and Jerry Lucas. (*Columbus Dispatch*)

The battle between the broadcasters, Chick Hearn (left) of Los Angeles and Johnny Most (right) of Boston, was as spirited as the games on the court. Radio and the written word were more important than television coverage, since the bulk of the televised games were blacked out in both markets. (*Dick Raphael/National Basketball Association/Getty Images*)

Los Angeles Times columnist Jim Murray (*National Sports Media Association*)

Boston Globe columnist Bud Collins (*National Sports Media Association*)

Home games were telecast in Los Angeles theaters.

Home court advantage held for Games Five and Six. Wilt had a large presence in Game Five, but Russell returned to form in Game Six. (*Associated Press*)

Johnny Egan, driving here against Sam Jones, had become a pest for the Celtics to handle. (*Focus on Sport/Getty Images*)

Don Nelson, onetime Laker, had become an even larger pest for his former team to handle. (*Focus on Sport/Getty Images*)

Havlicek lifts a jumper over Elgin Baylor's attempted block in Game Seven. This might be the prettiest basketball picture of all time. (*Bettmann/Getty Images*)

The finish (Los Angeles version): Jerry West leaves the Forum floor, his face once again looking as if he had witnessed a terrible accident. (*Los Angeles Times/Getty Images*)

The finish (Boston version): The Celtics, led by Russell, Bryant, and reserve Rich Johnson, leave the Forum floor, once again looking as if they had won a grand lottery prize. (*Bettmann/Getty Images*)

Balance Writes Happy Ending to Celtics' Cinderella Tale

Sam 'Glad to Finish as Champ'

By LEIGH MONTVILLE
Staff Writer

What had happened was what has happened over and over and over again

LAKERS RALLY TOO LATE AND TWO SHORT

Celts Hang On After Building 17-Point Lead

BY HAL FLORENCE
Times Staff Writer

The Celtics are greeted by a crowd at Logan Airport, a first in their long string of championships. Bill Russell accepts the congratulations of Massachusetts governor Francis Sargent. (*Boston Globe/Getty Images*)

A modest parade is held, followed by a celebration at Boston City Hall. These also are firsts for the Celtics. Russell does not attend either event. (*Boston Globe/Getty Images*)

Russell did retire. Sold the story to *Sports Illustrated* for $10,000. Chamberlain played for four more seasons, winning a second title in 1972. After twenty years of not talking, the two men became friendly again and appeared together on May 25, 1999, at a testimonial in Boston for Russell. Chamberlain died five months later at the age of sixty-three. (*Associated Press*)

Will McDonough became a national television presence as a football expert for CBS. (*George Gojkovich/Getty Images Sport/Getty Images*)

One year after the seventh-game drama, the bright young man found himself covering the Massachusetts Special Olympics on May 5, 1970, with a chance to talk to a young senator from Massachusetts. TBYM became a columnist and never covered the Celtics on a daily basis again. (*Leigh Montville*)

Things happened instead.

1. The Lakers did not call timeout—Emmette Bryant, intentionally fouled, had made his single free throw to cut the lead to a point, 86–85. A timeout would have given the visitors a chance to take the ball out at half-court and, more importantly, time to plan and decompose and think. Instead, they elected to take the ball out at the far end of the floor right away, the Celtics pressing, as the well-fortified, late-night crowd (9 p.m. start) of 15,128 bellowed in excitement.

This caused an immediate glitch. Van Breda Kolff wanted Elgin Baylor, tall and strong, to receive the inbounds pass. Baylor, instead, made the inbounds pass.

"Everyone else had headed down to the other end of the court," he said. "I had to take the ball out."

He passed it to Johnny Egan, the five-foot-eleven point guard from Providence College. Egan's work in the playoffs had been solid until now, his good shooting a surprise, but he was engulfed by Bryant and Bailey Howell. Double-teamed. Bryant spotted an exposed spot of basketball and swung his hand at it. The ball popped free.

Egan said a good stretch of his right arm was hit instead of that exposed part of the basketball. . . .

"He fouled me," Egan said, pointing to a spot on his right forearm where he felt the infraction occurred. "The referee didn't blow his whistle. They were double-teaming me—Bryant and Bailey Howell—and he fouled me out of desperation. He smacked me on the arm."

"It should have been a backcourt foul," Egan added. "Two shots."

Bryant, of course, said his hand touched only basketball. . . .

"I slapped the ball up, out of his hands," said the little man, whose defense was attacked by West for those 53 points in the opener. "For once I got the ball without a foul being called."

Howell agreed.

"We had Egan locked up," the Celtics forward said. "He had no place to go. Emmette's steal was clean."

Bryant passed the ball to Sam Jones. Sam took a jumper, which missed off the rim and then bounced off Chamberlain's hands, headed for out of bounds. That was when Elgin Baylor saved it. Or didn't.

2. Elgin Baylor didn't save the ball going out-of-bounds.—The man who once could fly jumped and grabbed the ball in midair, but landed

this time before he could get rid of it. Or he didn't land, but his foot was out-of-bounds when he took off. Or—third option—the ball had bounced out-of-bounds before the takeoff even started. Referee Joe Gushue did not indicate which malfeasance had occurred. He simply pointed at the end line and indicated that the ball now belonged to the Celtics with seven seconds remaining.

The man who once could fly was very upset by this.

"I didn't go out, nor did the ball go out," Baylor said. "I had the ball in the air and I know I didn't step on the line. But all he did was point to the line. He didn't say anything to me. You don't lose many games that way."

In the faraway future, the game would be stopped here and the referees (a third one added in the 1988–89 season) would gather in conference with some replay expert in Secaucus, New Jersey. After assorted angles were shown, again and again, everything slowed down and stopped if necessary, one human action dissected at its smallest molecular level—after announcers at the game, the network's own expert, plus fans in the arena and at home all were given a chance to comment, sandwiched around an advertisement featuring Flo from Progressive Insurance—the call would be judged correct or incorrect.

There was none of that here.

Gushue pointed. Celtics ball. Timeout.

3. The Celtics had a secret play.—Larry Siegfried often talked about how he and John Havlicek and everyone else on the bench helped coach the Celtics. He would tell the listener to think about the situation: How hard was it for Bill Russell to play forty-eight minutes against Wilt Chamberlain and coach the game at the same time? How could he slow down his thoughts when his body was just trying to take a break during a timeout?

"He'll come back to the bench sometimes and he can't even talk," Siegfried said. "He'll be just trying to breathe for the entire timeout. John and I call a lot of the plays. He's OK with that."

The secret play was part of the communal effort. In the faraway future, seven seconds left, down by a basket, this would be an analytic moment discussed by a head coach and his Mormon Tabernacle Choir full of sharp-eyed assistants. Computers would spit out tendencies for everyone involved at this particular time, space, phase of the moon. A defender would be attacked because he had .78 inches less in vertical lift, was troubled by an ingrown toenail on his left foot since last Thursday, needed a haircut, and had eaten a turkey club sandwich for lunch. A well-researched something

Here the play sounded as if it had been sketched out in the dirt in the second half of a schoolyard touch football game. You go here. You go there. You and you go there and there. Sam, you get the ball behind the triple pick and take your favorite jump shot.

A reluctant Russell had allowed the thing to be installed at that practice session in Melrose. (Down 2-0 in a best-of-seven series is always a fine time to add a secret play.) Havlicek, the perpetual fuss-budget, provided the historical details about how the play had worked twice at Ohio State. The Celtics walked through it, then ran through it, then ran through it again at speed. According to a stopwatch, the pieces were all assembled, the shot taken in seven seconds.

The Celtics had seven seconds now.

4. The play was a forerunner to the Picket Fence.—Seventeen years later the same play—pretty much the same play—would be run in the basketball film *Hoosiers*. Assistant coach Wilbur (Shooter) Flatch, an alcoholic on the mend, played by Dennis Hopper, would call for it in the last seconds of Hickory High School's big game against Dugger High. The score was tied at 58–58. Head coach Norman Dale (Gene Hackman) had been ejected, leaving Shooter in charge with his troubled past and odd-fitting new suit.

"Boys, this is the last shot we got," Shooter says in the huddle. "We're gonna run the Picket Fence at 'em. Merle, you're the swing-man. . . . Jimmy, you're the solo right. Everett, Jimmy should be open on the other side of that fence! Now, boys, don't get caught watchin' the paint dry."

The Picket Fence is three picks set straight across the foul line. Jimmy Chitwood (Maris Valainis) moves around to the back of the fence. Everett (David Neidorf) hits him with the pass. Jimmy, a troubled lad at the start of the film, squared away now, hits the jumper as the horn sounds. Hickory wins. Everybody hugs everybody else. Shooter has some damn good validation for living on the straight and narrow.

The Celtics' play, which had no name except maybe "that play from

Ohio State we ran at practice," also featured the triple pick across the foul line. There obviously was no Shooter, no Norman Dale, either, since Gene Hackman did not play Norman as a six-foot-ten famous black man, basketball legend coach who also was the starting center. There was a Jimmy Chitwood, though, one of the best last-shot Jimmy characters ever to dribble a basketball. Sam Jones had been Jimmy Chitwood for all his seasons with the team.

"At one point, we won eight consecutive NBA championships and six times during that run we asked Sam to take the shot that meant the season," Russell will say more than once in the future. "If he didn't hit the shot we were finished—we were going home empty-handed. He never missed."

Jones was a jump-shooting constant. He didn't have the reputation of West and some other NBA scorers, his star dulled by the excellence of the Celtics with their team-over-statistics approach, but his teammates knew how good he was. He was always the first choice in these situations. He had the resting heart rate of a house plant, the Celtics' version of "Mr. Clutch."

A large number of the Celtics' basic six plays and accompanying options were designed for the same result, shot by Sam to win the game, but for this one time, this moment, this was the variation. The Lakers had seen those other plays. Now they would have a new look to consider.

Russell and the players had agreed during an earlier timeout to use the play if the game clicked down to a last-shot situation, so they only had to nod again during this last timeout. Russell made a strategic decision. He took himself out and put Don Nelson into the lineup. The change was in case the Lakers decided to foul someone (one-shot foul under the rules at the time) and take the game into overtime. Nelson was a better foul shooter.

Everything evolved as if saltshakers were being moved against pepper shakers on a red-checked tablecloth at a place where basketball minds gathered. Emmette Bryant threw the ball inbounds to Havlicek, then moved immediately to the right side of the foul line, the right side of the fence. Nelson set up at the middle of the foul line. Bailey Howell set up at the left. Havlicek held the ball and waited. One Mississippi. Two Mississippi. Sam came around the left side. Jerry West, guarding him, was two steps behind as he tried to get around Howell. Havlicek passed the ball to Sam, who was free and clear.

Perfect.

Easy.

This was when Sam slipped on the parquet floor.

He had no traction and he was sliding and the clock was ticking down and everything was wrong, wrong, wrong, but he had no other place to go, no other thing to do, so off his left foot, the wrong foot, he heaved the ball toward the basket with the idea that if it missed—probably when it missed—Russell might be there to lay in the rebound. Front rim. Back rim. Net.

Celtics 89. Lakers 88.

Nobody got caught watching the paint dry.

5. Even was far, far different from 3-1.—Tommy Heinsohn, the retired Celtic, always talked about the gremlins, the leprechauns, the curators of pots of gold found at the end of the rainbow. The little guy with his green bowler hat and shillelagh and cocky smile, drawn and copyrighted by Red Auerbach's young brother, Zang, had made his debut as the team cartoon logo only at the beginning of the season, winking and spinning a basketball at the same time, but he had been part of the team's thought patterns for the entire championship run. Luck was a Celtics standby.

"Didn't you see that little gremlin sitting on the hoop when Sam shot?" Heinsohn asked again and again in the Celtics locker room. "I thought for sure you could see it."

"Those four-leaf clovers were all over the place," Emmette Bryant said.

This was a win that resonated. How could it not? The way it ended resonated. Familiar roles seemed to be distributed one more time.

The fact that Sam Jones took the shot thinking that Bill Russell could grab the rebound and win the game when RUSSELL WAS NOT EVEN IN THE GAME was a perfect footnote. One bounce, two bounces, through the net. Another perfect footnote.

"I was just plain lucky," Sam Jones said. "I didn't think I had a chance at all to make the shot. When it went in, I was the most surprised guy in the place."

"You know, I have confidence in Sam's shooting ability," Bill Russell said, "but not when he's slipping and shooting at the same time."

The shot. The shot. The shot.

"The ball hit the rim twice and just stuck there," Wilt Chamberlain said.

"It was a bad shot," Jerry West said. "It barely tipped the side of the rim. Their luck sometimes is unbelievable."

The shot.

"The loss has got to hurt us," he added. "If we won, no question we'd win in Los Angeles Thursday. It's hard to take a loss like that. I must be a loser. We played dumb basketball in that final minute. I don't want to talk about it. We got beat. That's all."

The shot.

The story written by the bright young man (appears at the start of this chapter) was on the front page of the *Boston Evening Globe*. This was another first for him. He never had been on the front page of the *Boston Evening Globe*. There he was now, "Off Wrong Foot . . . The Right Shot" by LEIGH MONTVILLE, Globe Staff, with a smiling two-column picture of Sam Jones above the headline. A story about possible Paris peace negotiations, "Cong Say They're Now Set for Direct Talks with Saigon," was the lead story, followed by a secondary story about how the stock market had jumped sixteen points with this news of a possible peace agreement.

The bright young man no doubt was pleased. I wonder if he has noticed that he missed the funkiest fact of the entire last play, the fact that RUSSELL WASN'T IN THE GAME when Jones thought he was. Every other paper had it, all editions. Why didn't he? Did he miss the interviews when the fact was mentioned? Sam said it. Russell said it. Did he think the fact didn't matter? This was the kind of stuff he liked, the little insider details. Everyone else was on the inside this time.

He spent too much time on Marvin Kratter. Marvin wasn't the owner anymore. Shouldn't matter. TBYM somehow was fascinated with this guy, the destroyer of Ebbets Field, saw him as a capitalistic villain walking around, right in front of everyone. Touch my stone for good luck? Isn't that a villainous act right there, having these basketball players pay some kind of tribute to the throne? Touch my stone?

Kiss my ass. The bright young man brought personal animosities into his account. Deduct more points right there.

I do see him happy, though, as he walked onto the plane the next day for the return trip to California. (And a third viewing of *Bullitt*.) The front page of the *Globe*? He would be looking for people who had the paper. See the front page? Yes, that would be my story, over there on the left. Above Sam Jones's picture. Yes, I'm the writer. That's me.

He would not necessarily want to see anyone actually reading the story. That would make him nervous. Is the person paying attention? Is he or she going to turn the page to read the slam-bang finish? Is he or she asleep? Watching someone read his words always would be an unsettling experience.

(Even now. Please put down this book if you see him coming.)

The worst reader/writer situations would arrive in a few years' time. TBYM would be shanghaied, commanded, ordered to pick the results of each week's National Football League games. Since he didn't know much about picking football games, he decided to make the column a humorous exercise. He would crack jokes about all the teams, make comments about pop culture, invent weird scores like 100–0 or 69–69 (wink).

The problem was he was covering the Patriots, who now were the New England Patriots. (The original change of names went from "Boston Patriots" to "Bay State Patriots." This change lasted for about a millisecond until the team realized that headline writer now would call the team the "BS Patriots.") The New England Patriots were terrible.

To maintain any credibility with the general football-watching public, the bright young man not only had to predict a defeat for the Patriots every week, he had to predict a humongous defeat that included some sort of sidesplitting description. The football-watching public did seem to enjoy this approach, but the football team did not.

Flying with the team, three-hundred-pound men already cranky because they had to ask for a seat-belt extension and were crammed next to each other two, three, four-five-or-six hours, the bright young man would notice some stares when he would pass on the way to the men's room. He also would notice a copy of the *Boston Globe* somewhere in the vicinity.

There would be a game somewhere, the mind shuts out the details, when the Patriots shocked everyone and recorded an upset over a very good opponent. When the locker room door was opened, reporters found the team in a circle, cheering as a newspaper page was burned in their midst. Yes, the bright young man could see that his name was on top of his football predictions, the flames consuming his words.

Anyway, there was no problem here unless, perhaps, Marvin Kratter was on the plane. I can see the bright young man heading toward his seat. Maybe various members of the Celtics are reading that front page story. Maybe Bill Russell is reading it. (Sorry, Bill. You'll find your own column back in the sports section.) Yes, that's my story. Yes, right over Sam's picture. Yes, yes, great game.

I can see it all, except I really can't. I see now that the flight to Los Angeles is at 9:30 in the morning. The *Boston Evening Globe* has not yet hit the streets. No one at all can have a copy of the paper. Not even the bright young man in his moment of journalistic glory.

Memory is funny.

Chapter 14

OFF DAY:
TELEVISION AND RADIO

By Leigh Montville
Staff Writer
LOS ANGELES—"If Sam Jones is in that limousine, would you please stop and leave him by the side of the road somewhere."

The words came over a two-way radio as the Boston Celtics were taken from the airport to the hotel here yesterday in preparation for tonight's fifth game of the finals of the National Basketball Association playoffs. The meaning was obvious.

Jones' off-balance, one-second jump shot had stunned the Los Angeles Lakers, 89–88, Tuesday night at Boston Garden. The best-of-seven series was tied at two games apiece.

Someone had lost money at the other end of the radio and everyone in this city—even if nobody would say it—was worried about the condition of the Lakers.

They had been so close to an almost insurmountable 3-1 advantage. Then they had blown it. One off-balance shot at the wrong time, and the Lakers had blown it.

The effects? Tonight at 11 o'clock at the Forum (TV-Channel 38) the effects will officially be measured.

Already, however, Laker coach Bill van Breda Kolff said
he has done some snooping.

"I'll tell you what, if we had to play another game 10
minutes after that shot went in, I don't think we could
have beaten anybody," van Breda Kolff said. "Now, I think
we're all right."

The coach led his team through a brief workout at the
Forum yesterday. He said he liked what he saw.

"I had planned to do a few things before the game
to help the attitude of everyone," van Breda Kolff said.
"But after seeing our practice, I don't think I'll have to do
anything.

"Everyone seemed all right."

The practice was low-key. Jump shots and running.
There were a few of the usual laughs and giggles and that
was what van Breda Kolff liked.

Perhaps, as he said, the memory of the game was gone,
part of the ghost of basketball past. Perhaps, however, it
still lingered.

A few of the Lakers mentioned bad dreams. Jerry West
said he hadn't had any dreams.

"I don't think I slept more than 40 minutes all night,"
West, the obvious standout of this series, said. "The game
kept bothering me.

"If it has an effect, it certainly can't be a good one."

"It has to have some (good) effect on us," Larry
Siegfried of the Celtics said on the other side. "It has to
help our older guys like Sam and Bailey Howell.

"Now we're even again. We have a lot more incentive
than if this thing was three games to one. It's easier."

Siegfried, as much as anyone, has been responsible for
the Celtics' comeback after falling into a 2-0 hole here
one week ago. Taped and slapped together with band-aids,
the 6-foot-3 guard has come off the bench twice in a row
for 20-points-plus performances.

Also, he has played a prominent part in the Celtics'
strategy against West. He has defensed the superstar
head-to-head, receiving help whenever West held the ball.

"You have to get help," Siegfried said. "You have to double-team West when you can. You don't want him to take any shot, easy or difficult.

"You'd much rather give up an easy shot to someone else than a not-so-easy one to West."

The "someone else" in Tuesday night's game was Keith Erickson, the 6-foot-5 forward-guard from UCLA. This time, at least, Erickson did all right, well enough for van Breda Kolff to say he will see even more action tonight.

"The shot they give you all alone is sometimes the hardest shot you take. It's psychological. You have time to think. You can worry about adjustments and situations and worry yourself into a missed shot."

Erickson hit eight of 16 open shots, played 32 minutes and scored 16 points. The reason he was in the lineup in the first place was defense—defense against John Havlicek.

Havlicek had run wild against the Lakers' usual starter, rookie Billy Hewitt. Erickson, almost the same size and physical build as Havlicek, was called in to stop the problem.

Again, he did all right. He held Havlicek (if held is the word) to 21 points.

"I can't stay up with Havlicek for the whole game, mainly because he has been playing a lot and I haven't been playing much in the playoffs," Erickson said. "If I get some rest, though, I'm all right."

Erickson will come into the lineup early tonight. Siegfried will come in early. Sam Jones, who was not left at the side of the road, will be in there all the way.

Boston Evening Globe
May 1, 1969

The Celtics' grand win sadly was seen in Boston only by the record number of 15,123 ticket holders stuffed into the Garden. The television blackout was in effect. The game was a 9 p.m. start, piped back to Los Angeles with a Chick Hearn and Rod Hundley simulcast

("Lakers on TV Tonight," a headline in the *Los Angeles Times* read), but Celtics fans saw none of it, restricted to Johnny Most's call of Sam Jones's shot on the radio.

Even there they had a problem listening to the entire game. WHDH, the station that broadcast the Celtics, also broadcast the Red Sox. The baseball team, the more lucrative tenant, had the priority in all scheduling conflicts. The Red Sox were playing the Yankees in New York, a 7:30 start, so the Celtics at nine were dropped to WHDH's FM signal while the proceedings at Yankee Stadium were on the more powerful, dashboard-accessible AM signal. The Celtics were switched to the AM when the Red Sox polished off the Yanks, 2–1, in a speedy two hours and fourteen minutes, Mike Nagy with the win, Sparky Lyle with the save, Mel Stottlemyre with the loss, but still there was a stain of indignity. Fourth game of the NBA finals? FM radio?

A positive development did occur the next day. An announcement was made at a luncheon at the Hotel Lenox in Boston while the Celtics flew to L.A. that tomorrow's fifth game of the series would be televised back to Boston after all. A group of local backers that included Northeast Airlines, American International Travel, Ballantine Beer, and Colonial Provisions, makers of the Fenway Frank, would cover the expenses of the Channel 38 production. Tommy Heinsohn, the former Celtic, would be the announcer. Red Auerbach would be his color man. The broadcast would start at eleven o'clock at night, Eastern time.

"We did the final game from L.A. a year ago, when the Celtics won everything," Heinsohn recalled. "When it ended, they told me to go down to the locker room to do the interviews. I thought Red would do that, but it was me. I went down and Russell kept the locker room closed for what seemed like forty-five minutes. Red was back in the booth on the air. He didn't know what to do, but someone gave him a box score. He read the entire box score out loud. Every statistic. The door was still closed. So he read the box score again. Every statistic. I don't know how many times he read it before Russell opened the door."

The Hotel Lenox luncheon went very well, all the principals posing for pictures with big smiles in front of a TV that featured the UHF circular wire antenna needed to pull Channel 38 to the screen. Auerbach, who had lived at the hotel for his entire tenure as coach, family back in Washington (stories about this arrangement always noted that he had a telephone installed in his Lenox bathroom because he liked to multitask), was a happy man, pleased with the outcome and his team's situation.

Then he opened the floor to questions. Jack Craig of the *Globe* had a few. Auerbach did not like this.

Craig was the first sports television critic in the nation, probably the world. A local guy who had graduated from Boston University on the GI Bill at the age of twenty-seven, spent some time at various suburban Massachusetts papers, then landed on the copy desk at the *Globe,* he had created the position in the past year and a half, defined its boundaries. People were watching more and more sports on television. The broadcasters had become more famous than most of the players. Monday morning discussions in offices were about Saturday afternoon games on television. Everybody had become a sports television critic. Forty years old, a veteran of the Korean War, Craig was the one who was paid for it. The first one.

His column, SporTView, would become a twenty-nine-year constant, copied by newspapers across the country. He was never shy, always forceful with his opinions. Television networks and stations, it turned out, paid much more attention to printed criticism than sports teams or even politicians did. He was given great access to broadcasters and executives and was not afraid to use it.

(He wound up in a public argument once with Howard Cosell at Fenway Park. The bright young man did not see it, but heard about it.

("How did Jack make out?" TBYM asked someone who was there.

("It was Howard Cosell," the someone replied. "That's like arguing against Jerry Lewis. What chance do you have?")

Here the opponent was Auerbach, someone also in the Jerry Lewis league. Craig congratulated him on the deal to televise the fifth game of the series, but bemoaned the fact that the fourth game and its dramatics had been blacked out. The game was a sellout. Interest was high. What was the problem with letting people see something that turned out so well? Wouldn't that sell tickets for the future? The blackout seemed counterproductive.

Auerbach answered with a gentle huff and a subdued puff. He said that removing the blackout would have been a breach of faith with the people who bought tickets, especially the ones who stood in line on the morning of the game. He said, too, that if the game had been televised, it might not have been a sellout. The third game was not a sellout and the fourth game became sold out only in the afternoon.

Craig said interest in the Celtics had lagged during the fourth-place finish during the regular season. Maybe a game like the last one, a thriller, televised, would rekindle interest, create new fans.

The huff and the puff from the general manager became more substantial. The Knicks, that team in New York, withdrew the black-out for the Easter Sunday afternoon playoff game against the Celtics. What happened? They were besieged with requests for refunds. The Celtics, too, had tried some home game television in the past when Walter Brown was the owner. Didn't work. The gate suffered.

But . . .

No buts . . .

The present owners of the Garden might ask for a share of revenue that was missed because people stayed home to watch on television. How would that be? Television hurt the gate. Unlike hockey, where the puck was hard to see, basketball was built for the screen. The ball was large. The people were large and in shorts. There might come a time when people who would have bought cheaper seats would stay home because they could see the game better on television.

But . . .

Auerbach delivered his biggest salvo at the end. When was the last time the questioner, Mr. Craig, sat in those cheap seats? When was the last time he sat in any seats at a Celtics game that he'd actually purchased? This was the Jerry Lewis moment. End of press conference. End of argument.

Craig decided on the way home, the way we all do, what he should have said. Before he ever worked at the *Globe,* even before the titles began to be accumulated, before Russell, he had paid to see a lot of games. He loved to watch Cousy. He thought it was the best bargain in sports. He loved basketball, quietly loved the Celtics.

He also could have said that he was absolutely right. There would come a time when it seemed every single game would be on television, games and more games from all around the league. There would come a time, get this, when the teams would play for a championship with no fans in the stands, not a one, all the games played in Orlando, Florida, inside a controlled environment in the middle of a pandemic.

He just wasn't sure all this would happen.

The sold-out fifth game, it should be noted, would be blacked out by the Lakers in Los Angeles. To protect the gate.

The importance of radio in these blackout, freeze-out situations could not be overstated. The gravel-voiced Johnny Most in Boston (it was almost a rule that local residents had to say the descriptive words every time, "gravel-voiced," when mentioning his name) and the staccato-delivery Chick Hearn in Los Angeles did not simply report the games, they were the games. If you followed the Celtics or followed the Lakers you had to listen to one of these two men.

The idea of radio as the main entertainment vehicle had largely disappeared by 1969. Radio dramas were long gone, no need to worry about Orson Welles scaring the nation with a report of Martians landing in Grovers Mill, New Jersey. Rock music, top 40, music of every taste and dimension dominated the airwaves. WBCN in Boston, Boss Radio KHJ in Los Angeles were favored examples. All-day news and the developing trend of phone-in talk shows also could be found around the dial. Television dominated. Radio was filler, background noise while the listener painted the living room or ironed shirts. That was the modern entertainment rule.

Except in sports.

In the downsizing of radio's importance, the grand retreat, sports were one of the few remaining strongholds. Walk a beach on Cape Cod in the summer and you could hear the uninterrupted voice of Ken Coleman blanket to blanket, transistor to transistor, broadcasting a Red Sox game. Go anywhere in Los Angeles and Vin Scully brought gentle poetry and observations of life along with descriptions of baseball activity from Dodger Stadium. The Bruins in hockey in Boston, the UCLA-version Bruins in basketball in L.A., any sport, any level of competition, if the game wasn't on television, radio ruled.

Most and Hearn were as important as any of the players on the court. More important. The game was not only delivered through their words, it was filtered through their perceptions, bent by their personal styles. The game was the game. The announcers were the show.

Most was forty-five years old. He had broadcast Celtics games since 1953, New York guy, World War II vet, tail gunner on twenty-eight combat missions in Europe, recommended by Marty Glickman, the prominent New York sports announcer. His reports had chronicled the Celtics' many championships as if they were conquests in the Crusades, opponents vanquished, Celtic heroes exultant, truth and decency preserved for future generations.

Hearn was fifty-two. He had broadcast Lakers games since 1961, joining the team near the end of its first season in Los Angeles. Midwest guy, World War II vet, ran a special services baseball team in the South Pacific, started broadcasting the games because no one else would do it. Found that he liked the sound of his own voice. Got a start-out radio job in civilian life, then another job and another and was the broadcaster for the USC football and basketball games when the Lakers arrived from Minnesota. Perfect. He loved the Lakers as much as Most loved the Celtics, no doubt about that, but allowed himself to criticize them when they needed it. The Lakers never would be the villains, of course, but they sometimes would make mistakes.

Tavern conversationalists and kids of all ages in Boston could do the Johnny Most voice, an impression that was so easy it wasn't even funny anymore. In Los Angeles, anyone who knew anything about basketball, who knew just the word "basketball," knew some of Chick Hearn's phrases. Slam dunk. Air ball. No harm, no foul. Ticky-tack foul. These were among the terms he invented, brought into the language of the game.

The matchup of voices—it had been going on for years already and would continue for years in the future—was as intriguing as any of the matchups on the floor. These guys were the best in the business and, yes, they were characters.

No one in the NBA was more intriguing than Most. Although TBYM was a tough judge of the written word, a firm believer in journalistic objectivity, blah, blah, he was a sucker for the spoken word. He decided Most was a preacher in the church of basketball. The man could say what he wanted, do what he wanted, as long as he could get those people clapping. There was no doubt he could do that.

As a new arrival from nowhere, sent on the road, maybe a little bit shy, TBYM found Most to be the most accessible member of the Celtics traveling party. He was an insomniac, always around, always available for conversation. He was a smoker, pulling one English Oval cigarette after another from a little cardboard box, forty and fifty and sixty and seventy times per day. The walls of a hotel room tended to close in on him, so he could be found in the lobby, the coffee shop, or the bar, maybe outside the door of the Airport Marina in the warm evening. If he wasn't working, he was just killing time.

He would talk about the haiku poetry he wrote, the politics of the day, his kids, his youth in the Bronx, anything. The Celtics. The games past. The personalities. He would sound the way he sounded on the radio, angry sometimes, ready for a fight against some injustice, making the fact the maid was late in cleaning his room as terrible as when referee Mendy Rudolph called a fourth foul on Russell. A fine seasoning of curse words was sprinkled through his conversation, something different from the radio.

The bright young man had read somewhere that Most was named after his grandfather, Johann Most, a famous anarchist in the nineteenth century who once said, "Whoever looks at America will see: the ship is powered by stupidity, corruption or prejudice." Johann would appear with Emma Goldman at huge gatherings of disgruntled workers, two hundred thousand people in Chicago, spouting his incendiary thoughts.

"That's amazing," the bright young man said to Most one night. "Your grandfather was a rabble-rouser and here you are, a rabble-rouser, too, but in a different way. What did your father, the guy between the two of you, do for a living?"

"He was a fucking orthodontist," Most said in his Johnny Most voice.

His broadcasts were pure theater, Impressionist renderings of what took place on the court. There was an element of truth in his descriptions—the baskets made, the score—but the picture was painted in the abstract, perhaps Picasso during his Cubism period. Most not only was a fan of the Celtics, he was an enthusiastic fan. Every game was a morality contest between right and wrong, cowboys and Indians, the Federal Bureau of Investigation and the associates of John Dillinger. He would describe the game through that set of glasses.

"Greer FOULS Havlicek!" he would shout at one infraction, Philadelphia's Hal Greer having the temerity to touch the Boston star.

"THEY'RE CALLING A FOUL ON HAVLICEK!" he would shout if the call was made after the same touch was applied by the Boston star on Greer.

The flip from active to passive voice was basic. Bad things might happen to the Celtics, but the Celtics never did the bad things they were accused of doing. Nicknames were handed to opposing players. If Chamberlain hated to be called "Wilt the Stilt," well, Most called him "Wilt the Stilt" all the time. If Wilt hated when Most said he was "unhuman," a made-up word to describe his feats of strength, his size, well, "unhuman" it was. Anybody from another team who complained about anything did not complain, he was "crying." Wilt always was "crying." Elgin Baylor was "crying." Van Breda Kolff was "crying" all the time. ("And now he's getting a technical foul," Most would shout in exultation.) Even Jerry West sometimes was "crying." Everybody in the wrong shirt was a crybaby.

The oft-told tale was that wives and children, parents and friends of Celtics players would greet them after a road trip—Johnny on the mike a night earlier in the family home—and ask about the fights and the mayhem they had heard. Was the player all right? Had anybody been left behind in the hospital? The player would not know what his relations were talking about. What fight? What mayhem?

"Is there any other sport you would like to broadcast?" the bright young man asked Most one time.

"Auto racing," he said. "The smell of death hovers over the track tonight. . . ."

A young Catholic priest, Father John Creed, a Celtics ball boy before he went into the seminary, would sit next to Most at many of the games, keep statistics for him.

"Johnny didn't like stats at all, didn't think they meant much, but sometimes he'd use some of them," the priest said. "People would tell me they knew the games I was working because Johnny used some stats."

Most had large ears and a wrinkled face that looked like last night's melted candle. He was not a handsome man, a fact that he would sometimes mention in his conversation. Weird things would happen to him. He would complain about losing his hearing and Celtics doctor Thomas Silva would find an earplug that had been lodged for a month or so in one large ear. He would drop a cigarette on his polyester pants during a broadcast and would have to put out the fire while he continued to talk. He would be talking another time and his upper dental plate would fly out of his mouth in the middle of some fierce description. He would catch the plate in midair, shove it back into his mouth, and keep talking.

He was an acquired taste, perhaps, but he had been acquired by a whole city. He was a unique kind of star.

"Some professor sits back in a university somewhere and says, 'Thou shalt not be prejudiced,'" Most told *Sports Illustrated* once in a description of his approach. "I wanna know why not? Why can't I be with a bunch of guys day in, day out, year in, year out, and not have affection for them. And if you don't broadcast that way, you're lying."

Chick Hearn's prejudice was printed in public in any list of Laker executives. He was an assistant general manager for the team as well as the announcer for the games. When Jack Kent Cooke bought the Lakers, he never had seen a professional basketball game. He was Canadian, had made a fortune in Canada, loved hockey. The basketball team was part of the investment to get into hockey. He needed a basketball adviser, so he promoted the man who attracted customers, the man who broadcast the games and was as popular as any of the players.

Hearn was the opposite of Most in a bunch of ways. He was handsome, for starters, tall and television friendly. His voice was neutral, not a broadcasting-school baritone, but not an ongoing gargle like his counterpart in Boston. It was a durable voice, something that could be heard over the long haul, eighty-two games plus exhibitions and playoffs, not too excited, but certainly not bored. Durable. The staccato approach allowed him to keep pace with the action on the floor. His turns of phrase, the different things from the normal play-by-play man that he said, were verbal jewels.

Lakers faked opponents "into the popcorn machine." Someone

whose shot missed everything "threw up a brick." "The mustard's off the hot dog" was when someone tried a flashy play that did not work. "My grandmother could guard him and she couldn't go to her left" was said about a defensive mistake against a usual non-scorer. The court was a "ninety-four-by-fifty hunk of wood." Someone wouldn't score a layup after a rebound, he would "pick up the garbage and take it to the dump." A miss on that layup would draw the comment that "Marge [his wife] could have made that shot." A player didn't chew gum, he "worked on his Wrigley's." The Lakers, if they were playing badly, were "just standing around."

The words seemed to fall out of his head in a grand rhythm. (Late in his career they would be put into a rap song.) A Chick Hearn game never was a normal, expected blow-by-blow account. There always were the verbal jewels. Pay attention and you heard them.

"The game's in the refrigerator," he would say when the Lakers were ahead by enough to feel they had won a game that still had to be finished.

The phrase was the Laker equivalent of Red Auerbach lighting a cigar on the bench or in the stands when the Celtics had a big lead in the same situation. The thought was so positive, so strong, such happy news, that he would expand it during the years, a verbal snowball gathering size as it rolled down the hill.

"The game's in the refrigerator," Hearn would say. "The door's closed, the light's out, the eggs are cooling, the butter's getting hard, and the Jell-O's jiggling."

The dark clouds that Most saw daily—meals that were cooked too much or not enough, cabs that were late, assorted inconveniences—didn't appear as often with Hearn. He was a happy character on the road, a practical joker, a man with a hearty laugh. In *Chick: His Unpublished Memoir and the Memories of Those Who Knew Him*, by Hearn and Steve Springer, published in 2004, two years after his death, various Laker people told stories about the practical joker's sense of humor.

Jerry West said he sat near Hearn on a plane and could hear him talking to a woman, telling her how he had been a pilot in World War II and had downed fifty enemy planes. This included the time he was surrounded by four enemy planes and had to maneuver to shoot all four out of the sky, one after the other. Hearn then excused himself and went to the lavatory. The woman turned to West and said, "What a brave American."

Elgin Baylor told how Hearn would come up to him at the airport and tell him that not only had the flight been canceled, but the game had been called off. Trainer Frank O'Neill talked about terrorizing bus drivers, how Hearn teamed up with Wilt Chamberlain. They passed a billboard for dog food that everyone could see. Hearn asked which kind of dog food Chamberlain liked. Chamberlain said he ate them all. But which do you like? Chamberlain said they all tasted a little different. The bus driver almost drove off the road.

Hearn told a funny story himself. He noted that one of the things Wilt did that made van Breda Kolff angry was he brought fried or broiled chicken into the locker room to eat every night before a game. General manager Fred Schaus relayed this opinion to Chamberlain. The next game, Chamberlain brought a dozen hot dogs with him to the locker room.

"Nobody said anything about hot dogs," he said, working his way through his dinner.

A sad truth was that many of the broadcast words spoken by Most and Hearn—most of them, in fact—disappeared into the air not too long after they were spoken. The games were one-shot appearances, same as a night at the opera. The broadcasts were taped, but seldom saved, the tape used again and again, tonight's game obliterating the game from a month ago. Radio stations went out of business or ownership changed, and tapes also disappeared that way.

An effort was made to get tapes for this book from the entire series, but the idea fell apart in a hurry. (No doubt some reader has all the games, stuffed in an old cardboard box from Thom McAn shoes somewhere.) The next idea was to get whatever was available, first from the series, then if necessary from any time in the broadcast history of the two men.

This idea led to John Miley, eighty-nine years old, in Newburgh, Indiana. When he was sixteen years old, he began taping baseball games off the radio. That was 1947. He never stopped. He added basketball and boxing, horse racing, just about any sport that came along. The result was a large collection of tapes, better and better in quality as the years passed and technology improved. A story was written about the man and his collection in *The Sporting News* in 1972 that brought him into contact with collectors from around the country. This gave him the opportunity to collect more tapes. Thousands more.

When he made a deal in 2011 to send six thousand of his tapes to the Library of Congress, a small percentage of his catalog, he ensured there will be a long-term home for a lot of words. Some of them belong to Johnny Most, some to Chick Hearn.

Between the library and Miley, looking through the inventory in his garage and basement, we were able to find at least parts of the remaining games. In addition, there were a couple of games from previous seasons, samplers of both men.

Johnny Most screamed again. . . .

"Havlicek with the ball. He stops and pops. And it's good. . . . The Celtics defense has been murder out there. Just murder . . . A tremendous emotional battle going on right here . . . And that's it! It's all over. Havlicek has the ball and he's mobbed!!!"

Chick Hearn spoke in his version of tongues (basketball-related). . . .

"He went up so high, his head came down wet. . . . He's colder than a delicatessen turkey. . . . You could call that one with brail. . . . He did the bunny hop in the pea patch. . . . Oh, how exciting can it get? This series has to go down in history. It can never be matched. . . ."

The excitement still was there, saved in acetate or whatever the material for the tape was. Johnny described the menacing threat everywhere, the assaults on Boston virtue. Chick described the action in front of him, good or bad, never a doubt on which was which.

Back in 1969, four games had been played.

The two men were on the job.

Best two-out-of-three.

The local populations couldn't help but listen.

Chapter 15

GAME FIVE

LAKERS: JUST 1 MORE
WEST HURT IN 117–104 WIN

BY DOUG KRIKORIAN
Herald Examiner Staff Writer
Despite the biggest conquest in their nine-year Los
Angeles stay that puts them a game away from destiny,
the Lakers today are a worried team.

Jerry West, on an evening when he and Wilt
Chamberlain tore apart the Boston Celtics, pulled up
lame with 2:44 remaining, and the diagnosis afterwards
was a pulled hamstring.

"It will be a day-to-day proposition," said Dr. Robert
Kerlan, the Laker physician. "These types of injuries are
very unpredictable."

If you go on past history, West will be unable to play
when the series resumes tomorrow in Boston. He never
has made particularly rapid recoveries from hamstrings.

Twice before this season, West, who scored 39 points
in a 117–104 victory, has incurred such an injury, missing
four games the first time and 11 the second. In 1963, he
missed 24 games.

"Emmette Bryant bumped me while I was dribbling, and I took a big step and pulled it," explained West, whose 28-point second half provided the Lakers with a 3-2 edge in basketball's World Series.

"It just doesn't seem fair at all," continued the magical West Virginian, who has totaled 197 points in the series for a 39.7 average. "It was such a meaningless part of the game.

"Sometimes I just can't understand why things like this always happen to me."

West was asked if he would be able to perform in tomorrow's nationally televised game.

"I won't know until I run on it," he said. "I do know this: If I get up tomorrow and it feels all right, I definitely will play. I've waited too long to miss an opportunity like this."

Someone wondered if the injury was painful.

"If it wasn't, I would have never come out," he said.

Immediately after a game in which West controlled the offensive tempo and Chamberlain the defensive, Dr. Kerlan wrapped and administered medication to Jerry's left leg.

"If it is at all possible, Jerry definitely will play," said Kerlan. "After all, he has all summer to rest."

West will make the trip East with the team this morning accompanied by Dr. Vincent Carter of Kerlan's staff.

If West doesn't recover, this would be possibly a fatal setback to a Laker club that depends too much on the leadership, scoring, and defensive talents of their all-star guard.

Clearly, they aren't a very good team without West, whose masterpiece was witnessed by 17,553 last night at the Forum.

Afterwards, in the dressing quarters, the Laker players were solemn. The mood compared favorably with Tuesday's one-point heartbreaker in Boston.

Chamberlain, his right eye half-closed as a result

of third-period contact with the busy Bryant's hand, summed it up best when he said:

"I can't explain how much West's loss would mean to us."

Bill van Breda Kolff, the saddest winning coach in basketball history, indicated he would start Keith Erickson if West couldn't make it.

That famous VBK sense of humor still slipped out, though, when a reporter wondered if West would be ready to play.

"I'm a terrible doctor," said Princeton Butch, "and even a worse coach."

Chamberlain last night made up his mind that he would outplay his longtime adversary, Bill Russell, and he did—badly.

Wilt aggressively crashed both boards all evening, winding up with 31 rebounds and also blocking seven shots. He continually afforded the Lakers extra shots with his offensive rebounds.

"He was tremendous," said VBK, who felt the Lakers played better in the opening game.

Russell, in perhaps his most pitiful Los Angeles exhibition, had just five rebounds at the half and 13 for the game. Those 35-year-old legs just couldn't get off the Forum floor.

Chamberlain frightened the crowd when he had to come out of the game in the third quarter for treatment of his eye. However, Wilt, gallant soul that he is, was in there a minute later although he wasn't seeing things too clearly.

"I could only see out of one eye the remainder of the game," he said. "They put drops in my eyes and this could have caused the blurriness."

"Wilt suffered a slight abrasion of the cornea," said Kerlan. "He'll be all right, though."

Another key to the victory was the tough defensive pressure applied on John Havlicek, who has been averaging 33.7, by Erickson and Tom Hawkins.

Havlicek finished with only 18 points, 12 of which came when the Celtics were out of reach.

Erickson started on him at the game's outset, holding him to a pair of field goals in the first quarter. Hawkins allowed him a free throw in the second and another one in the third.

"I attempted to keep him away from the ball," said Hawkins, who has proved to be a valuable reserve during the playoffs.

"I just tried to play him tight," said Erickson, who took advantage of the Celtics double-teaming of West by scoring 16 points.

So did John Egan, who threw in most of his 23 points with no one harassing him.

Anyway, the Lakers are a game from their cherished goal today. It would look much closer if Jerry West's hamstring responds to treatment.

Los Angeles Herald Examiner
May 2, 1969

The voice of Chick Hearn could have been at the other end of a late-night phone call instead of coming from the kitchen radio. Something bad had happened. No, nobody had died, no, but something bad had taken place. You should know.

"Jerry West has hobbled into the locker room followed by Doctor Kerlan and by trainer Frank O'Neill, and the way he hobbled it did not look good," Hearn told his listeners along the Lakers Radio Network. "You can't be an alarmist, but you have to be a reporter."

What?

The tone of Hearn's voice told as much as his words. This was serious. Forget any euphoria about the 117–104 Lakers win that was being finished for the final two minutes and forty-four seconds with a fat lead in stripped-down expedience. Don't dwell on the thoughts and happy possibilities that arrive with a 3-2 series advantage over the Celtics, mountain almost climbed, one more win needed now for that championship that had been so elusive for so long. Listen to Chick. Listen to Hot Rod Hundley, the color man. They were the experts.

This was serious.

"As much as this victory means to Los Angeles, much of the starch is taken out of it with this injury to West," Hearn said, the game still not finished, but the Lakers in charge. "He only has 48 hours until the next game and it's going to take the brilliance of Dr. Kerlan and a little prayer from heaven, I think, to get him back. Let's hope it's not as serious as it looks."

Hearn had spotted the injury almost as soon as it happened. The start was the collision with Emmette Bryant as Bryant pressed in the backcourt, the Celtics trailing by thirteen points with less than three minutes left. West looked like he might fall, but didn't. Bryant did fall. ("No harm, no foul," Hearn reported.) The ball went over to the Celtics. Bailey Howell hit a twenty-foot jumper. Hearn saw West was in trouble.

"Jerry West is hurt," the announcer reported.

"Jerry West is hurt," he reported again for emphasis.

"He's holding the back of his left leg," Hearn said, not shouting any of this, talking as if he were phoning in the details of a bad accident that happened in front of him on the 405. "That always indicates it could be a muscle."

A pulled hamstring. That was the obvious diagnosis.

Depending on the severity, a normal slow-pitch softball player who overextended his out-of-shape self in trying to stretch a single into a stand-up double would be out of action anywhere from four or five days (mild) to four to eight weeks (medium) to three months or more (severe) with a pulled hamstring. The prescription would include ice and rest.

"Well, Chick, it does not look good," Hundley said. "It's definitely the back of his left thigh in the hamstring area, which is the worst injury Jerry ever has had. He's had that two or three times."

West always had to be watched for injuries because he had been a fragile commodity throughout his career. The four games he missed from the first hamstring pull during the 1969 season, the eleven games from the second pull and the twenty-four he missed in 1963 covered the hamstring spectrum from minor to medium to severe.

In nine seasons in the NBA, he had missed 128 games, the equiva-

lent of a season and a half, with injuries. His last three seasons had
been his roughest. He missed fourteen games in 1967, thirty-one in
1968, twenty-one in 1969. He broke his left hand in the first minute
of the first playoff game in '67, never played again as the Lakers were
swept. In the 1968 finals against the Celtics he was troubled from the
start with a pulled groin that had kept him out of action at the end of
the regular season, then added a sprained ankle in the fourth game.
Now this injury in the fifth game of the 1969 finals. There seemed to
be no end.

He had missed three of the Lakers' six games during the season
against the Celtics, first with the flu, then a pulled groin muscle, then
one of his two pulled hamstring muscles. He also suffered a pulled
thigh muscle and a charley horse during the season. He estimated
that during his career he had broken his nose eight or nine times and
had sustained injuries to his fingers, ankles, feet, wrists, hands, fingers, and ribs. He was a Stradivarius, wound tight to perfection, that
often needed to be tuned. He had shown reporters a swollen thumb
earlier in the series, just one more thing.

"I hate it when people say I'm injury prone," he would write in *Mr.
Clutch: The Jerry West Story*. "But it's time to make a confession. I
now admit what I've denied, not only publicly, but to myself, for so
long: I think I am injury prone.

"I do play aggressively, but I like my life and limbs and I don't think
I do things many other athletes don't do, yet they don't get hurt as
often as I do. Maybe it's just chance that I've had so many injuries
and I'm just unlucky."

One important asset he had with the Lakers—simply by playing
sports for money in Los Angeles—was the presence of Dr. Kerlan. Not
only was the forty-six-year-old orthopedic surgeon the house doctor
for West's employer, he also was the doctor for the baseball Dodgers,
the football Rams, the hockey Kings, and the jockeys at Hollywood
Park, Santa Anita, and Del Mar. In the increasingly important field
of sports medicine, he and his partner, Dr. Frank Jobe, not only were
pathfinders, they pretty much were the inventors.

Specialized medicine for athletes had become more and more
important as salaries grew larger. Getting a player back on the field,
back into the gym, back on the ice or on top of that horse was differ-

ent from sending a patient back to work in the department store or the office cubicle. Dr. Kerlan had become the expert of experts. He estimated that one year he had gone to 240 athletic contests.

"In 10 years on the job," former Dodgers general manager Buzzy Bavasi said to writer Alfred Wright in *Sports Illustrated,* "he was my most important signing."

Kerlan, an athlete and a sports fan before he became a doctor, was waiting when the Dodgers arrived in L.A. from Brooklyn in 1958. He and a friend, Dr. Robert Woods, an internist, had volunteered a few years earlier to treat players on the Pacific Coast League California Stars simply to be involved in baseball. They now applied to do the same work for the Dodgers.

Bavasi thought at first they were looking for jobs to help fans at the ballpark, to take care of the cardiac cases and drunken brawlers in the crowd. That was how unique the idea was, doctors with the team to help put players back on the field. It turned out to be especially important here. The Dodgers lineup, transported from Ebbets Field to the West Coast, was filled with familiar names attached to aging bodies. This was perfect for Kerlan, a chance to study his craft, try out ideas on a daily basis. This was also perfect for the aging Dodgers like Duke Snider and Ed Roebuck and the rest of them.

The patient who changed Kerlan's life was Sandy Koufax. The transcendent left-hander, best pitcher a bunch of experts ever had seen, showed up in 1962 with an arterial blood clot in his left hand. Kerlan cured this condition, but in 1964, late in the season, a larger problem arrived. Koufax had developed traumatic arthritis.

Kerlan knew exactly what to do here. He had become an expert on arthritis because he also had arthritis, had suffered its effects since his final year of medical school. His condition had grown worse and worse. A big man, six feet three, he now was hunched over as he walked, steadying himself with canes. He could tell Koufax, flat out, that there was no cure for traumatic arthritis, but that there were ways to deal with it.

Kerlan kept Koufax on the field for the next two seasons. Arthritis? Koufax never pitched better. He won twenty-six games in 1965, twenty-seven in '66, led the majors both years in innings pitched, strikeouts, and ERA. He won the Cy Young Award in both years, pitched in the World Series both years, then retired at the end of the second one at the age of thirty due to the arthritis pain.

Kerlan's contribution was noted, praised. He developed a national sports medicine reputation at a time when there were no other national sports medicine reputations. He was the man. He had been involved in virtually every injury to every famous athlete in Los Angeles in the past decade. He was a national voice for other doctors to call for advice.

One day earlier, the day before West was injured, Kerlan was part of the medical team that put the pelvis of jockey Bill Shoemaker back together after a horse fell on him in the paddock at Hollywood Park. This was after he had put a pin in Shoemaker's fractured thighbone only a year ago. Now he was trying to put West back on the floor at the most important time of West's career.

"If he's physically able to play against Boston, he'll play," Kerlan said in the no-nonsense way of doctors everywhere, adding the part about how the patient would have all summer to rest.

A cortisone shot was administered in the locker room before West left for home. Ice and more ice was in his present and immediate future. There would be another shot, an anti-inflammatory, in Boston before the game. Fingers crossed. There were a plane ride and two restless nights to handle before that.

What next?

"The only thing that matters now is the condition of Jerry West," Chick Hearn said near the conclusion of his broadcast. "If West misses this last game, it'll tear the heart out of his chest cavity."

The unlucky part here was that the Lakers had the game won when he was injured. He owned the fourth period—"the bread and butter time," in Chick Hearn's description—until he was hurt. He scored 13 points in a row in the first four minutes of the quarter on the way to his 39 points for the game.

This was the game the oddsmakers in Vegas had imagined when they made the Lakers such big favorites. This was the whipping a first-place team in the West should administer to a fourth-place finisher in the East.

"We were really ready to play," West said. "They knew it when we were warming up. I think they knew we were going to beat them. You feel those things."

Wilt demolished Russell. The first four games had been a cold war sort of standoff, my nuclear weapon against your nuclear weapon, the two big men even in most statistics, but this time the Los Angeles nuclear weapon was detonated. Russell was bothered with early fouls, bothered through most of the game. Chamberlain controlled both backboards, 31 rebounds to Russell's 13, and Lakers rolled to the basket for one layup after another.

Russell, the player, was so frustrated and Russell, the coach, was so frustrated they kept the locker room door closed for forty-five minutes after the game to discuss life and basketball with the troops. Russell, the coach, then talked to no one with a notebook and told Russell, the reporter, to take a hike.

"Some things are better left unsaid," the reporter/coach/superstar wrote/phoned/mumbled under the *Globe* headline "Russell Reports." "So regarding Thursday night's game against the Lakers I have no comment."

(Did the *Globe* pay the obligatory $200 for a single paragraph? The bright young man did not know, but he wondered.)

John Havlicek also was locked in a cabinet for this one by Keith Erickson. The Lakers had tried different players to guard the Celtics' perpetual-motion basketball machine in the first three games, but they all had been torched as the machine kept humming, quietly outscoring West in two of the first three games, challenging him for any most valuable player honors. In the fourth game, the mishmash of turnovers and missed shots by everyone except West, Erickson did nice work on Havlicek, helping to hold him to 21 points by keeping him scoreless in the fourth quarter. Was this a quirk, part of the general basketball malaise that had landed for a day? Or was this the answer?

Butch van Breda Kolff wanted to know. ("The way Keith played, we have to use him," the coach said. "He made some good plays defensively.") The result was Erickson started for the first time in the series, replacing rookie Billy Hewitt. At six feet five, 195, he was the closest match to the six-foot-five, 203-pound Havlicek. Like Havlicek, he had a multi-sports past, a gold-medal experience with the U.S. volleyball team in 1964 added to NCAA basketball titles with UCLA and John

Wooden. His size meant he could do many of the things Havlicek could do—play in the backcourt, play up front, interchangeable—but the hard part was doing them at Havlicek's robo pace.

"In the last quarter I only took one shot," Havlicek said, not sounding worried. "Larry [Siegfried] was going so good that we let him take most of the shots. I really don't care who's going to cover me. My game is a running one and he's going to have to run to keep up with me."

The keeping up was very good in Game 5. Havlicek was held to 18 points on 6-for-21 shooting, 11 of the points coming during the six minutes of mop-up time at the end of the game. The Celtics star said he shot "terribly," the reason for his numbers, but Erickson's performance certainly gave the Lakers some confidence.

Their general manager, Fred Schaus, had spent part of the flight from Boston complaining about Auerbach and the Celtics complaining to the league office about the officials all the time, trying to gain an advantage, which he said always worked, year after year. His complaint about the Celtics' complaints seemed to have worked. The Lakers wound up with six more foul shots (33–27) and a staggering seventeen more shots (106–89) from the floor.

So Wilt outplayed Russell. So Erickson held down Havlicek. So the referees were kind. So the Lakers were within one game of the championship.

Any other good news?

Jerry West felt pretty good when he awakened in the morning.

The pulled hamstring appeared to be minor, the least painful choice on the spectrum. Trainer Frank O'Neill said he thought maybe the Lakers had gotten lucky and treated the injury fast enough to control it. Dr. Vincent Carter, sent from Dr. Kerlan's office to Boston with West and the Lakers, concurred.

"The injury is lower than the usual hamstring," the doctor said. "Jerry says he feels good, but hasn't put much stress on the leg. He is much better, though, than he was last night. We'll wait until game time for a proper decision."

"It really doesn't feel too bad," West said. "I really want to play. I'll see how it feels tomorrow, but I won't play if I don't think I can be any help to the team."

How would he decide if he should or should not play?

"If I can crawl," he said, "I'll be out there."

—

Some holes appear now in the accompanying saga of the bright young man. He covered this game—he was in L.A. to write the advance, so obviously he was there to cover the game—but the evening edition of the *Globe* for Friday, May 2, 1969, apparently has been lost in the historical movements from the printed page to the microfilm roll to the digital cloud. This is too bad, because TBYM definitely must have recorded Jerry West's postgame angst with the soap opera significance it deserved. Or at least thought he did.

The blackout of TBYM will continue from here, too, no record of his efforts for the Saturday evening paper, either, a vestigial edition, slim and usually so forgettable that it never was saved half the time by the *Globe*. Then, too, the next game also is missing because it will be a Saturday afternoon game and there is NO evening paper on Sunday. He would not cover that game.

I squirm with the bright young man about all this from afar, knowing how pissed he certainly was, not covering a possible close-out game at the Garden. I can't even remember if he went to the game, if he sat in the press section, maybe sat in the actual stands with his wife. (Tickets were available a day before the game.) I'm sure he was eager to see West's condition, eager to see if the Celtics could turn the aged ship around one last time to force a seventh game (and one more trip across the country) on Monday. There was, remember, no television in Boston, the national ABC broadcast blacked out.

While the possibilities are good that he was at the Garden (but why doesn't he remember it if he was?), there also is the chance that he spent the day at the headquarters of the Massachusetts Army National Guard on Commonwealth Avenue, a brick building across from Atamian Ford. He was a Pfc in this operation, too, this time with the single chevron on his fatigues to prove it.

Finishing up the fourth year of a six-year commitment that saved him from the perils of the military draft at the height of the Vietnam War, he still owed the military one weekend per month, two weeks every summer. The days and weeks were mind-numbing stuff, typing out stories about Guard projects (one, I remember, was a campaign to make team handball a popular sport in the United States, a plan that went nowhere) and press releases about promotions for officers around the state. The alternative to this was still not good, the war pumping along, 543 dead in the last month alone. The lottery system for the draft would not be added until 1970. Everyone was eligible.

Almost everyone.

"What are you doing about the draft, Toby?" the bright young man had asked Toby Kimball, a six-foot-eight balding basketball Adonis, star of the team, when they both were seniors at the University of Connecticut.

"Too tall," Kimball said.

"Too tall?"

"The cut-off is six feet six," he said. "Too tall."

"Too tall," the bright young man, five feet nine, 1-A, said.

This took care of the big men and power forwards in the NBA, but left the quick forwards and backcourt standouts vulnerable, not to mention the young sportswriters. (The bright young man would think about the too-tall rule while crawling under barbed wire with his M-15 rifle during basic training at Fort Jackson, South Carolina. Kimball, drafted by the Celtics, not the United States Army, would spend a year playing in Italy, then one season in Boston before being taken by San Diego in an expansion draft. He would play nine years in the NBA.) The quick forwards and the backcourt standouts, if they weren't married or if they didn't have a surgical history to make them 4-F, would be left with the young sportswriters to consider the National Guard option. Many took it.

Don Chaney, the six-foot-five number-one draft choice this season for the Celtics from the University of Houston, had spent the first half of the schedule at Fort Polk, Louisiana, taking care of his six-month active-duty obligation. Mal Graham, the six-foot-one number-one draft choice from NYU a year earlier, had spent most of his first season at Fort Dix. The draft board didn't fool around. Bill Bradley of the Knicks was in the Air Force reserves. Elgin Baylor had missed a big part of the 1962 season doing his active duty with the Army Reserves, only played in the playoffs on a pass. Elgin had joined before Vietnam, advised to do this after Elvis Presley was drafted.

There were ongoing scandals where teams used undue influence to slide their stars to the front of National Guard and Army Reserve waiting lists, but famous names did put on the uniform and did crawl under the barbed wire with their M-15s. (Red Auerbach had just waded into appropriately heated water when he selected guard Jo Jo White with the ninth pick of the NBA draft in April during the series against the Knicks. Teams had stayed away from White because he apparently had been drafted by the military, off, gone for two years, except . . . wait a minute . . . there might be an opening in a Marine Corps reserve unit in Boston.) Various teams would run into trouble.

The bright young man saw assorted athletes in his military travels. Carlton Fisk and Bill Lee of the Red Sox were in local units. Alex Johnson and Bobby Tolan of the St. Louis Cardinals both came through the office where TBYM worked at Fort Leonard Wood, Missouri, in on-the-job training. The most exciting moment at that office, he was told, had been when Howard (Butch) Komives of the Knicks and then the Pistons had visited. TBYM spent one weekend day in some armory with Fran Healy, who was a catcher for the Yankees and later became one of their announcers. And one day, at summer camp at Fort Dix, when he was with his first unit from New Haven, he was in the barracks when another fine young citizen soldier arrived with the breathless information that Cazzie Russell was playing basketball in the post gym.

"Nicky," the citizen soldier said to Nick Brunetti, a local New Haven basketball legend. "Go down and kick his ass."

Nicky thought about it for half a second.

Nicky nicely declined.

The military obligation—again, the draft board didn't fool around—pretty much trumped whatever other activity a person might plan. You could say, hey, it's the NBA finals and the Celtics might be eliminated and it's my job and I have to be at the game. No one would pay attention. Or you could call in sick, bogus, and go no matter what. You also could be discovered and fall into big trouble. There were stories of guys who did. These were not stories with positive results.

A year later—OK, one year and eight days to be precise, May 10, 1970—the bright young man would be faced with another big-game dilemma. This time it was the fourth game of the Stanley Cup finals against the St. Louis Blues, also at the Garden, an afternoon game on a Sunday booked for the National Guard. The Bruins were going to complete the sweep, win their first Stanley Cup since the Dawn of Creation. All of Boston was agog. (A word to be used only in very special agog circumstances.)

The bright young man did the right thing, put on his uniform and went to headquarters. He was pissed again, of course, missing another once-in-a-Boston-lifetime moment, but he did what he was supposed to do. The game was scheduled for a 2:05 start. So somewhere around 2:05 was when he became antsy. The Bruins! The Stanley Cup! Bobby Orr! This was also when Sp4 John Premack, a camera man at Channel 5 in his day job, also became antsy.

"We have to sneak out," Premack decided. "We can go to my apartment in Brighton to watch the game."

"We have to sneak out," the bright young man agreed.

Done.

Premack's apartment was pretty nice for a bachelor. He had a large-sized television, maybe twenty-one inches. Color. He also, on the other side of the room, had a large fish tank. The tank, I believe, contained only one fish. The fish was maybe the size of a silver dollar. Maybe a little bit larger. Premack asked the bright young man if he ever had seen a piranha before. The bright young man said he hadn't.

The game was a corker, the Garden crowd waiting to explode at the end, but frustrated by the Blues, who finished regulation time tied, 3–3, with the home team. Premack served up a couple of beers and maybe some pretzels during the action, and somewhere late in the proceedings, maybe during the intermission before the start of overtime, he went to the refrigerator and came out with a plastic bag containing water and two cute goldfish. Premack said it was time for dinner for the piranha. Had TBYM ever seen a piranha eat dinner? Premack undid the bag and poured the two goldfish into the tank.

Jesus.

The bright young man watched the goldfish swim around and swim around while the piranha also swam around and swam around. Everybody seemed to get along. Nothing happened. The bright young man turned to the television for a little hockey commentary. He turned back to the tank and the two goldfish still swam around and swam around except, wait a minute, one of them was missing a large part of his torso. His stomach was completely gone.

Jesus.

The game resumed and the bright young man tried to watch, but found he had a bigger desire to watch the fish tank. The second goldfish also was missing his stomach now and the piranha was swimming around and swimming around and carnage certainly was going to occur and of course Bobby Orr scored that goal. You know the one. Forty seconds into overtime. He scored on goaltender Glenn Hall and was tripped by St. Louis defenseman Noel Picard and flew through the air, looked like a smiling Superman in the most famous hockey picture of all time and of course the bright young man missed it because he was watching a piranha eat a couple of goldfish.

It was not his fault. It was the fault of the United States government.

That was what he said.

That is what he still says.

Chapter 16

OFF DAY: FACTS AND FLAIR

Five-Game Statistics

Boston Celtics (2-3)

Player	MP	TRB	A	PTS	AVG
Havlicek	240	59	24	150	30.0
Russell	240	108	28	49	9.8
Bryant	144	21	11	39	7.8
Siegfried	131	11	15	79	15.6
Nelson	93	26	5	42	8.4
Howell	147	30	3	61	12.2
Jones	165	16	14	98	19.6
Sanders	30	4	1	11	2.2
Chaney	10	1	0	2	.4
Totals	1200	276	101	534	107

Los Angeles Lakers (3-2)

Player	MP	TRB	A	PTS	AVG
West	220	16	37	197	39.4
Chamberlain	240	130	14	56	11.2
Egan	174	14	22	90	18.0
Baylor	178	47	20	82	16.2

Erickson	119	25	9	49	9.8
Counts	104	28	5	46	9.2
Hawkins	72	15	2	14	2.8
Hewitt	93	22	2	4	0.5
Crawford	1	1	0	0	0
Totals	1200	297	111	548	109

The series has been pared down to essentials. The rookies—Billy Hewitt of the Lakers and Don Chaney of the Celtics—are now seated at the ends of the benches with the noncombatants, the added players who fill out the roster to fill out the practice floor. They will not be seen again. Veteran Tom Sanders of the Celtics, bothered throughout the series with a cranky back, may be called in emergency circumstances for emergency minutes, but not for much more.

These basically are seven-man teams now. Havlicek and Russell have played every minute of every game and will be expected to do that the rest of the way. Chamberlain has played every minute. West, who missed twenty minutes with his different injuries, will play every minute that he can. The rest of the time will be divided pretty equally between the remaining five players on each side.

The individual stats show Jerry West is having a wonderful series: 39.4 points a game, 9 points better than John Havlicek (30.0), 20 points better than anyone else on the score sheet. Wilt Chamberlain has an edge on rebounds (130–108) against Bill Russell, another edge on points (56–49), but the two men largely balance each other out. Sam Jones (19.6 points per game) and Larry Siegfried (15.6) pretty much are equal to Johnny Egan (18.0) and Elgin Baylor (16.2).

The Celtics have complained about a disparity in free throws, the Lakers with eighty-three more (284–201) in the six games. The Lakers' lament about bad free-throw shooting (182-of-284, 63.3 percent) is justified, but the Celtics (159-of-201, 79.5 percent) still haven't been able to make up the difference. The Celtics have taken sixty more shots from the field, made ten more baskets, but operated at lower percentage (.419 to .443).

Some of the most interesting statistics, alas, are not being recorded. No differentiation is made, for example, between offensive and defensive rebounds. The Lakers have outrebounded the Celtics by twenty-one (297–276), total, but if the Celtics have taken more shots, then they might have collected more offensive rebounds. No one will know. The extra shots also might have come from steals or from the wider statistical term, turnovers, which covers all sorts of mistakes and infractions. Those numbers also are not recorded.

The most glaring statistic that is missing is blocked shots. In the pairing of Russell and Chamberlain, the blocked shot is probably at an historical high point. The game—as opposed to what basketball will become—is focused on driving to the basket. Since there is no three-point shot, which will not arrive until the 1979–80 season, twenty-three feet, nine inches from the basket, a different sort of mathematics is involved. The best shot is the closest shot, starting with a dunk, and extending outward. A four-footer is better than a five-footer, which is better than a six-footer, simple as that. All baskets are worth two points.

There is no reason to take a longer shot that counts as much as a layup if you have the option. Players drive past defenders and arrive deep into the three-second lane (expanded from twelve feet to sixteen in 1964–65 solely due to the presence of Wilt) as if they were on a production line. Chamberlain or Russell ship back their efforts—Rejected! Wilsonburger! Not today!—at an astonishing clip.

Everybody applauds, gasps, flat-out cheers. And then the moment disappears. How many blocks is that? How many blocks for the game, the series, the year, a lifetime? A few writers try to keep track, but even they have no guidelines. What is a block? What looks like a block, but maybe is not? The writers have different ideas. The writers have days off when they do not keep the stat.

The statistic "blocks" will not be added until the 1973–74 season. (Spoiler alert: the year after Wilt retires.) The all-time blocks leader (3,830) will be Hakeem Olajuwon of the Houston Rockets. The most blocks in a game (17) will be by Elmore Smith of the Lakers. The best block per game average (3.5) will be recorded by Mark Eaton of the Utah Jazz.

There is no doubt that Russell and Chamberlain are operating at paces to beat all these numbers. Russell is airmailing assorted efforts off his left hand to his teammates already on the fly. Chamberlain is blasting weak shots as far into the stands as he possibly can, bouncing balls off the fat cats and B-level celebrities, driving his coach to say bad words on the sideline. None of it matters in any of the history books, only in the memory bank.

Unwritten history is being unwritten in full view every night.

Russell started all these statistical/artistic problems. He was the inventor of the blocked shot. He discovered it on his own, perfected it on his own. He should have gone to the U.S. Patent Office and stood in line behind Thomas Edison and your uncle who always thinks up weird stuff in his basement. The get-that-weak-shit-out-of-my-house rejection did not exist before Russell.

The same way managers in the long ago tried to convince Babe Ruth that hitting home runs was a mistaken approach to his craft, coaches tried to tell Russell that blocking shots was a fool's errand. See? It was right there in the textbooks. A player was not supposed to leave his feet on defense. Leave your feet and your man would go past you to score. Be smart. Stay on the ground.

Russell loved to describe the moment, eureka, when this thinking fell apart. He would do this many times in the future, one of the best in a three-hour interview in 2013 with Taylor Branch, his coauthor of *Second Wind,* as part of the Civil Rights History Project for the Library of Congress.

"We were playing Cal-Berkeley and their center was a pre-season All-American," Russell said in the interview. "The game starts and the first five shots he took, I blocked. And nobody in the building had ever seen anything like that. So they called a timeout to discuss what it was I was doing, because they didn't know what I was doing. So, again in our huddle, my coach says, 'You can't play defense like that.' 'What? [I said.] I just stuffed him five times in a row.' 'That's not the way to play defense.' So he showed me on the sidelines how he wanted me to play defense. So I try it and I go back out there and the guy shoots layups three times in a row. I said, 'This does not make sense.' So I went back to playing the way I knew how. [The coach] was really insulted by that. He was trying to help me and I was hard-headed and stubborn, and didn't know what I was doing, and he was trying to help me figure out what I was doing and I rejected it. So he never liked me as a player from then on.

"Basketball was taught differently then," he said. "I mean, some of the things people wouldn't be familiar with was that you weren't supposed to leave your feet. Yeah, no good player ever leaves your feet. Well, basically, what I was doing in retrospect was bringing the vertical game to a game that had been horizontal. And this was, we get a new element. See in high jump, which I had participated in in track and field, I can jump over my head. Well, in basketball, we should do an exercise where you take chalk and put it on your finger and run and jump as high as you can and put a chalk mark on the wall. Well, I can put a chalk mark 13 feet above the court. Which is the height of the backboard. And that was going to waste.

"So the coach did not like me. But I made up my mind that I was going to see how really good I could be. So I really worked at developing the game. Part of my game was logistics. So I learned how to cover long distances in a short period of time. So I developed how to play."

So USF won fifty-five games straight in his junior and senior years. So he pulled down 27 rebounds in the NCAA championship game as a senior, an 83–71 win over Iowa, 50 rebounds in the two games of that championship weekend, records that would remain untouched forever. (Or at least through 2020.) So nobody counted the blocked shots. How many did he have? Who knows? They disappeared in the statistical air, deemed not worthy of notice, no different from the numbers for how many dribbles were taken by the point guards, how many shoelaces were tied on the bench, how often the cheerleaders said the word "fight."

He brought this new idea with him to Boston. Auerbach, who worked out of his own head instead of a textbook, the same way Russell did, encouraged him. The blocked shot bred running and running won games and that was that.

Along the way, that tall kid from Philadelphia—the one Auerbach tried to convince in the Catskills to go to Harvard and be a territorial pick, that one—saw Russell's success and adopted the blocked shot as a defensive standby. He had the perfect architecture to make it work. A reporter from the *New York Times* counted that the kid had 17 blocks in his first professional game against the New York Knicks.

Nobody ever had blocked more shots than Wilt Chamberlain. Except, maybe the man in front of him every other night now. The inventor.

—

The bright young man did not keep a personal count of blocked shots. He also did not keep a count of offensive rebounds, steals, or turn-overs, a term that Jack Barry, his luncheon companion at Toots Shor's, created and used in the *Globe* before anyone else. The bright young man was not much of a statistics guy.

The new coach of the Boston Patriots, a contentious character named Clive Rush, hired in February 1969, would have a question for TBYM when they met some time in the following summer. The question was a first indication of how the sportswriter-coach relationship was going to proceed.

"Fact or flair?" the thirty-eight-year-old coach would ask.

He wanted to know how the twenty-five-year-old sportswriter would characterize his approach to a story. The twenty-five-year-old sportswriter never had considered this, never thought of it at all. He thought about it now.

"Flair," he had to admit.

Not that facts were a problem. He went after facts. He checked facts. He wanted to be right about everything. He knew, though, that he liked style. He liked the different story, the story that would read like the pages from a good novel instead of the minutes from the meeting of the local town planning commission.

Someone else could have the exclusive about the latest stadium proposal, the rancor over a new contract, the breakdown of the strengths and weaknesses of next week's opponent. The bright young man wanted the human aspect, the story about home life or bad dreams, incidentals that provided a link between the famous guy and the rest of us. Anecdotes.

"Do you have a dog?" was the kind of hard-hitting question the bright young man liked best.

"Does the dog do any tricks?" was the kind of follow-up that would come next.

Let someone else write about whether you're going with the 4-3 on defense or the 3-4, coach. Tell me about how you get your kids to go to bed on time at night, what your favorite television show is, why you come off the practice field and pour yourself a large belt of scotch before you start your press conference.

(Which Clive Rush did. Which was a solid indication of why he would not last two full seasons, leaving with health issues and a 5-16 record.)

Talking to players, coaches, front-office executives, getting them to tell stories, was a luxury that would disappear in the interview-controlled future. Too many people would get on the train. Too much attention would be paid. Television would become more and more important. Money would control the interview stage. Thirty reporters, semi-analysts, and frauds would be around the star of the game. Fifty. A hundred. Two hundred. The questions weren't built for anecdotes anymore. They were built for sound bites. Explain the obvious. We can run some action tape behind the words.

The "Do you have a dog?" answer would not fit into the postgame gridwork, not even a little bit. The "Does he do any tricks?" follow-up would be worse. The idea of a conversation, not an interview, would be gone.

Not so for the bright young man in 1969. The beginnings of over-kill might have started in these playoffs, too many people around for too much of the time, but there are still moments. The bright young man can show up early, hang around late, go to practice in the morning. He will find someone just for bullshit. Just to talk.

All the Celtics—take away the always-busy Russell—are pretty good in this department. Funny guys, earnest guys, quiet guys, city guys, country guys, they cover the range. The Lakers, in this small playoff sample of contacts, also seem to be very good. If he covered the Lakers, the bright young man would follow West and Chamberlain everywhere. They were smart, these two, had opinions, were fascinating by their skills alone. The coach, van Breda Kolff, was also interesting. He always had the look like he was going to explode. Maybe it would be a good explosion, laughter all around. Maybe it would be a grumpy explosion, hellfire and outrage, find cover. He is the colorful uncle in the family, the one who has traveled to interesting places and has stories to tell. Be ready.

The best of the Celtics for conversation is Havlicek. He listens to a question, thinks about his answer, and delivers it without many filters. He has anecdotes, is available and friendly after wins, losses, and after his eye was swollen shut when Keith Erickson poked him by mistake in the third game of the series.

The big thing he has to explain during this series—will have to explain for his entire career—is where he gets his endurance. He is always moving, weaving through the big bodies, coming through screens, taking a shot. ("He stops. He pops.") Sometimes it seems as if he has been wound up by a key sticking out of his back or operates on a battery that no one else has found. He is big enough to move inside for rebounds, fast enough to cover guards. He is the robo-perfect player.

"Maybe it's God-given," he says about his stamina. "I don't work on it consciously any more than I did when I was a kid. I'd run everywhere . . . to the school, to the store, to the post office. I had it timed getting home from school. I could do it in 45 seconds."

He grew up in Bridgeport, Ohio. His parents owned a general store. He worked in the store—would sit on top of the freezer and eat a quarter-pound stick of butter as if it were a popsicle—played the three big sports in high school and was good in all of them. Phil and Joe Niekro, who would become knuckleball pitchers in the major leagues, were neighbors. He had two sisters, Rose and Marilyn, and a brother, Fred.

"Was your brother like you?" the bright young man asks one day. "Did he run everywhere, too?"

"He never liked sports that much," Havlicek says. "He liked playing cowboys and Indians, cops and robbers."

"What's he do now?"

"He works for a rifle company. So I guess it worked out for both of us."

The fact that Havlicek hangs up his socks is noted by teammates often. He is tidy, controlled. Everything has to be in its right place. He is frugal in the extreme. Everyone says so. He agrees. The measured approach to money probably comes from working in the general store. He tried out as a wide receiver for the Cleveland Browns when he first got out of college, famous story, would have tried to play both pro football and pro basketball, but was cut on the last day of training camp. He wasn't a great shooter when he arrived with the Celtics, never had been asked to be, but Red told him not to embarrass himself by not taking shots. ("Red didn't have to tell me twice.") He was a good shooter now.

Conversations can be about anything. He says getting through college, Ohio State, was a grind.

"Jerry Lucas was one of my roommates," he says. "I'd be study-ing all night for the big test. I had all my pencils lined up, my books, all my notes, clean sheets of paper. Jerry would come in, turn on the radio, leaf through the book for half an hour and go back out again. You know how it went. He'd get the A. I'd struggle home with the C."

This was the stuff the bright young man loved. Jerry Lucas! Turn-ing on the radio! TBYM never considers himself friends with any of the players—there is a journalism-school line he doesn't want to cross—but friendly is fine. He would be glad to find out some player's taste in music, experiences in gardening, troubled past in a troubled neighborhood.

"Remember this," a friend, Jack Benoit, said when the bright young man left New Haven to take the job in Boston, "I don't care who won the game. I want to know what they had for breakfast."

OK.

TBYM's favorite "Do you have a dog?" moment would arrive at the 1984 Olympics in—yes—Los Angeles. He was writing a column now, and his subject of choice for a particular day was Canadian boxer Shawn O'Sullivan.

A light middleweight, O'Sullivan was seen as a possible star, a twenty-two-year-old redheaded guy climbing the same ladder that Sugar Ray Leonard had used to become rich and famous. This was the first public rung. All of the boxing insiders said he had a bright future if his chin didn't betray him.

Talking to a circle of maybe twenty-five reporters, he detailed some of his previous bouts and his hopes and expectations, nothing great in the way of anecdotes. The bright young man threw out a dog ques-tion.

"Have you ever been to Boston?" he asked, thinking about the Irish-American population, the number of Sullivans, O'Sullivans, and guys named "Sully" that he would meet every day.

Stan Hochman, a columnist from Philadelphia, did not like this.

"Oh, sure, ask the local question," he said, indignant but with a smile. "There are reporters here from around the world and you ask the guy about Boston. Think about everybody else, not just yourself, will you?"

"Well, I've never been to Boston," O'Sullivan said, answering the question anyway, "but I've been close. I went to Walden Pond, just outside Boston. I got lost at Walden Pond."

He explained that his father, Willie, a bus driver in Toronto, was a great fan of Henry David Thoreau. Read and reread all the books. Loved Thoreau's way of thinking, loved the written and spoken word. He read *Bartlett's Quotations* every day during his lunch breaks. Wanted to go to Walden Pond. Put the plan in motion.

There were seven kids in the family and Shawn was six years old and Willie piled everyone into the 1962 Chevy, all seven, plus his wife and himself, and took the big trip. There was a quick stop at Ralph Waldo Emerson's house in Concord, then Walden Pond. Willie was exultant.

A dirt path ran around the pond, maybe for a mile, maybe two, and the kids took off and there was another path off the main path and Shawn took the turn all by himself and that was how he got lost. Willie did some family accounting a little later and came up one short. Luckily the kids all were wearing the same outfit, blue shorts and blue shirts, so they went around and around the pond asking strangers if, excuse me, you might have seen anyone dressed like me?

Eventually Shawn came back to the main trail by himself, was found, even though he never really felt he was lost, and everyone went back to Toronto. Happily ever after.

"And that's how I got lost at Walden Pond," Shawn O'Sullivan said.

There was silence, as everybody wrote down the details of the story.

More silence.

"Shawn," Stan Hochman asked. "Have you ever been to Philadelphia?"

The best facts writer in the *Globe* sports department is Will McDonough. He is a gatherer of news, a breaker of scoops. He is the 180-degree opposite of the bright young man. He wants the fat headline and the buzz that comes with it.

A late addition to the roster, he has joined the *Globe* effort in covering the finals. Bob Sales has other business to handle. McDonough is on the case with the morning paper. This is the no-nonsense start of his effort for today:

The Celtics go back into the trenches this afternoon, wondering about what type of attack the Los Angeles Lakers—and their walking wounded—will throw at the Boston champions.

"I don't care how banged up Jerry West is," says Celtic Capt. John Havlicek. "The only way he won't hurt us is if he's on crutches or in the hospital."

West, who suffered a hamstring muscle pull in the Lakers victory Thursday night in LA is neither.

He, Wilt Chamberlain (ailing eye) and Tommy Hawkins (sprained ankle) will suit up for the Lakers charge at the NBA title that will get underway at 5 pm (that's right) in Boston Garden.

The game will be blacked out locally on TV, but can be seen nationally on ABC-TV. Those shut out from the Garden—and it is a sellout—can listen to the radio broadcast over WHDH. . . .

Thirty-three years old, a graduate of both the ballfields of South Boston and the classrooms at Northeastern University, McDonough already is a strong character in the *Globe* sports department. He is a throwback master of the Walter Winchell front-page kind of scoop, the movie-style reporter who calls the office and says, "Get me rewrite."

He courts friends, destroys enemies. He always is on somebody's side, against somebody else's side, 180 degrees away from any lessons in objectivity. His working principle is "I can write better than anyone who writes faster and I can write faster than anyone who writes better" and he probably is right. (This is a great journalistic motto, first proposed by A. J. Liebling in *The New Yorker*. It can be used by different people and each of them can be right.) McDonough takes no notes, but gets the facts right. His goal always is to be first to report the story, to startle the morning reader.

He was an athlete, a quarterback at Boston English High School, then a quarterback at Northeastern until he was injured. He started at the *Globe,* part-time, when he was eighteen. He has contacts at all levels of Boston sports, all levels of Boston life. This is the strength of a city kid, Old Harbor Housing Project, grown older. One of the sidelights of his résumé is that he was the first campaign manager in a race for state representative for Billy Bulger, who later would become powerful and famous. He also was friendly with Whitey Bulger, Billy's older brother. Whitey Bulger also would become famous as a gangster on the run, accused of nineteen murders.

"I was the only one to visit him in Leavenworth," McDonough said, talking about Whitey's first round of incarceration. "I was covering the Red Sox in Kansas City. Took a bus on an off day. There were three different prisons in Leavenworth. Didn't know that. Had to find the right one."

The South Boston stories—". . . and then the can of beans exploded and all these guys dove onto the floor and pulled out their guns"—are cards McDonough will play throughout a career that later will establish him as a national football expert, a television voice on CBS and NBC. He will have a Chuck Norris quality to him, larger with every year, a streetwise mix of charm and hard edges that people in power will admire. He will sit at his phone and talk with Lamar Hunt and Al Davis and Pete Rozelle and Bill Parcells and a long list of his geniuses. He will trade information and laughs. It all will work.

High on the list of 1969 geniuses is Red Auerbach. McDonough is a very good tennis player. Auerbach also is a good tennis player, but not as good as McDonough. He loves to play McDonough, hoping to improve, hoping to win. Sometimes this happens. In the winter, McDonough is a very good handball player. Auerbach is a good handball player, but not as good as McDonough . . . and so it goes. The matches, the games, are followed by lunch and conversations.

Sometimes headlines are the final result.

Chapter 17

GAME SIX

LIVE FROM THE BOSTON GARDEN: Organ music in background. Tune indistinguishable. Ambient crowd noise, mixed with some cheering. Chick Hearn and Hot Rod Hundley begin their night's work on KNX AM1070.

CHICK: Chick Hearn with Rod Hundley . . . And Rod, I have been around the NBA, like you have, for many, many years, been involved with the World Series before, and I have never seen a club as tense or as dedicated as each individual Los Angeles Laker appears to me to be today.

ROD: They're ready for the game, Chick, and I think for the first time this ballclub realizes what's ahead of them, what they have in their grasp, only one game away from being a world champion. I believe they're all prepared for it mentally coming into this basketball game and I don't think you'll see the bad start they've had in the last couple of games. They're ready to play . . .

Player Introductions. Stuff.

CHICK: The Celtics are standing at the rim of the Grand Canyon. They have their backs to the big pit and the Lakers want to push them in. Can they do it?

Stuff. The game is ready to begin.

CHICK: Ninety-four by fifty. Down below us. Lakers will drive. Northern goal to our right. Southern goal to our left. Celtics in white against the Forum Blue Lakers. Jerry West takes off the sweat trunks and you can see the extent of the bandage now on his left thigh. It extends just about from the back of his left knee and under the bottom part of his trunks. . . . Incidentally the Lakers have a heating pad on the chair in which West will sit any time he is not in the game or even during timeouts or even here before the game. And Jerry sits on that heating pad with his left leg. Right now he's doing some squatting exercises in front of the bench. He checks with trainer Frank O'Neill and vice-versa. Jerry says, "I'm going." You couldn't keep him out of this game if his leg had been amputated. Believe me. He is the kind of a guy who wants this title so badly he can taste it. Each and every Laker does. Each and every Celt does. That's why when these two great clubs meet year after year the pandemonium that breaks through in Boston and Los Angeles can be heard over the three thousand miles that separates those two great American cities.

Stuff.

CHICK: If the Lakers win, they stay here overnight. Come home tomorrow, United Airlines Flight 191. Arrive at International Airport around 12:07. If they lose, they come home tonight. Arrive at International Airport at 1:52 a.m. in the morning.

Game begins.

Sorry, Chick. The bus to the airport would be leaving straight from the Garden after the game.

The series now was tied, three games apiece in fairly perfunctory fashion. The heating pad worked well enough and Jerry West worked well enough—26 points in thirty-nine minutes on the floor—but he wasn't the 100 percent Jerry West, and the Celtics took advantage. Boston 99. Los Angeles 90.

"If I could have played a normal game, we would have won," West said. "I'll definitely play Monday. I won't be in top shape, but I'll be better than I was today. I just couldn't move around very well and [the leg] bothered me when I drove to the basket. I had at least three good opportunities to drive and I couldn't do it. There wasn't any power in my leg."

He played the first ten and a half minutes of the game, scored 10 points despite the fact that his leg felt stiff. He left with the Lakers trailing, 26–22, for a dose of that heating pad. Chick described his exit as "one-legged, limping so badly you want to go down there and lift him off the court."

When he came back early in the second quarter, the Lakers were trailing by 11, 37–26. The rest of the game was played trying to escape this hole. With his hamstring loosened simply by being used so much, West led a small comeback in the fourth period, but the Lakers never came closer than eight points.

"We just played a very bad game," coach Butch van Breda Kolff said. "We didn't do much right."

The distress from West's left thigh radiated through the rest of the Lakers' lineup. The game seemed to be played in a smoky fog for the visitors. (OK, it was the Garden, no air conditioning, no ventilation, and the temperature in Boston was 77 degrees.) They committed 26 turnovers leading to 20 of the Celtics' points, seemed to need a guidebook to operate when their superstar was not a superstar.

The persistent double-teams the Celtics unleashed to try to slow down West in the past few games had disappeared. Emmette Bryant was able to pay full attention to Lakers point guard Johnny Egan. John Havlicek was able to play man-to-man, no fooling around, against Keith Erickson. Egan and Erickson had combined for 39 points on 39 shots when they were left open, handed invitations to shoot in Game Five. In Game Six, invitations rescinded, each scored 7 points on a combined 20 shots. Egan was 3-for-14.

"With Bryant not switching onto West, this didn't leave Egan free," van Breda Kolff said. "Or Erickson, either, as Havlicek sometimes switches off to Jerry. Bryant guarded Johnny closely and tired him out."

Without West's drives to the hoop, the other Laker hope on offense was that Wilt Chamberlain would expand his offense, become a modest reincarnation of the legendary Man Who Scored 100 Points. That did not happen. The Man Who Scored 100 Points did that seven years ago. His dour look-a-like now scored 8. He made one basket in five attempts, went 6-for-10 from the foul line. Eight points.

A familiar plot line was explored: Lakers lose, Wilt to blame.

"We got the ball into him at times," van Breda Kolff said, delivering Complaint No. 751 about his highly paid famous center. "But he didn't do anything with it."

"We just didn't adjust," the highly paid famous center replied, Retort No. 751. "This is the first time I've played with Jerry when he's been hurting like this and we couldn't do the things we usually do. I'd say we have to make some adjustments before the next game."

The Celtics also had some problems. Sam Jones, who guarded West tight, without any help, picked up three fouls before the Laker star left for that rest in the first period. After a minute-and-a-half standing ovation during the pregame introductions for his last appearance at the Garden, Jones played only fourteen minutes in the entire game, scored only 8 points. Havlicek, who admitted he was suffering from a pulled groin muscle that had slowed his activity for the past three games, had another bad shooting night, 8-for-26, scored only 19 points. Russell, who outrebounded Wilt by one, 19–18, also only outscored him by one with 9 points.

The pace and style of play could be attributed to tired legs and tired bodies, ground down by the every-other-day basketball or trip across the country. Minutes had accumulated into noticeable piles for the starters on both teams. A two-hour takeoff delay had made the Celtics' latest return home an extended grind. Both teams were looking for a spark, a surprise, an unexpected source of energy. The Celtics received it from two of their more rested sources: Don Nelson and Emmette Bryant.

The twenty-eight-year-old Nelson, a six-foot-six reserve forward who had played a total of ninety-three minutes in the previous five games, 18.5 minutes per game, lowest among the seven players the Celtics used every night, entered this one with 4:13 left in the first period. He came out firing.

"If we need scoring, my job is to score," he explained. "If Sam and Havlicek are going good, that's not my job. You've got to evaluate the situation and see what the team needs."

Sam already was on the bench with the three fouls. Havlicek, despite scoring 10 points already, was an offensive question mark the rest of the way with that pulled groin muscle. So Nelson fired. He hit jumpers from the outside. He created space for himself on the inside.

Not the tallest player, not the greatest jumper, he was a master of tugs and pulls, subtle elbows and good leverage. He used a head-and-shoulders fake as a basic weapon. One fake. Two fakes. Three. A defender had to choose when to commit, when to jump. When he did, Nelson would slide past for the score, collect the and-one foul shot as the defender crashed on top of him. He had 5 points by the end of the first quarter, 25 by the end of the game on 10-of-19 shooting, 5-for-5 from the foul line.

Bryant, the thirty-one-year-old point guard obtained in a trade with the Phoenix Suns for a second-round draft choice before the season started, played forty-seven minutes, locked up Egan on defense, scored 18 points on 7-for-18 shooting. This was the longest he ever would play in an NBA game in an eight-year career. Part of the reason was that Sam was on the bench for so long, the three-man guard rotation reduced a lot of the time to the two on the floor. Another part of the reason was Bryant's defense on Egan. The largest part, though, was that he simply was playing great, scoring, distributing passes, stealing the ball on defense. He was a backcourt tornado.

"I've never seen Emmette Bryant play better," Chick Hearn said.

The one minute that he missed was the last minute of the game. With the win assured, the Garden crowd started chanting, "We want Sam, we want Sam," asking for a final curtain call for Sam Jones in his final Garden game.

Russell gave the call, Sam came onto the floor, hit a seventeen-foot jumper to seal the final result. The locker rooms were filled with perfunctory words after the perfunctory win/loss. Perfunctory words about how West will be better after some more rest and treatment. Perfunctory words about the Celtics' storied history in no-tomorrow, back-to-the-wall situations. The one moment of passion came when some young guy snuck into the Celtics locker room and started to ask players for their autographs. Public relations man Howie McHugh spotted him, asked to see a credential, saw none, and whacked the guy in the ear, hard, causing him to leave holding that ear in pain. The public relations department issued a short comment on the incident.

"The little *&^###@&*," Howie McHugh said.

—

Nelson and Bryant, the evening's heroes, were favorites of the bright young man. He thought they represented this edition of the Celtics as well as anyone. This, again, was the team largely built from spare parts, constructed in Red Auerbach's basement from some diagram printed in *Mechanics Illustrated* (you can look it up) or something, changes made here and there according to what was available. Everything clinked and clanked, whirred and fluttered, but somehow worked.

Russell and Havlicek and Sam Jones were the stars, bona fide and road tested by now, but even they had not been seen as defined commodities when Auerbach brought them to Boston. Russell couldn't shoot and Havlicek couldn't shoot, maybe was going to play football anyway, and Sam was from North Carolina Central, an historically black college. Red had never seen him play in person and no player from a historically black college ever had been drafted on the first round, but Bones McKinney, the coach at Wake Forest, had seen him and called Red and look at how it all had worked out. Or listen. The ovation still might be taking place.

The rest of the team pretty much was found by driving around the sidewalks of the NBA on the designated morning for refuse pickup. Bailey Howell, who did have a pedigree because he was drafted in the first round from Mississippi State, was traded from his second team in five seasons, his star diminished a bit, for Mel Counts. This was a rare Red trade. Siegfried, of course, was signed as a free agent after he was rejected by teams in two leagues. Nelson came off the waiver wire—"for $1,000," Chick Hearn reminded his listeners just this afternoon—from the Lakers, who had not used him much in two years. Bryant came in that trade for the second-round draft choice from Phoenix, who had selected him from the New York Knicks in the expansion draft.

This was the least-talented Celtics team ever to challenge for a title—especially if you looked at Russell's age and Sam's age—and Nelson and Bryant were probably the least talented players who drew important minutes. They were better than they were supposed to be. That was why the bright young man liked them. They were the ones who were easiest to approach for conversations.

There usually weren't a lot of other people around.

—

Emmette Bryant never played high school basketball. That was a fact TBYM learned during a conversation during the season. The little guard never played because he was five feet three when he was sixteen years old and never showed up at the high school very much. The five feet three might have been a problem, but the bigger problem was that he never showed up at the high school at all after a while. He just quit.

"I was a dropout," he said. "A high school dropout. I lived in Chicago, the West Side. The kids would be going to school and I'd be across the street in the playground. Where I came from, going to school wasn't the hippest thing to do."

His mother cured this situation after a short while when she took him to an Air Force recruiting station, signed the papers, and sent him off to basic training, which was followed by the next four years of his life. He grew up in assorted ways. Became ten inches taller. Earned a high school degree. Learned how to operate radar equipment. And played a lot of service basketball.

"You're pretty good," someone told him after some game somewhere. "You should go to college to play."

"I should?" Bryant replied.

This new direction led to Crane Junior College, then DePaul University on a three-year scholarship. He was the seventh-round draft choice by the Knicks in 1964, picked so late because of his age. Made the team even though he would be almost twenty-six years old on opening night. Played four years in New York. Selected by Phoenix in expansion draft. Didn't want to go. Traded to the Celtics. Auerbach wanted a guard because Mal Graham, who had been drafted a year earlier to replace K. C. Jones, had developed a debilitating blood condition that sapped his energy and eventually would end his career. Bryant was excited about the move.

"There's a difference playing with the Celtics," he said. "It's something you feel when you walk into an arena. People expect you to win. When you lose, people are surprised and make a big deal out of it."

In his time with the Knicks, Bryant had followed the flamboyant fashion lead of fellow guard Walt Frazier. He wore Edwardian suits, leather vests, shoes with extravagant heels. He had the big mutton-chop sideburns, a couple of gold medals hanging from his neck, did everything as if a Marvin Gaye song was playing in his head. Everything he did was cool. The bright young man noted Bryant was wearing a pair of green velour pants and one of those Sherlock Holmes hats during one interview.

Stories circulated about how he had brought a pet jaguar with him to Boston, had the exotic pet living in his apartment, but now the jaguar was gone. Bryant was left with his two German shepherds, Cleo and Bruno. Bruno had been a gift from Knicks center Willis Reed.

"The jaguar was getting too adventurous," Bryant explained. "I'm sticking with the dogs."

He was the third guard on the roster, the backup, for most of the season. He'd played about half as much as Siegfried, averaged 5.7 points per game to Siegfried's 14.2, but late in the year Russell started to call on him more and more. He'd replaced Siegfried in the starting lineup, then been replaced by Siegfried, back and forth. That pattern continued until this game, where Bryant played the forty-seven minutes in the sixth game of the NBA finals.

He wouldn't have done this in Phoenix.

Don Nelson was the opposite of Bryant, a farm boy, a child of Rock Island, Illinois. He went to a one-room school, liked to shoot a basketball at a spokeless bicycle rim nailed to a shed, grew tall, did OK in high school, somehow wound up at the University of Iowa on a good team that would have been wonderful if Connie Hawkins, another freshman in his class, hadn't been ruled ineligible. Nelson was drafted by the Chicago Zephyrs on the third round in 1962, traded to the Lakers after one season.

He was quiet—dressed quiet, talked quiet, acted quiet—but he was an observer and a thinker, qualities that would be large in his future in a thirty-one-year second career as a head coach of four different teams that would send him to the Basketball Hall of Fame. There was a confidence about him, the idea that whatever needed to be done would be done.

The most important playoff game he ever played probably had been four years earlier in the 1965 finals between the Celtics and the Lakers. He came off the bench, same as this time, scored 9 points, added a couple of rebounds and a couple of assists in a 126–105 win. The difference was that he did it for the other side.

"I think that's when Red noticed me," Nelson said of his standout game with the Lakers. "I played point guard for a lot of that game. We had a lot of injuries. Both our back-up point guard and our back-up back-up were not available. They had me bring the ball up and pass to Jerry West."

West scored 43 points. The Lakers won their only game of the series. Red remembered.

Nelson was released at the end of training camp in the following season. He waited by his phone for an obligatory couple of days— there were no agents, nobody had an agent—and when the phone did not ring he returned to Moline, Illinois, to figure out his future. If basketball was not going to be part of it, what would he do? His father always had encouraged him to be a watch repairman. Good money. Clean work.

The phone rang.

Auerbach asked if he wanted to join the Celtics. Nelson was in Boston the next day. The career of a tall watch repairman was finished before it began.

The defending world champions needed help. Tom Heinsohn had retired. First-round draft choice Ollie Johnson, a six-foot-seven forward from Russell's alma mater, the University of San Francisco, had been a bust, released in training camp. Second-round draft pick Ronnie Watts from Wake Forest had made the team, but his movements were stiff. Auerbach was not a fan. There was room for immediate advancement in the frontcourt on either side of Russell. Three days after he was signed, Nelson was playing in a 105–100 win over the Baltimore Bullets.

"He's a solid player," Auerbach said. "He's the type of player who won't hurt you. I can put him into a game and know he'll hold the status quo. He'll give some guys a rest, which is what I was after. I know some of my guys always thought Nelson battled them when he was with the Lakers."

He now had the unofficial designation of "sixth man." This was an Auerbach invention, an added bit of status (but no money) to the first man off the bench every night, sort of a nonstarter with status, able to give the team a quick lift. The job first had been held by Frank Ramsey, then given to Havlicek, who made it famous before he moved into the starting lineup. Now Nelson had it, watching the first eight or ten minutes of every game, coming off the bench, trying to add whatever the team seemed to need. He usually wound up playing half the game, but sometimes less.

The bright young man had stumbled upon an unusual sight involving Nelson during the Eastern finals against the Knicks. An optional practice had been called at the Garden and the busiest Celtics on game nights had taken the day-off option. Two of the un-busiest had not.

In the empty arena, background noise provided only by guys who cleaned the cramped spaces around the seats, Nelson and rookie Don Chaney were at work. Hard work. They played one-on-one against each other full court. Neither felt he was playing enough during the games to keep in top-grade physical or basketball condition. This was their answer to the problem. They had done this workout in the past, but not often.

"No stopping," Nelson declared, listing the only real rule. "You could take the ball out of one basket and start driving towards the other basket. You didn't have to take the ball out."

The game was frightening to behold. Each man wanted to work a full-court press against the other on defense. Each wanted to drive to the basket, coast to coast, on offense. This was the basketball version of a 220-yard race on an Olympic track: too long to be a sprint, too short to be a distance race. No stopping.

Chaney had a couple less years in age on his side, less weight to carry. Nelson had more height and bulk for rebounds. The action went up and down the court, a lot of thumping and breathing hard, maybe ten times up, ten times down, maybe twelve times and twelve times until one of them scored that final basket. Then they both deposited their breakfasts at the side of the court.

"He got sick and I got sick," Nelson reported later. "Then we went back and ran up and down about eight more times. Then we got sick again and then we played a little half-court basketball, just to help our shooting."

The next night, Nelson scored 15 points in twenty-two minutes against the Knicks. Those were solid sixth man numbers.

—

Nelson would show up every now and then for a workout at the Newton YMCA. He was friends with a Newton guy, Bill Barry, lived in
Barry's house the first year with the Celtics, and they showed up
together. Nelson sometimes went up to the indoor track to run. The
banked track overhung the old gymnasium, twenty-eight laps to the
mile, sort of like putting yourself into a centrifuge if you were running
any distance at all. A single basketball court took up most of the gym,
a thousand layers of shellac covering the bruised wooden floor, pickup
games every noon, no jump shots from the corners because you'd hit
the bottom of the track.

Nelson could watch the action while he thumped out his distance.
The action went back and forth while he went round and round. A
few grunts. A few warnings. "Pick." "On your left." "I got him." A few
calls for the ball. Celebrations. Disappointments. The bright young
man often was one of the players.

Not very tall, not very fast, not able to jump very high, not able to
do one constructive thing with his left hand, TBYM had a forlorn
passion for the game that never would be requited. He had played it
all his life, played it at the Y in New Haven, played it in the dirt backyard at Bobby Montgomery's house in a three-on-three league that
featured blowout-patch basketballs, shoves into a rosebush behind the
basket, games timed by a wind-up alarm clock that rang at the oddest
moments.

TBYM scuffled here at the Newton Y with a collection of business-
men, day laborers, teachers, former high-school heroes and present-
day fathers of four, everybody on a first-name basis, no more than
that, first come, first served, games of only five baskets, winners stay,
losers go to the end of the line. There could be as many as thirty
people waiting to play.

Everybody was attached to a scouting report from other games,
other days. Gerry would really hurt you physically. Watch out for
Gerry. Herbie, the minister at the Congregational church, would hurt
you, too. Watch out for Herbie. Hank liked to drive to his left. Big
Warren, six feet eight or so, played on the freshman team at Notre
Dame. Watch out when he gets a head of steam. He'll either make
a basket or call a FOUL!!!! There were three guys named Steve. Big

Steve played at the University of New Hampshire. Very good. Little Steve worked at a publishing company down the street. Pesky. Liked to drive. Steve the Cult Deprogrammer was a cult deprogrammer. You might see him on some television show rescuing some kid from a Hare Krishna house somewhere. Steve the Cult Deprogrammer also could really hurt you.

The bright young man would play basketball here for the next thirty-plus years, three and four and five times per week. He would get to know the changing characters, a few of them in the real world, actual friends, but most only on the court. It was ritual, exercise, fun. Bad words were allowed. Fistfights did occur. The bright young man would break his nose twice within a week at one point. Sort of like Jerry West.

An interesting thing would happen when Nelson arrived on these disparate occasions. The bright young man noticed that the intensity of the games increased. Nobody said a word, nothing like "Hey, there's Don Nelson jogging up on the track," but everybody knew. Guys would start diving for balls that were going out-of-bounds. Fouls became harder. Boxing out became more important. Arguments got louder. It was as if someone had turned a switch. The real basketball player was here. Everything was more important by a multiple of at least two, maybe three or four.

The bright young man mentioned these Newton Y visits to Nelson one day after a Celtics practice. He had never bothered him at the Y, not once, but now he mentioned that he had seen him up there on the track running. Those games on the court? The bright young man was one of the participants.

He was not sure what response he wanted. Something like "I saw you hit that jumper from the key" would be wonderful. Something like "You're playing in those games? They're pretty good" would also be fine. "Looks like fun" would not be bad.

"You play with those little fat guys?" was what Nelson said.

Sigh.

Yes.

The little fat guys.

Heading now to the seventh game of the NBA finals, backs to the wall, no tomorrow, all that good stuff, TBYM wonders what that would feel like. How crazy would it be? What would the game be like?

Seventh game. The bright young man's only true frame of reference is the Newton Y, game tied, 4–4, losers sit, everything more intense because Don Nelson was running laps on the track above the court and occasionally noticing the little fat guys.

Sometimes distance can be measured in light-years from what will happen in one place to what happens in another. Sometimes not.

Chapter 18

OFF DAY

Pre-Game Show

By Leigh Montville
Staff Writer

LOS ANGELES—Emmette Bryant, the Boston Celtics guard, is 30 years old, but he doesn't let it bother him. He is still a child of the modern world.

He wears bellbottoms. He wears the Edwardian suits, the granny glasses, the good colognes. He wears the ruffled shirts and the silk scarves and, of course, he wears the rings—a lot of rings.

"Emmette," a sportswriter asked him yesterday, "if you win the championship, what are you going to do? You don't have room for a championship ring."

A smile broke out between the mutton-chop sideburns and over Emmette Bryant's Dr. Faust beard.

"Are you kidding?" he said. "I'd sell my soul to win this thing now. There'll be room for another ring. I'll make room."

That is the way it is tonight. One game. One ring. One more time.

The Celtics try for their 11th National Basketball

Association championship in the past 13 years. They meet the Los Angeles Lakers in the seventh and final game of the championship playoffs at 10:00 PM (TV Channel 7) at the sold-out Forum.

For Bryant, who played his other four years of professional basketball as a New York Knickerbocker, this is a new story, a first chance for a ring. For the Celtics, it is an old, old story.

Here they are again. Bill Russell is the center and all his help is supposed to be old. Even Bill Russell is supposed to be old.

The championship is down to one game. Wilt Chamberlain is supposed to be a problem. Elgin Baylor and Jerry West are supposed to be problems.

It is the same old situation, even though this time West and Baylor have joined forces with Chamberlain. No one wants to bet against the Celtics.

Nine times they have been in playoff series that have gone to the seven-game limit. Nine times they have won.

Nine times, Russell has battled Chamberlain somewhere along the round-robin like that leads to the finals. Eight times Russell has won.

Five times the Celtics have played the Lakers in the finals. Five times the result has been the same.

"I just know we're going to do it this time," West said after the Lakers held a short shooting practice.

The slender guard is an optimist, but like everyone else he knew the Lakers have problems. The biggest problem, he knows, is Jerry West's left leg.

His pulled hamstring muscle, which kept him at about 75 percent efficiency in the Celtics' 99–90 series-tying win Saturday at the Garden, still hurts. Perhaps the muscle didn't hurt as much as Sunday, but it did hurt.

"There's no way you're going to keep me out of that game," West said. "No way at all. I know the leg won't be 100 percent, but I'll be able to play."

The Lakers, with a limping West, were sloppy

Saturday. They hesitated and stuttered and stood around on offense. They didn't do what most people thought they should have done. They didn't ask Wilt Chamberlain to score.

"I've been playing one style against the Celtics all year and we've been winning," the big guy said. "But now I guess I'm going to have to change and try to score more."

Nevertheless, it is the same. Chamberlain, for the first part of his career, concentrated on scoring. Russell didn't have any more problems than he does now.

"When Wilt does more on offense, the other people do less," said Celtic captain John Havlicek with obvious logic. "They can't drive as much when Wilt handles the ball.

"And remember, Russ did all right when Wilt was trying to score all those years."

Boston Evening Globe
May 5, 1969

A quick read here: the basics are covered. A little offbeat lead: the case of Emmette Bryant, looking for his first championship with a team that has won so many of them. A recitation of the historical facts: the Celtics' nine-game unbeaten string in seventh games, the Lakers' five failures in the finals, Wilt's failures in eight of nine play-off series against the Celtics on assorted teams. A nod to the present situation: West's hamstring injury, the always-present questions about Russell's age, the uncertainty about Wilt's scoring.

Only one important ingredient is missing.

The oomph.

The oomph is missing.

A brass band of metaphors should be playing. Some Technicolor, brand-new anecdotes should be unfurled. A parade of excitement should be high-stepping to this cataclysmic finish—on a Monday night, no less—in an arena called "the Fabulous Forum," movie stars and other Hollywood high rollers in attendance, history and money on the line, ONE NIGHT ONLY, a national television audience added to the mix.

The oomph.

How do you put everything into a 609-word newspaper advance?

The printed word always struggles to describe this kind of situation. Too much is happening at once. Fed by the senses, the mind can capture the scene—the smells, sounds, colors, jostles, bumps, communal roar—but even the most nimble fingers can't communicate all this to the printed page. There aren't enough words, and the words that are available are tired.

What is each player thinking as he gets ready for this game? What are the coaches thinking, the referees, the owners, the writers and broadcasters, each and every one in the stands? What are the variables? Dinner? Breakfast? Lunch? Sleep? Lack of sleep? Issues at home with wives and children? Issues not at home? Mistresses? Old friends? Previous coaches? Money? Bills? What music is going through every head? Who is listening and who is not?

A traveling salesman's monotony has intruded here at the very end. The two teams' playoff schedules began on March 26, 1969, the Celtics on the road in Philadelphia, the Lakers at home. The two teams have played seventeen playoff games in thirty-nine days, a game almost every other day. The Celtics, with their fourth-place finish in the regular season and with an alternate-game playoff schedule in the East, have made nineteen plane trips. The Lakers have made ten. The 2-2-1-1-1 format for the finals has been brutal. The Celtics have now flown across the country five times in twelve days, the flights sandwiched around the six basketball games.

Russell demanded that the team switch airlines, moving from United to American for this trip. He said he had watched *Bullitt* four times. He wanted a different movie for this last trip to the final. That was his sole reason for the change. (Alas, the name of that new movie apparently is lost to history.) Steve McQueen could not be reached for comment.

The bright young man is exhausted. The zip-a-dee-doo-dah joy of a first visit to California two weeks ago has disappeared. He made most of the trips in the first two rounds of the playoffs and all of them for the final. He feels he is as worn down as any of the athletes could be. (The fact that he doesn't really know how worn down an athlete might be contributes to his judgment.) This part of the professional athlete's life, this grind from day to day, on the plane, off the plane, cab to the hotel, traveling, waiting, coffee shop food, traveling, waiting some more, all of life based around a two-hour highlight, was something TBYM never really had recognized.

In New Haven, he once wrote a story about the roller derby, which made a local stop. A young guy, a derby star, Mike Gammon, detailed the gypsy life. He would help unload the pieces of the track from the trailer truck, help set it up in the arena, skate on it during the show, then help take it down and put the pieces back in the truck. The derby had a deal with Holiday Inn. Every night at the end of all this work, he would stay at a Holiday Inn.

"Do you know how much the same these Holiday Inns are?" he asked. "I'll wander all over the place, looking for the room I stayed in two nights ago. Then I'll wake up in the morning and not know what city I'm in."

This was the travel bubble that now existed for the Celtics and the Lakers. The Fabulous Forum was the final Holiday Inn.

The normal insider look at a seventh-game situation would ignore or touch very lightly on results from previous years. Rosters change, players age, new coaches arrive with new ideas, nothing is the same. The Celtics' perfect 9-0 record in seventh games would be a pleasant statistical note, signifying almost nothing. Except this situation is different. The history hangs over the Fabulous Forum as if it were a sad and persistent cloud.

The people involved in this seventh game are far from new. They have been characters in big swathes of that streak. Both sides of it.

Bill Russell, of course, has been part of every one of those nine wins. Enough said. He is the heavyweight champion of this world and has the belts around him when he steps into the ring. Sam Jones has been his sidekick for eight of the nine, his jump shot a deciding factor in a bunch of them. John Havlicek has been around for five.

On the other side, Wilt Chamberlain had been involved in three seventh games, never won once. (He has met Russell in the playoffs ten times, won once.) Jerry West and Elgin Baylor have lost seventh games twice, also have lost the five playoff finals to the Celtics.

This seventh game is the remake of an old story, hyped with the idea that anything can happen, but burdened with the knowledge that in the past anything did not happen. The Celtics won every time.

1. April 13, 1957 Finals: Celtics 125, St. Louis Hawks 123 (Two Overtimes): The standard was set in the first winner-take-all game Russell or the Celtics ever played. He was a twenty-three-year-old rookie and Heinsohn was a rookie and Frank Ramsey was a rookie and the finish was a doozy. Doomed now to black-and-white fuzzy obscurity in the modern video archives, the game still stands as a scholarly contender in all arguments about the greatest NBA game ever played.

The lead changed thirty-eight times and the score was tied twenty times during the fifty-eight minutes of action. Russell flew down the court with thirty-nine seconds left in regulation to block a fast-break layup by Jack Coleman that would have given the Hawks the lead. It was the type of defensive play seldom seen in the league until his arrival, a picture of the basketball future inserted into the basketball present.

In the second overtime, the Celtics led by a hoop with one second left. The Hawks seemed dead because they had to travel the length of the court to the Celtics basket at the far end. After a time-out, player/coach Alex Hannum unleashed a mighty out-of-bounds heave that traveled end to end, hit dead in the middle of the far backboard, and bounced straight to the foul line and into the hands of the Hawks' leading scorer, Bob Pettit, who already had piled up 39 points. It was a brilliant play, diagrammed by Hannum in the huddle, and it worked. (It was better than that last-gasp pass from Grant Hill to Christian Laettner to defeat Kentucky 104–103, in a 1992 NCAA Eastern Regional final called "the best college basketball game ever" by *Sports Illustrated*.) It was perfect.

Except Pettit missed the shot from the foul line to tie the game.

The horn sounded.

The Celtics and Russell had their first championship.

"Let's see," Russell said in the locker room, "that's three championships in a year for me. The NCAA, the Olympics and now with these fellows."

2. April 1, 1959 Division: Celtics 130, Syracuse Nationals 125—The picture at the end was a dribbling exhibition by Bob Cousy. The Celtics had trailed by as many as 16 points in the first three quarters, charged to the front early in the fourth, then squandered their success toward the end when Russell fouled out. With the lead down to three points with 1:09 remaining, Cousy took an outlet pass from Heinsohn and went into his act of keep-away. The Nats chased, but couldn't catch him. With two seconds left on the twenty-four-second clock, he stopped and lifted one of his set-shot one-handers from fifteen feet. When the ball came through the basket, the Celts were ahead by five points and only forty-five seconds remained.

"Seemed like I was dribbling for hours," Cousy reported.

3. April 9, 1960 Finals: Celtics 122, Hawks 103—This was a back-and-forth series, the two clubs alternating home-court wins with the Celtics at the Garden in the end for a final advantage. They took full advantage of that advantage as they stormed to an eighteen-point lead at the half and never let the slower, taller Hawks within fourteen points the rest of the way.

Russell was everywhere on the backboards, collecting 35 rebounds to add to his 22 points. Normally quiet Hawks star Bob Pettit (Robert Lee Pettit Jr. of Baton Rouge, Louisiana, and LSU) was awestruck by Russell's performance.

"I'll take my hat off to Bill Russell as a basketball player and man any time I'm asked to," he said. "He's a lot of man in my book."

4. April 5, 1962 Division Finals: Celtics 109, Philadelphia Warriors 107—The Celtics had the ball with twenty-five seconds left in the

game. The score was tied, 107–107, on a five-point run by Chamber-lain, three of the points—stop the presses—on free throws. Cousy told Sam Jones to hold for the last shot, a forever-prudent strategy at the end of games.

Sam held and held, thought he held too long when he heard Auer-bach yelling at him to shoot. He dribbled to the left, figuring the Warriors expected him to go right. He tossed up his fifteen-foot jump shot, hoping that he threw it high enough to clear the onrushing Chamberlain. The idea was that if the shot missed, Russell possibly could grab the rebound and score. The shot did not miss. Celtics 109, Warriors 107. Final.

5. April 18, 1962 Finals: Celtics 110, Los Angeles Lakers 107 (Overtime)—The big moment came at the end of regulation time at the Garden and involved Hot Rod Hundley and Frank (Franklin Delano) Selvy, a pair of shooting guards for the Lakers. Selvy had scored the last four points in regulation to bring the Lakers into a tie, 100–100. Hundley, later to become a Laker broadcaster, said he had dreamed a night earlier that he would hit the shot that would make the Lakers the world champions.

The ball was passed to him from out-of-bounds in the closing sec-onds. His first choice was a pass to Jerry West, but West was covered. Hundley faked his own defender, Carl Braun, into the air and the dream was possible, right there, but he saw Selvy open at the same time. Selvy once scored 100 points (still a Division! record today even with the addition of the three-point shot) in a college game for Fur-man (41-of-64 from the floor, 18-of-22 from the line). Selvy was a better shooter. Selvy had a better shot than Hundley, left side, maybe eighteen feet from the hoop. Hundley passed the ball.

Selvy missed the shot.

The game went into overtime, where the Celtics pulled ahead by five points and hung on at the end for their fourth straight title, fifth in six years.

6. April 10, 1963 Division Final: Celtics 142, Cincinnati Royals 131— Sam Jones woke up nervous. Not that he had slept much during the

night. A sense of foreboding had come across the Celtics for this version of a seventh game. The Royals were a surprise. They had beaten the higher-seeded Syracuse Nats in a best-of-three qualifying series and now had beaten the Celtics three times, twice in Boston, to reach this final contest for the right to move to the NBA finals.

To occupy his thoughts, the Celtics guard had his wife drive him to Boston Garden at nine o'clock in the morning. He walked around the city, went to a movie double feature. (*Five Miles to Midnight*, starring Sophia Loren and Tony Perkins, was at the top of the bill. He couldn't remember the second film.) He hung around Red Auerbach's office for a little bit. He went upstairs to the Garden and shot baskets, something he rarely did on the day of a game. He worried some more. Fretted.

Then he played the best basketball of his career.

He scored 47 points, a Celtics record for a regulation game, on 18-for-27 shooting. He said this was the most points he ever had scored in the NBA, college, high school, or practice.

7. April 15, 1965 Division Final: Celtics 110, Philadelphia 76ers 109—Havlicek stole the ball. This was (and still is) the most famous play in Celtics history. Part of the fame came from the drama of the moment. A bigger part, the lasting part, came from Johnny Most's gargled radio description.

The Celtics were ahead by a point, 110–109, but had surrendered the ball and what looked like a certain victory when Russell tried to throw an inbounds from the end line and the ball hit a guide wire attached to the basket. This gave possession at the same spot to the Sixers and guard Hal Greer with five seconds left and a chance to win the game.

"Greer, putting the ball in play," Most told his listeners. "He gets the ball out . . . and Havlicek steals it! Over to Sam Jones. Havlicek stole the ball. It's all over. It's all over. Johnny Havlicek is being mobbed by the fans."

8. April 28, 1966 Finals: Celtics 95, Lakers 93—This was Auerbach's final game as head coach. He already had announced his retirement

at age forty-nine. Russell already had been named as his replacement. This was the going-away present. Or the welcoming gift. Whatever.

The Celtics galloped to a seventeen-point lead at the half, still were ahead by ten with forty-five seconds left in the game, then weathered some mistakes to let the Lakers close to within a hoop at the end. In the locker room, a photographer asked Russell to kiss Auerbach or Auerbach to kiss Russell. That would be the perfect picture of the transition. Russell declined.

"Red and I are close," he said, "but we're not funny."

9. April 19, 1968 Division Finals: Celtics 100, Philadelphia 76ers, 96—This was a game and a series the Celtics were not expected to win. They meekly had surrendered the Eastern Division and the eventual NBA title to the Sixers and Wilt Chamberlain a year earlier, the end of a record eight straight championships. (This is the longest championship streak in U.S. professional sport.) The "Russell is old" talk had begun in earnest, paired with the "Russell is not much of a coach" talk. When the Celtics finished second in the East during the regular season and then fell behind, three games to one to the Sixers in the playoffs, well, there it was. No team ever had recovered from a 3-1 playoff deficit in NBA history. No team. Ever.

Then the Celtics won a game in Philadelphia on a Monday night, the Sixers ready to celebrate. . . .

Then they won another game in Boston on a Wednesday night, to tie the series. . . .

Then they played the Sixers on Friday night, back in Philadelphia, seventh game, no tomorrow, for all the marbles, blah-blah-blah, the Sixers still ready to celebrate. . . .

"It's like the Peanuts cartoon," Sixers coach Alex Hannum, a victim again, said after the 100–96 loss. "It's like dropping an ice cream cone. There it is. But what can you do about it. You can't pick it up and eat it. It's gone."

Wilt Chamberlain scored 14 points, 11 of them in the first half. He took only two shots during the second half. He was off to Los Angeles three months later.

—

10. May 5, 1969 Finals: Celtics vs. Lakers. Score to be Determined—So now it happens again. Check the schedule. No tomorrow. Yadda-yadda-yadda. The best-of-seven is now the best-of-one.

Suppose Sam Jones's shot didn't fall in the fourth game. Suppose Jerry West's hamstring hadn't been tweaked, just a little bit in Game Five, slowing him down for Game Six. Suppose the Celtics could have won one of those two very close games way back at the start. Suppose. Suppose. Suppose.

Didn't matter. None of it mattered.

Tired bodies will be dragged to the floor one more time. This will be the game that will be remembered. This is the only game, in the end, that counts.

> Four More Copters Crash in Vietnam, Killing 10. IRA
> Ready if Civil War Comes. Princess Anne Has Influenza
> and Will Not Be Able to Set Off with Her Parents,
> Queen Elizabeth and the Duke of Edinburgh, for a Six-
> Day State Visit to Austria. American Civil Liberties
> Union Launches Draft Fight. No Increase in Social
> Security Planned Until 1970. *Boys in the Band* Blends
> Waspish Wit, Loneliness, and Need. Red Sox Four
> Games out of First in the American League, Dodgers Two
> in the National. No games today.

Lakers vs. Celtics. Celtics vs. Lakers.

That is the news that matters.

"We're going to win," Jerry West says on page thirty-three of the *Long Beach Independent*. "I've never been so sure of anything in my life."

"The way I figure it, we'll be drinking champagne about nine o'clock," Johnny Egan says.

"I'm a former Celtic and I know their great traditions, but this is our year," Mel Counts says.

Seventh game.

Chapter 19

GAME SEVEN

CELTICS CINDERELLA TALE, 108–106

BY LEIGH MONTVILLE
Staff Writer

LOS ANGELES—How many times had they done it? A million times? Maybe. It seemed like at least a million.

John Havlicek put his pale white arm around Sam Jones' brown shoulders. The green shirts on both men were wet and stuck to their bodies.

"Sam, old man, I just want to take one more picture with you," John Havlicek said, disregarding a cold sore and breaking into a grin. "Give them that Colgate smile."

Sam smiled. Havlicek continued to smile. Lights flashed. Cameras recorded.

This was the last time. This was the best time. It was Sam Jones' last locker room scene. It was the Boston Celtics' 11th National Basketball Association championship in 13 years.

It was the annual celebration. Another championship. Another flag for the top of Boston Garden. This was the toughest one. It was the best one.

The Celtics had won the title again with a 108–106 victory over the Los Angeles Lakers at the sold-out modern Forum. The formula had been familiar—balanced scoring, defense, the fast break, work from Bill Russell—but the situation had been alien.

The Celtics, since the playoffs had begun 18 games ago, had been underdogs. They had been the fourth-place finisher in the regular season, the ugly sister invitation to the playoff ball.

"Every year people used to talk about how we'd win the playoffs because of the home-court advantage," Jones said. "Well, this year it was different. This year we didn't have the home-court advantage once.

"We had to win a game away from home in every series and we did it.

"On paper, the Lakers had the greatest team, no doubt about it. But we had the greatest bench. Me? I'm glad to finish as a champion."

Jones, who scored 24 points to match his jersey number in the final-game win, started to take off the green uniform for the last time. The trunks, he said, would go back to Bailey Howell.

"They're his," Sam said, showing the label and the stitched-in No. 18 for corroborating evidence. "We switched pants early in the season. Maybe it's superstition, but they do fit me better than my own."

Havlicek, standing next to Sam, backed against a wall, tried to undress his own emotions. He couldn't do it.

"Some day, when all this is over, I'm going to sit at home and try to figure all this out," he said rapidly. "The feeling now is something I just can't explain.

"I don't want to think about next season or anything like that. I want to sit down and enjoy what has just happened."

What had happened was what has happened over and over and over again in the NBA. The Celtics had done the big job at the big moment.

In the first five minutes of the game they had taken a 13–6 lead. They had nursed it, given away chunks of it, then nursed it again. When there were only nine minutes of basketball left, the lead had grown to 100–85.

"We wanted that early lead," Havlicek said. "In this series, it always seemed that the team that went ahead early was the team that won the game."

Then, as often happens, the Celtics hit a dry spell. A dry spell? The Gobi Desert was not nearly as barren as what the Celtics did in almost the next eight minutes.

They were outscored, 19–3. Suddenly the margin was 103–102. The Celts' lead was down to one point.

Then, Don Nelson picked a basketball off the floor and took a jump shot from the foul line. The ball hit the back of the rim, the inside of the rim.

"A shot that hits the inside of the rim should never go in . . . but it did," Lakers coach Bill van Breda Kolff said.

The ball bounced up in the air. Swish. It came back down through the net.

"What can I say?" Nelson said. "It was a lucky shot— the luckiest shot of my life."

Neither team took advantage of opportunities the rest of the way, until Larry Siegfried was intentionally fouled with 24 seconds left. He hit both shots, the score jumped to 107–102. The title stayed in Boston.

"We didn't have champagne in the dressing room," Havlicek said. "I never drank a glass of champagne in a Celtics locker room.

"We just don't have it—it's not superstition. We just don't have it."

Down the hall, at another, quieter dressing room, there were five cases of unopened champagne. There were eight unopened bags of balloons at the top of the Forum ceiling and an unsliced victory cake in the Laker press room.

"That's the Celtics' strength—balance," Lakers coach van Breda Kolff said. "Don't get me wrong, it's nice to have Jerry West to go to, but it would be nice to have four guys with him.

"You can't beat balance. The Celtics' balance was only getting old, that's why we stayed close.

"Four years ago? Sam Jones and those guys would have run away from us."

Van Breda Kolff, gave a wistful smile at the thought, drank a soda. It was an old story.

Sam and John were having their pictures taken. The Celtics were the World Champions again.

Boston Evening Globe
May 6, 1969

The voice of Chick Hearn described the desolation to the Laker faithful. He was his staccato self, but without emotion, without fun. He was like someone forced to apologize, to write the final line of an accident report, to tell the family that the refrigerator, alas, was empty again. He said what he had to say.

"That's all she wrote," he said with fifteen seconds remaining, the Lakers trailing by five points. "For the 11th time in 13 years, the Boston Celtics are world champions. What a tremendous heartbreak for the Lakers, who fought 'em all the way down to the wire. . . ."

Grrrrrrrr.

The 108–106 finish—a few meaningless points distributed at the end—was wonderful if you were a Celtic, a validation of truth, justice, solid personal hygiene, three square meals per day, crossing on the green, not in-between, and a strong belief in the enduring abilities of William Felton Russell. The finish was terrible, terrible, the pit of pits if you were a Laker. Money had been thrown out the window. Hope had been destroyed. How much pain were human beings supposed to endure? It was synthetic pain, of course, the result of an athletic contest, no one dying or dead, but it certainly felt real.

All those multicolored balloons, blown up by office staff, stuffed in bags and placed in the Forum rafters to be part of a grand celebration, would never be dropped. The champagne, cases of it, stored in the Lakers locker room, never would be opened. The championship cake . . . what would happen with that? The University of Southern California band, hired to play just one song, "Happy Days Are Here Again," would never march onto the floor. Happy days, it would be remembered, never had been here in the first place.

"Never in my life have I been so sure that we'd win," Jerry West said in the quiet of the Laker locker room.

He was Greek-tragedy heroic to the end. His left hamstring taped again, he was great even though he limped noticeably through the game's final stages. He scored 42 points, had 13 rebounds and 12 assists. A triple double. (Before the accomplishment became a big deal.) He had averaged 37.9 points per game for the series and almost immediately was awarded the series Most Valuable Player Award by *Sport* magazine. Still, there were a couple of turnovers, a few missed shots, all the nagging pieces of another loss. What if he had been 100 percent healthy? What if? More than fifty years later he still would say this was his most disappointing defeat.

"The day of the game, I took a ride to Marina del Rey," he would say four days after the loss. "I was thinking of all the happy faces that I'd see after the game. That's how sure I was that we were going to win. 'This is going to be some night,' I said to myself. It was some night. It was a nightmare."

"We were all so positive that we were going to win," owner Jack Kent Cooke said. "We know that we're the better team but we didn't show it in the series."

Hearn's radio voice, the words delivered in his basketball shorthand, had dipped and risen with the Lakers' fortunes inside the heads of an entire city as the game progressed. Tense from the start ("I've never felt like this before in the basketball history of Los Angeles," he said. "I've never been this on edge."), he never was allowed to run free. It was not that type of game.

The Lakers were in trouble from the start. Then they were out of trouble, pretty much, down by three points at the half. Then they were ready to take the lead. No, then they were in trouble again. They were in big trouble. They were dead, done, finished, out of time, but wait, wait a minute. They were not dead. They were back. They were ready to take the lead! No, they were dead.

Hearn chronicled it all, heartbeat by heartbeat. The rest of the nation—Boston, included—watched the drama play out on ABC television, the first prime-time broadcast of an NBA game. The news-caster neutral duo of Chris Schenkel and Jack Twyman delivered a balanced Walter Cronkite commentary. Hearn talked as if his children were playing. His heart was attached to his mouth.

"Will the Lakers get the lead?" he asked when they trailed, 60–59, in the third period, their first chance to get the lead in the game. "If they do you'll hear it all the way back in Boston without a transistor."

A foul shot by Keith Erickson tied the score, 60–60.

"If you're driving a car, you better stop and park and listen," Hearn said. "This is very exciting."

The Celtics then proceeded to score the next twelve points in a row. The Lakers didn't score for six minutes. They missed sixteen straight shots. Hearn counted off the misses, starting with nine. That's ten. That's eleven. That's twelve, all the way to sixteen. The Lakers had become discombobulated at the worst time. They couldn't do anything right.

"The Celtics are running patterns," Hearn declared. "The Lakers appear to be ad-libbing. The Lakers are just standing around."

The Celtics had a 15-point lead, 91–76, at the end of the third quarter. "The fourth-place team in the East!" Hearn mentioned the fact with a mixture of admiration and disgust. Probably more disgust. The fourth-place team in the East. The lead was soon stretched to seventeen points in the final quarter.

"HOWELL TAKES THE JUMP SHOT AND IT'S GOOD!" Johnny Most shouted from a different broadcast spot in the Forum to the people back in Boston, many of whom had turned down news-caster neutral from the television feed to listen to their familiar, hysterical version of the action. "IT'S 98–81, BOSTON LEADING BY 17 WITH 10:06 TO GO IN THE GAME!"

Fourth quarter. Seventeen points. The game was done, the Lakers finished, just about time for the fans to find their cars in the asphalt desert with six minutes to go. Disappointment seemed assured when, yes, assumptions were flipped again. Down by eleven now, the Lakers scored the next ten points. The Celtics went as cold as the Lakers had been in the third period, missed seven shots in a row. Hearn counted off the misses, one by one. The Lakers trailed, 103–102, with 2:30 left.

"We want it so bad we can taste it," Hearn blurted in the middle of his description. The noise could be heard all the way in Boston without a transistor. The Lakers assuredly were back. Cue the USC band.

A curious subplot had developed in the early part of this comeback. Wilt Chamberlain came down awkwardly with a rebound and twisted his right knee, which had given him problems in the past. He grimaced, shouted. There was little doubt that he was hurt. Hearn spotted the injury, noted the severity, said Wilt might have to leave the game. Wilt would be "bitterly disappointed."

The big fellow came down the court, slow and in pain. The Lakers got the ball and called timeout. He limped off the floor.

"CHAMBERLAIN IS HURT AND HE'S LIMPING AROUND!" Johnny Most shouted. "THERE'S 5:32 LEFT IN THE GAME AND BOSTON IS LEADING 103–94! CHAMBERLAIN IS COMING OUT!"

The curious part happened next in stages. The Lakers played better. Mel Counts, the seven-foot journeyman, once a Celtic, now a Laker, took Chamberlain's place. He had done this at times during the season and van Breda Kolff usually liked what happened next. The offense ran better, was faster when Counts was in the lineup. Nobody had to wait for The Load to come up the floor. The Lakers could fly, create mismatches in the forecourt when other teams couldn't set up their defenses. This was what happened here.

West took over the fast break offense. He had scored the last basket before Chamberlain left, and now he scored three more in a row. ("A FANTASTIC SURGE BY WEST AND THE LAKERS!" Most reported.) Counts connected on a foul-line jumper, a shot Wilt would never take, to drop the score to 103–102. The Forum was a color-coordinated kettle of noise.

On the Lakers bench, the subplot had become even more curious. Chamberlain, after icing his knee, told van Breda Kolff that he was all right, that he could go back into the game. The coach told him either "No," or "We don't need you," or maybe "Go fuck yourself," according to the account a listener might believe. The Lakers would win or lose with Mel Counts in the game.

This was prime soap opera stuff. The final blowup between two combustible men came at the most important moment of the entire year. The $250,000-per-year superstar, the physical marvel, the holder of most of the individual records in the league, would not play the final few minutes that would decide the Lakers' fate. This negated the whole reason he had been brought to Los Angeles. The obstinate, opinionated coach had delivered a final obstinate opinion. If the Lakers won, he would be a strategic genius, his gamble praised in words and deed forever. If the Lakers lost, he should pack his possessions in his traveling bag this very night because he never would be back to his office again.

No one in any of the broadcast booths knew any of this was happening. Hearn made the same wrong assumption that everyone made.

"Wilt apparently won't come back," he said. "Because he would if he could."

Almost two minutes passed after Counts's basket, no score at 103–102, fouls called, foul shots missed, nerves stretched. The Lakers had a chance to take the lead at last, but never did. Baylor missed a shot. Russell batted away an Erickson pass to Baylor. West had his dribble slapped away and stolen by Siegfried. The Celtics did no better. Havlicek missed a foul shot. Nelson was called for charging into West. Everything seemed to happen in a frenzy.

Then Don Nelson hit a crazy, loopy shot that won the game.

"HAVLICEK GETS MAULED, BUT HE GETS RID OF THE BALL TO SIEGFRIED," Johnny Most screamed. "NELSON FIRES UP A SHOT AND IT'S GOOD! 105 TO 102 WITH A MINUTE FIFTEEN TO GO! MAN, OH MAN, THE TENSION AND THE EMOTION!"

This was not exactly what happened. Siegfried was forced into a corner, double-teamed by West and Keith Erickson, who shifted to the job from guarding Havlicek. Siegfried fought through the double-team to make a pass to Havlicek, who was open. Erickson rushed to cover his man.

The Celtics star, dribbling, tried to move to his left, but exposed the basketball in the process. Erickson swiped at it from behind, knocked it free toward the foul line. Which was where Nelson was standing. The ball came at him low, maybe like a bouncing ground ball to a shortstop. He fielded the ball on the bounce just about at his belt line and in one motion, worried about the twenty-four-second clock, lifted up a shot with his right hand.

It was not a great shot. It was a heave, a prayer . . . but it was a soft heave. Nelson always used an exaggerated shot-put motion for foul shots, different from anyone else, before or after he played. This was the same type of shot put. His hand waved good-bye, the way all the basketball teachers teach. The ball hit the back of the rim, bounced high in the air—higher and higher in every retelling since— and dropped back down through the hoop, soft and perfect as Santa Claus coming down the chimney.

This was Sam Jones's shot at the end of Game Four all over again. Magic. Luck. A tribute to clean living and crossed fingers and toes. Bigger and better. The Zang Auerbach gremlin in green was at work for one last time in the 1968–69 basketball season.

Celtics 105. Lakers 102.

"It was a garbage play all the way," Hearn exclaimed, the Los Angeles version. "After a good play by Erickson."

The Lakers had a couple of chances to move back within a point, but West missed a jumper on one possession and Counts, on another possession, tried to come off the baseline and shield Russell with the basket to make a layup. Russell was too quick for that. He blocked Counts's shot and when Siegfried, the top foul shooter in the NBA for 1969, was whacked on purpose by Egan and converted twice, the score was 107–102 with twenty-four seconds left. The Forum was emptying as if there was a fire drill.

"One of those things that won't happen four times a year," Hearn repeated about Nelson's pivotal shot in his wrap-up, his eulogy.

"The Lakers had four men around the hoop," color man Hot Rod Hundley said. "The ball bounced as high as the top of the backboard and came back down."

"AND IT'S OVER!" Johnny Most shouted in triumph back to Boston. "THE BOSTON CELTICS HAVE WON THE WORLD CHAMPIONSHIP FOR THE ELEVENTH TIME IN THIRTEEN YEARS! THE CINDERELLA TEAM! I BELIEVE THAT'S THE FIRST TIME A FOURTH-PLACE TEAM HAS EVER COME ON TO WIN THE PLAYOFFS. THEY HAVE DONE IT AGAIN! A SPECTACULAR FINISH!"

"The Lakers were not humiliated here tonight," Chick Hearn concluded, sounding as if he were at a wake, deciding how the mortician had made the subject look lifelike. "They were simply outshot."

In pretty good seats, but certainly not courtside Forum seats, former training-camp Celtic George Plimpton reported his version of the ending. The author said that the Nelson shot bounced "SEVERAL FEET straight up and then dropped down into the net." He then reported what happened next.

"I sat next to Red Auerbach in the stands," Plimpton wrote for *The Boston Celtics: A Championship Tradition,* a coffee table book published in 1996 to celebrate the team's fiftieth anniversary. "When Nelson's shot went in, he leaned back and lit his victory cigar—that famous signature gesture of his. He took a puff or two. Just then, a Lakers fan, her face contorted with the agony of watching her team go down to defeat—I got a good look at her—raised an aerosol can of shaving cream and doused the cigar with a quick glob of white foam. It was the only time I ever saw Auerbach slightly flustered."

The storied general manager had recovered from this attack by the time he reached the floor after the game ended. Where should he go next? He immediately found the important action. Jack Twyman, a microphone in his hand, an ABC director's words in the plastic gizmo in his ear, first prime-time telecast, remember, was trying to interview Sam Jones in the midst of chaos. Young males, mostly wearing ties and sports coats and good six-beer buzzes, waved at the camera and shouted and tried to be seen by someone, anyone out there in the world. They seemed to be Celtics fans. They were at least happy. Twyman tried to talk. Jones tried to answer. Auerbach stood in the middle of them.

"What are they going to do with the balloons?" Auerbach interjected.

Twyman paid him no mind. Sam paid him no mind.

"What are they going to do with the balloons?" Red asked again. Louder.

A mischievous smile crossed Auerbach's face. An evil twinkle came from both eyes. He could have been another one of those kids.

Waving to the people back home.

A crowd waited outside the Celtics locker room door, far and away the biggest crowd of these playoffs. Glad-handers and friends, plus people-who-assuredly-knew-people were added to the waiting journalists. Russell took his time inside. He asked Bailey Howell to say a prayer. He talked to the players he had coached for this long and eventful grind, men who also were teammates. There was shouting, of course, celebration, but also a pause for a satisfied deep breath of accomplishment, the view from the top of the mountain again, something to remember forever.

The situation outside the door was quite different. The glad-handers were excited, hoping their credentials or supplications would work to gain admittance. The print and broadcast journalists, people on the job, mostly grumbled and fretted. The journalistic clock had become very important. Time was running out. Deadlines beckoned. Worries were piled upon worries. The work was beginning just now, not ending. Got to get in there. Got to get going. There was some jostling, some antsy movement while trying to stand still. Nervous conversation. Forced jokes.

The bright young man, part of this group, was a certified mess. He was caught in his own inexperience, overwhelmed by the moment. His mind was clicking and clacking, shooting in far too many directions. The game still was a freight train of plays and colors, noises, heroes and villains, emotions. The immediate future was a wall of uncertainty.

Who would be available? Who would want to talk? What time was it on the East Coast? Two in the morning? Jesus. Isn't that War-ren Beatty over there, waiting to get in, too? Never mind. What's my story? What time is it?

(The movie *Goodfellas*, which of course comes along much later, has a stretch toward the end that encompasses the paranoia and the worries of this locker room moment. Ray Liotta, playing gangster Henry Hill, strung out on cocaine, is convinced—and rightly so—that a helicopter is following him as he makes his deliveries, talks with assorted women, frets about both his immediate and distant futures, tries to teach his little brother to make a perfect Italian sauce at the same time. Everything is done with the helicopter overhead, with too many drugs pounding through his system, with way too many balls of attention and need in the air at the same time. Henry is strung way, way out. He could be a sportswriter in this moment.)

The first story that screamed to be done was the weird finish and disappointment for the Lakers. Why did Wilt never come back into the game? Was he really hurt? What was van Breda Kolff thinking?

Wilt surely will be pissed. His teammates will be . . . what? Befuddled? Bemused? Van Breda Kolff will be . . . defensive? Jerry West certainly will be distraught. How much does West have to do to win this thing? Good Christ Almighty. Did someone say he had been chosen MVP? Should have been, yes. Was he? For sure? The losers' locker room was where the story was. Every great sportswriter, from Grantland Rice to Paul Gallico to Red Smith to whoever was featured in the local *Daily Bugle,* knew this axiom. This Lakers locker room would be an all-time exhibit A. This would be the losingest losing locker room imaginable.

The bright young man, sad to say—Wait a minute! Are those people going into the Lakers room already? Why aren't the Celtics open?—could not write this losers' story for a lead. He was from Boston. His reading public wanted to hear about the Celtics' glorious win, the eleventh flag to be added to the Garden heaven. This was a time for Boston dancing, not Los Angeles pathos.

OK, fine. The angle for that story also could be pretty good. It had to be something to do with the balloons that never dropped from the Forum ceiling, the University of Southern California marching band that never marched. "Happy Days Are Here Again"? Not this year, baby. The Celtics' victory over the Lakers could be painted as total destruction. See how Jack Kent Cooke had been so sure that his team would win? See how everybody in L.A. had been so cocky? Well, they could eat those balloons for breakfast, those suntanned surfboard layabouts. How does that rubber taste? This would be a devastating takedown of the Southern California team, the Southern California culture, rich and famous Southern California names from that Hollywood Walk of Fame. The bright young man could do this.

Except he couldn't.

The balloons story belonged to Will McDonough for the morning *Globe,* not for the second-in-command for the afternoon *Globe.* At least that was how the situation seemed. McDonough was his proprietary self. Red Auerbach had handed him the story before the game—handed him a copy of the memo on Lakers stationery about the balloon drop. The memo contained a moment-by-moment schedule of what would happen. It mentioned the immediate release of the balloons, the moment the high-stepping band would come onto the floor, the champagne that would be served, the victory cake that would be cut. Or at least that was what the memo supposedly said. McDonough never shared it. He treated it as if it was the only copy of the Zapruder film of the assassination of JFK, hush-hush and exclusive.

Asking to see the memo was against the unwritten rules of the sportswriting business. The memo was McDonough's scoop. At least that was how the bright young man felt. And it certainly was how McDonough, the king of exclusives, the king of scoops, felt. There was a competition between the a.m. and the p.m. *Globe* as well as with the other Boston papers. This was his story. Stay away.

TBYM could have, should have done some different things. Wouldn't other people also have this memo? He could have, should have tracked them down, could have, should have seen the thing for himself. He could have, should have worked around McDonough. Except he couldn't and shouldn't. McDonough was the strong personality, the alpha male. He had first claim on stories that he received from his contacts. Everyone from the *Globe* stayed away. That was the unwritten rule.

The young man had to figure out a different story.

Nelson might be a start. He hit that crazy shot. Havlicek. Always good. Sam. Last game ever. Russell would be good, but what was the point? He presumably would be writing his own story, too, for the *Globe*. Maybe TBYM could do a general story. Get quotes from a lot of people. Maybe find out some weird anecdote. Maybe. Something.

"Do me a favor," Will McDonough suddenly said.

What? He had been standing here all along? He had just appeared?

"What?" the bright young man asked.

"Wait until Russell is all alone," McDonough said, "then ask him if he is going to retire. I heard a rumor. Ask him."

The rumor also must have come from Auerbach. Of course. The tennis. The handball. Russell is going to retire. McDonough always was ahead of the story. While everyone was celebrating the accomplishment of the moment, he was looking at the day after tomorrow and the day after that. It was a talent, an art. The bright young man did not have—and never would have—this talent.

"Why don't you ask him yourself?" he said.

"Russell hates me," McDonough said. "Wouldn't talk to me. You ask him."

Would the story belong to the bright young man if he asked

the question and confirmed? Probably not. Would it belong to McDonough? Probably so. What? Bzzzz. Another electric worry was added to the pile.

The locker room door was opened. The crowd squeezed past the security check, expanded into the room. Let's see, TBYM had to wait for a moment when Russell was all alone. Ask him if he was going to retire. Check. TBYM also had to tell him to remember to call the *Globe*. Important business. Check. Relations with Russell hadn't improved, but also hadn't diminished during the five weeks and five days of this playoff slog. TBYM still was the private first class. The decorated general was still the decorated general, except he had another large decoration now. Check.

The balloon story—the one the bright young man could have, should have been pursuing—still was off-limits in his mind. (McDonough, it turned out, did lead with the balloons, but didn't have much detail. There would have been a lot of room for a p.m. balloon story.) The Lakers story still screamed to be written. Did TBYM have time to go to the Lakers locker room to find material for a sidebar? One of the first tips he ever received, straight from some writer from Toronto at a track meet in New York, was always to try to write a sidebar. The facts were in the main story. The drama that people remembered was in the sidebar. Always write the sidebar.

That was what he wanted to do here, write the sidebar, but first he had to ask Russell about the retirement, remind Russell about the *Globe,* then had to find a Boston angle, had to, had to, had to get moving.

Warren Beatty walked by him again. Warren, thirty-two and famous, straight from *Bonnie and Clyde,* was celebrating, shaking hands, exchanging big hugs, seemed to be as happy as if he had played in the backcourt, guarded West and triumphed. Good for Warren.

The bright young man's head hurt.

By Leigh Montville
Staff Writer
LOS ANGELES—On one side of the room, Jerry West talked to a small, bespectacled man from Sport Magazine who wanted to give him a car.

On another side of the room, Wilt Chamberlain talked about the coach. The coach, Bill van Breda Kolff, sat in the back of the room and talked about Wilt Chamberlain.

It was a loser's room. It was the Forum basement home of the Los Angeles Lakers last night after they had lost their sixth NBA title to the Boston Celtics.

"Every year gets more difficult to sit here and talk about it," West said intensely, after telling the man he would accept the car for being the most valuable player in the playoffs.

"It gets more difficult after hearing those guys yelling and celebrating in that other room . . . I guess it's just not my fate to be with a champion.

"I don't think I can take it much longer. To be honest with you, I don't think I will play many more years."

West had scored 42 points despite a pulled hamstring muscle. He wasn't a winner. He wasn't happy. Neither was Chamberlain.

Chamberlain had scored 18 points, grabbed 27 rebounds. But he had missed the final five minutes and 19 seconds of the game.

That was the main reason he was upset.

"Is this the worst loss to the Celtics?" he said. "It is to me because of not being able to do anything about it."

Chamberlain had left the game with an injured knee. He had leaped for a rebound and felt the pop. He had limped and left and never returned.

"I asked to go back in," he said sullenly. "Sure, I felt better. That's why I asked to go back in."

The future? Chamberlain has a contract for two more years with the Lakers and some said certainly there is no question about him coming back.

"Right now," the big guy said, looking towards van Breda Kolff, "there are questions about a lot of things."

"All I know," van Breda Kolff said, "is that after Wilt came out we scored some points (six in a row, to close within 103–102 of the Celtics).

"Mel Counts was playing extremely well. He gives us

another outside threat and if he gets fouled he makes the foul shots.

"It is a little bit of a strain if you get fouled all night and don't make the foul shots. (Wilt was four for 13.)

"If we made some shot, it would have been a great move. We didn't . . . but we came close, didn't we?"

Close, but not close enough.

"We are all aware there is a certain amount of luck in basketball and life," Chamberlain said. "Usually it evens out. Sometimes it takes a long time."

There was no happiness. The Lakers' room was the loser's room.

Time obviously did exist for the bright young man to visit the Lakers for a sidebar. He learned in the Celtics locker room that Sam Jones had worn Bailey Howell's shorts for the entire season (hey, a small exclusive right there), consulted the always-helpful Havlicek, learned that the Celtics never had champagne to celebrate any of those championships (another exclusive), and checked Russell, again and again, as the coach/player/correspondent talked with reporters, still in his uniform. There was time to visit the Lakers, come back, talk to Russell. Maybe.

The switch from the winning locker room to the losing locker room was strange at any time, like going from a wedding celebration to the funeral for a favorite uncle, but this one was a mammoth pressure drop. The relieved Celtics had cashed a winning lottery ticket at the last possible minute and were set for life. The Lakers had declared bankruptcy, unable to pay off their many creditors in the seats. Noise filled one room. Music. The voices in the other room could have been used to check out the writings of Edna St. Vincent Millay at the Los Angeles public library.

The bright young man was in the third, fourth, fifth wave of Lakers interviews. The same questions were being asked for the third, fourth, fifth time and brought out the same answers, but muted. The highest emotions had been strained out by now. This was a business transaction, dutiful sadness repeated for public consumption.

Doug Krikorian of the *Los Angeles Herald-Examiner* flat-out won the sportswriting sweepstakes for the night. He had been in the room from the beginning. He knew his subjects personally. This was the true story of the game. He wrote the heck out of it.

"Their faces were wreathed in agony, their words were solemn and their bearing was somber," he would write in his lead. "Always, the outcome is the same for Wilt Chamberlain, Elgin Baylor and Jerry West.

"This was a different season, and they played on a team with superior talent, but again they came up losers against the Boston Celtics."

West answered reporters' questions "in hushed tones while his eyes reddened with tears." Baylor was "twitching nervously." Chamberlain "realized he must endure at least another year with the stigma of being a guy who couldn't win the big one at the end, a stigma that clearly gnawed at him."

"Wilt Chamberlain doubtless was as dejected as he's ever been during his thirty-two years on this planet," Krikorian would write. "He stood in front of a mirror and furiously brushed his hair as the lone reporter [which had to be Krikorian] vainly attempted to console him.

"He kept shaking his head sadly and saying, 'How could it happen . . . How could it happen?'"

The bright young man, who could not concentrate on this one room as Krikorian did, bounced from Lakers star to Lakers star, two questions each, little time to take down description. His favorite quote was from West, the part about hating to listen to the celebration coming from the Celtics next door. West was a story by himself, the tragic hero at his most tragic moment. He knew it. He knew what he was. He hated what he was.

"They are a fine team, but I think we were the best team," he said. "I had no idea that we'd lose—even in the last quarter when we were 15 points behind. I guess it's just not meant for me to play on a championship team."

The bright young man scribbled down words—wait a minute, let me get a few more from van Breda Kolff, who surely would be fired in the next few days—and hurried back to the wedding celebration. Would Russell still be there? Had to be. He was both the groom and the father of the bride. Checked his locker.

Yes, there he was.

He had showered and was almost finished getting dressed. He was wearing a tan suit with a lavender shirt. He was tying his tie. The reporters had left, questions answered, but he was not alone. Jim Brown was sitting at the next locker talking with him. Jim Brown, the certain Hall of Fame football player. (Three years after his early retirement from the Cleveland Browns.) Jim Brown the actor. (Two years after *The Dirty Dozen*. One year after *Ice Station Zebra*.) Jim Brown, the civil rights activist. He was thirty-three years old, still seemed close to his perfect football height and weight at six feet two, 232 pounds. He was wearing a dashiki.

The bright young man faced a situation. He wanted to talk to Russell alone, but that did not seem to be possible. Jim Brown looked as if he was going to accompany the coach/player/commentator to whatever celebration was planned. The bright young man had to ask his Will McDonough–based question not only to the two greatest players in the history of their respective sports, but to the two most prominent black activists in sport if you didn't count Muhammad Ali. He only had to ask . . . he had to interrupt their conversation.

(I have told this story countless times in the many years that have passed. I always mention here that 1. I was five feet nine, far from a robust athlete, and probably the whitest white person possible with red hair and freckles and the skin tone of Johnny Winter in a snowstorm. I also mention 2. that I have a somewhat squeaky voice, at least to my ear, and that in times of stress it rises an octave or two. I deliver my parts of the ensuing dialogue in a falsetto.)

"Uh, Bill . . ."

(He was in the finishing stages of buttoning up, ready to roll.)

"Yes . . ." (Deep voice.)

"I just wanted to ask: Are you planning to retire?" (Definite falsetto.)

(Dramatic pause.)

Jim Brown chose to answer for Russell.

He looked up from his seat at the locker. Stared straight at TBYM. A potter's glaze of incredulity came across his *Dirty Dozen* face. Perhaps with a touch of disgust.

"Retire?" he said. (Deep, deeper, maybe deepest voice.)

"The man just won the world championship," he continued. "You're asking if he's going to retire?"

The bright young man wanted to say, "No, of course not, I wouldn't ask you that. Will McDonough wanted me to ask you that, maybe heard it from Red, because Will couldn't ask because, you know, Bill hates him," but of course the bright young man didn't. He nodded. Of course it was a stupid question.

"Uh, Bill . . ."

"Yes?"

"The *Globe*, uh, don't forget . . ."

"Right." (Deep voice.)

Bill and Jim presumably went off to do cool Bill and Jim things in Tinseltown. The bright young man went to his seat in the stands to write. There were cigarettes to smoke, words to find.

He hoped to Christ Bill would call the *Globe*.

By BILL RUSSELL
Player-Coach, Boston Celtics
Copyright, 1969, Boston Globe

LOS ANGELES—Well, another chapter is over. I still can't believe it.

After 100 games we're champions again. I honestly didn't think it could be done, but here we are with another flag.

It was awful hard getting here. Even when we had that big lead in the fourth quarter (98–81), I felt it was too early to count anything as won.

We had to keep it up and we did. We came up with the big plays and held on for a two-point victory.

Well, let's talk about my players, my friends who made this championship possible.

Guys like Bryant, you know this is his first championship. I guess he's the most thrilled guy of all. He's been in the league for five years. He's really made a contribution, you know.

Bryant's sort of a story within itself. Last year he was expendable, put up for expansion and picked up by Phoenix. He said he wanted to retire. So they gave him to us for a Number 2 draft choice. And he ends up starting on the World's Championship team. That's pretty good traveling for one year.

This kind of thing has happened to guys before, but it's always nice to see.

I'm real happy for the guys, especially for the others on their first championship team.

Let me talk about Sam Jones for a minute. I think Sam finished a brilliant career in brilliant fashion. He had a great shooting night. He shot 10 for 16, which is good for anybody. He had 24 big points. He got seven rebounds, a couple of assists. I think he went out in great fashion. That's the way to end a career. He did a great job.

Siegfried—Larry had a hamstring pull, as we all know. But I don't know if everybody knows he pulled it again tonight. And in the last quarter it was really, really hurting him. He told me it was hurting him, but he wanted to play. He said he could do four or five minutes and cut it off. So I put him out there and I thought he did a good job. He brought the ball down well and he had to guard West. I was just so proud of him the way he conducted himself. Until you've done something such as play basketball in real pain, you can't appreciate what it's like.

I've had the same injury and it's like having a real bad toothache in your leg. I could appreciate what he was going through. It gave me a thrill to see the guy want to play.

And John Havlicek had his usual good game. He shot well, as usual, played good defense, and rebounded well. Made come clutch baskets.

Speaking of clutch baskets, let's talk about Don Nelson. He made the biggest basket of the night. It was a bouncer—the kind that gives you three heart attacks before it goes in. It hit the back rim, went straight up and looked like it would bounce out, but it bounced straight in. That was the key basket. It locked it up. I think that was the basket that broke their backs. And a difficult shot.

Now Bailey Howell didn't have what you'll call an outstanding series—for him. And Bailey is a worrier, which is something most people don't realize. You have no idea what agony he's been going through because his shooting was off. But it's hard to convince him—or anybody on the outside—that despite his shooting, he played very well. Like I tell all the guys, shooting is only one part of the game. There are other parts of the game which are just as important. Playing defense, keeping your man off the boards, setting picks, giving a guy the ball when he's free and you're not, all these things.

He worried so much about his shooting, though, that I felt really bad for him. And we did everything we could to get him up for it, but it was tough for him. When you win a championship, anyway, all that goes out the window.

It's hard for me to believe that it's over. When I went into the game I didn't know what was going to happen. And after it was over, I kept saying "it's really over." And finally it is over. We played 100 games and, like I told somebody before the game, I wouldn't trade this bunch of guys for any bunch in the world.

Then again at halftime I told them, "You've got another 24 minutes out there. Whatever we're going to do, win or lose, let's do it together. And I think this is one of the outstanding things about playing on a team like the Celtics. We play together, live together, take care of each other. Worry about each other and I would feel the same way about these guys if we lost.

We see each other as men and we judge a guy by his character, not by how well he plays or anything like that. Strictly on character, because we are not awed by a man's reputation. We are a bunch of men that work together and we judge each other solely on character. Reputation has nothing to do with it. You can see the things we've achieved as a group and it's definitely thrilling.

In a sense, it's strange to say, but we really identify with each other because we know each other. If one guy has a good night, we're all happy because the guy's a friend of ours. We are proud of each other.

If Sam has a good night, we're proud of Sam and if John has a good night, that's the way we feel about John, or Emmette or Bailey or Satch, or anyone. And so this is why it's always such a thrill for me because that's the way of the Celtics since I've been with the team. And, as far as I know, it's always been that way.

Chapter 20

A SMALL PARADE

By LEIGH MONTVILLE
Staff Writer

Bill Russell read a copy of Lakers' Illustrated, the program from the night before, and watched the United States slide underneath him.

John Havlicek slept and almost missed his meal. Tom Sanders talked with George Plimpton, the author, and Sam Jones sat and looked out the window and talked about a future of playing tennis and golf and coaching basketball.

The World Champions returned home yesterday. The Boston Celtics, on American Airlines Flight 43 from Los Angeles, brought their 11th title back to the Boston Garden.

Eighteen basketball games in the playoffs, 82 games in the regular season and 12 more exhibitions were welded into one long fast break, one continuous full-court press. The final result was Tuesday night's 108–106 seventh-game win over the Los Angeles Lakers for the National Basketball Assn. title.

"I'm going to Puerto Rico," Russell said. "A friend of

mine has just built a $250,000 house down there. It must be a nice place to stay.

"The money? I'm going to spend it. I still haven't figured out a way where I can send it ahead or take it with me, so I'm going to spend it."

The total playoff earnings figure for the team was $93,000. The split will be made sometime today or tomorrow when the Celtics hold a small breakup dinner, just the players and their wives.

If they follow past procedure, the Celtics will hand out a few gifts to office personnel then split the pot 13 ways—the 12 players and trainer Joe DeLauri. Each man should earn over $7000.

"This is the greatest thing to ever happen to me," little guard Emmette Bryant had said before he left on his own for Chicago. "This is the world championship.

"Before last night I had played that game 100 times. All in my mind. We had won every time."

That's how it was—with everybody. There was a little shock, a little disbelief. How many times can you go to the well and still find water?

"We're a very fortunate bunch of guys," said Bailey Howell, who did not have a spectacular series. "People say the only way we win is luck, that it is a crime we win.

"If it's luck, then that's all right. I'll take it. I'll take all the luck you can give me."

Howell said he probably would be back to play another year of basketball because it is hard to quit on a champion. Russell, also rumored as a retirement candidate, also said in a roundabout way he would be back again.

"My contract still has one more year," he said. "Will I be back? I signed the contract, didn't I?"

Nobody talked much about next year. Nobody talked about the NBA draft today in New York, where the Celtics will try to find a replacement for the retired Jones.

The Celtics relaxed and watched the United States and

an in-flight movie they had seen before. They ate a meal
and they were satisfied.

"Golf," said Sam Jones, looking out of the window. "I
always have liked the game of golf. I'm not very good, but
now I think I'm going to take a couple of lessons . . ."

Boston Evening Globe

May 7, 1969

There was a victory party after the game back at the Airport Marina
Hotel. The bright young man took forever to write his accounts of
the Celtics' grand finish to the game, the season, the championship
decade. (Did he do this from his seat at the Forum? Or did he return
to the room? Can't remember. Probably the Forum.) Someone had
told him the name for the ballroom, restaurant, whatever the loca-
tion was where the party would be held. Should he check it out? He
was exhausted, whipped, wrung dry. The time was three o'clock in
the morning. Maybe four. The plane would be leaving in a few hours.
Would anybody still be there? Should he check it out?

He was twenty-five years old.

He splashed water on his face. He combed his hair. He weaved his
way to the back of the property. Went past the pool. He had never
been past the pool in his three separate stays at the hotel. The night
was lovely. Palm trees. Warm. California! The Lakers were dead. The
Celtics were champions again.

A small feeling of accomplishment had arrived. It was silly, of
course. TBYM hadn't scored a basket, hadn't done a thing except follow along like one of those beer cans attached by string to the bumper
of some newlyweds' car on the way to the honeymoon, clinkety-clank,
a noise in the background, but following along somehow gave him satisfaction at the end of the trip. He had put in the time, traveled the
miles. He deserved the satisfaction.

The party would be good. He was thinking ornate. Late as he was,
the large ice sculpture of the swan probably would be melting, but
still would be impressive. The band might be done, then again might
not. There certainly would be some kind of music. Dancing. Famous
people. Maybe now there would be a good conversation with that
Warren Beatty, maybe Candice Bergen. Bartenders, waiters, food.

Cocktails. Balloons and party hats. This would be something to see, something to remember.

No.

The ballroom, the restaurant, whatever it was, turned out to be a suite. An OK-sized suite, perhaps, but an average suite in an average hotel. There was a little kitchenette where you could mix a drink or find a beer, a place where a number of drinks already had been mixed and a number of beers already had been found. The lights were turned low. Quiet and unmemorable music came from a radio stereo. Jazzy music. Conversations were subdued. No dancing. No celebrities. No food. The party was done.

Havlicek was still there. Don Nelson was there. They were talking with people they knew. Rich Johnson, the rookie backup center from Grambling who played a total of two minutes in two games in the playoffs, none and none in the finals, was there with some young friends from Louisiana. Eddie Gillooly wasn't there. George Sullivan wasn't there. Johnny Most wasn't there. Nobody from the Los Angeles press. This was like the aftermath of a Thanksgiving dinner, most of the guests gone, the few survivors talking about how it all went.

The bright young man slid quietly out the door. He said nothing to anybody. He shouldn't have gone. No. This was a night of many lessons. This was a final one.

The aftereffects of the party could be seen at the airport the next morning. Havlicek, never a drinker, came onto the plane, put a towel over his head, and never took it off on the cross-country trip. Siegfried, his Ohio State teammate, was worse. Far worse. He had to be wheeled up the ramp, looking as if he was a survivor of a natural disaster, a significant automobile accident, maybe fifteen rounds in the ring for the heavyweight title. Three nuns watched him pass. George Plimpton watched with them.

"Look at that poor child," a nun said.

"He is a member of the basketball team that won the championship last night," Plimpton told her.

"What a brutal game it must have been," the nun replied.

The breakup after the final win had begun almost immediately for the recrowned champions of the world. Bailey Howell, Don Chaney, and Jim Barnes flew back to Boston on the overnight red-eye, which left a few hours after the game. Red Auerbach, who had escaped being tossed into the showers this time, took a red-eye to his home in Washington, D.C. Emmette Bryant and Mal Graham took morning flights to Chicago. Don Nelson went to Florida.

The rest of the players were scattered around Flight 43. They were not separated from the normal passengers at all, same as always, could have been those tall salesmen returning from that big conference on the West Coast. The bright young man bounced around the plane to collect his quotes (note that he even asked Russell one more time about possible retirement plans), settled down in his seat, fired up a succession of Lucky Strikes, and typed out his dispatch on the Lettera 32, hoping that the sound of the keys and the bell and the continuous thumping on the tray table didn't disturb the unlucky passenger in the seat in front.

A surprise waited at the landing at Logan Airport in Boston. The pilot came on the intercom and said a crowd had gathered at the American Airlines terminal. An arrangement was made to allow the other passengers to disembark. (Did they leave first? Last? Can't remember.) Then the Celtics—OK, the six of them who were on the plane, plus trainer Joe DeLauri—would be released into the midst of their fans.

This was a new situation. Russell had turned to Johnny Most in the descent and said—a joke—that "now I suppose we'll have to fight our way through a crowd at Logan." The returns from the previous world championships won on the road had been subdued affairs. There had been no special crowd a year ago when the team returned from Los Angeles. Now there were over two thousand people, including Governor Francis Sargent, stuffed in the corridor from outer gate D-8 to the lobby at 5:50 on a Tuesday night, cheering and singing. Twenty state troopers had arrived to control the situation. Ropes had been strung to make a corridor for the team's exit.

"I didn't expect this kind of a reception," Russell admitted while he shook the governor's hand.

"This is exciting," Beth Havlicek said as she greeted her husband and they went into the crowd.

Why was there this sudden outpouring? Had it been the excitement brought into the local homes by network television? Had it been the closeness of the final game, the closeness of the final series? Had it been the upset, the too-old underdog beating the glamorous over-dog? Was there a feeling that this was the last wonderful gasp of this dynasty?

No survey was taken. All of the above.

The bright young man, veteran transcontinental traveler, followed the players and their families through the packed corridors, watched the players sign autographs, talk into microphones. He could feel the heat from the bodies around him. He hung on to his Lettera 32 and finally broke free.

He needed a cigarette.

The better story still involved the inhabitants of the losers' locker room. The morning after the night before had arrived back in Los Angeles and the headache was even worse. Jack Kent Cooke's dream had been dismantled, deconstructed, destroyed. There was no easy way the pieces could be put back together. The backbiting could begin.

This meant a visit to Wilt Chamberlain. Though he was preparing to go back to Philadelphia to visit his mother, he did have time to talk on the phone with Milton Gross before he left Los Angeles. The subject, of course, was van Breda Kolff.

"The thing that kills me is that we had a chance to win and he wouldn't put me back in," he said to the columnist from the *New York Post* and the North American News Alliance (probably in a whisper). "I don't see how he could have left me on the bench. I asked him about 10 times. The first time he said, 'Wait, wait.' The next few times he didn't even answer. He could have left Counts in and put me in. We had the ball three times when we were one down and I had a chance to rebound and go against Russell."

The subplot had overwhelmed the plot, a situation not unknown in Hollywood. Despite the fact the Lakers trailed by nine when Chamberlain left and came within a point of the Celtics with Mel Counts in the lineup, the narrative now turned heavily toward the idea that Wilt could have been the difference in those final few minutes.

The negative possibilities had materialized from van Breda Kolff's breathtaking gamble. What was the coach thinking? Benched the greatest scorer in the history of the game! A shot blocker! The super-star of superstars, the man who makes all that money! How could Wilt be sitting at the end?

Animosities were dragged out of the locker room, placed under a spotlight and magnified. If the Lakers had won, the problems between the coach and his elongated star would have been casual bumps on a championship road. Jokes. Now they were mountains. Van Breda Kolff couldn't stand Chamberlain from the start. Chamberlain couldn't stand van Breda Kolff. There never had been a chance of success. Not if you thought about it.

"You have to have direction," Chamberlain said. "You can have the greatest horses in the world, but if you don't have the rider you're going nowhere. They didn't beat us. We beat ourselves. You don't mind too much being beaten by a really superior team, but to go out and beat yourselves, it's a shame."

He clearly had gone over the game summary, basket by basket. The six-minute scoreless stretch in the third quarter after the teams were tied at 60–60, the sixteen missed shots in a row, stood out to him. None of those shots were his. The shots mostly were jumpers. The ball was not going into the middle to the most prolific scorer of all time.

Why didn't van Breda Kolff call timeout to stop the trouble? That was his question. Why didn't the coach say, "Get the ball into the big guy?"

"They should have come right to me," Wilt said. "I could have gone to the basket."

"Why didn't you suggest it?" Gross asked.

"You suggest something, he doesn't take it kindly. He's not like other coaches. All you can do is keep your mouth shut. I don't have control over everything. I wish sometimes I did, but I've got to go out and keep things harmonious. I've got to take what people are saying. I'm a loser, I know. How many times have I heard that tripe [probably said 'shit'] before?"

Van Breda Kolff, alas for reporters and columnists, did not and would not join the argument. He flew to New York the day after the game, a trip that had been scheduled in advance because the second round of the NBA draft would be held on Wednesday at the

Baroque Room in the Plaza Hotel. When he finally was contacted, he only repeated what he said after the game about his dealings with his famous big man.

"I told him that we were doing well without him," van Breda Kolff said. "I would have put him back in if I thought he would have made a difference."

The coach would elaborate a bit in years to come, talk about how he had troubles with Wilt from the beginning. ("First day of practice, when he showed up, I thought he was amazing. He was running, cutting, blocking shots. The second day he didn't move at all. The third day he said he couldn't practice.") The year had been a grind, beginning to end. No fun. No fun at all. The coach had been so bothered by the experience he knew in the middle of the season he was going to quit at the end, no matter what happened. Perhaps that had made his decision in the last minutes of the game easier.

"I don't know," he said in New York. "Maybe someone else could have done a better job of coaching Chamberlain."

Jerry West also was in New York City on the day of the draft. He appeared at a luncheon at Mamma Leone's restaurant to receive a Dodge Charger R/T as the Most Valuable Player for the series from *Sport* magazine. This was a big deal at the time, the presentation of the car, a promotional forerunner of the "I'm going to Disneyland" celebration of the future. (The fact that he was the first and only playoff MVP from a losing team, noteworthy in 1969, is even more noteworthy now. He still is the first and only playoff MVP from a losing team.) He said he was taken aback by the color of the car— green!!!—and admitted that he still was numb from the result of the final game.

"Today is the first time I've smiled since Monday," he said.

He was his normal interview self, sometimes embarrassingly candid. The New York writers painted him into a hypothetical corner when they asked if he needed one man on his team to win one game would he take Chamberlain or Russell. He said that this was a loaded question, but . . .

"For the one game that you want to win, there's nobody like Russell," he said. "The man is incredible. As soon as he gets on the floor he gives the Celtics guidance and encouragement. He doesn't have to score. He's quick and agile for a big man and has a very sure pair of hands. He just lights that team up.

"Chamberlain is a better all-around player than Russell. He's a better scorer and rebounder and I think he even blocks more shots than Russell. But for the one game, I'd have to pick Russell. His record speaks for itself."

West considered the inconsistencies in his words. Why would he not take the best player? What kind of judgment is that?

"You'd have to be an athlete to understand," he said.

The story about Wilt and the coach and the final few minutes would wind down, but never disappear. It was one of those odd historic sports moments that always will be worth comment, debate, analysis. Fifty years, one hundred years later, it still would be a topic. Van Breda Kolff, as expected, did resign two weeks after his grand gamble. Two days later was named as head coach of the Detroit Pistons. ("I'm not one to look back," he said. "I'd just as soon not go into the past. Let's look at the future. That's what I like to do.") Wilt would seek a small measure of reconciliation right about that time.

"If we had won the game, it would have been a Laker victory," he said. "Not a Wilt victory. Not a Jerry West victory. Not an Elgin Baylor victory. Not a van Breda Kolff victory. We lost out as a Laker team. All of us—not one man—lost that game."

Oddly enough, the most divisive words came from Bill Russell. Three weeks after the game, on a forty-seven-day trip around the country to give thirty-one speeches at colleges, he made one of his first stops at the University of Wisconsin in Madison at an event on race relations sponsored by the school's Pan-Hellenic Conference. He talked to an audience of two hundred kids, all white, for fifty minutes about a range of subjects, none of them involving basketball. He talked about the Black Panthers, black studies, the Olympic boycott, the Oakland police department (he didn't like it), plus the fact that he would never enter politics because politicians in 1960s America did not tend to live too long. He talked about "the establishment," which he thought "has to be altered."

"In the 100 years since they said they abolished slavery, we [the black man] have survived in a very hostile atmosphere," he said.

"We've reached a stage where we won't take anything less than the best. All we want is all there is and we don't mind working.

"It's hard to believe in law and order, the establishment, the proper way of doing things. You can't use a system that was created to exclude something to include it."

A question-and-answer session followed. It lasted an hour. Basketball finally entered the discussion. A student said that Chamberlain "obviously" had better basketball abilities than Russell but also had a more troubled public image. Why was that? The question, the way it was presented, Chamberlain obviously better, awakened an inner voice that Russell mostly had kept quiet for his years on the court against his tall friend.

He unloaded.

"I think he copped out in the last series in the last game," Russell told his student crowd about Chamberlain. "Any injury short of a broken leg or a broken back isn't good enough. When he took himself out of that final game, when he hurt his knee, well, I wouldn't have put him back in the game either, even though I think he's great."

The inner voice sounded pretty good. The circumstances were different from the normal interviews Russell had handled in his basketball life. College kids. Middle of nowhere. He had put two conditions to his appearance: he would not pose for pictures and there would not be any press conference.

He kept talking.

"I never said Chamberlain didn't have talent," he continued. "But basketball is a team game. I go by the number of championships. I play to bring out the best in my teammates. Are you going to tell me that he brought out the best in Baylor and West?"

And finally . . .

"I'd have to say yes and no about whether criticism about Wilt is justified. No, because people see his potential as greater than it is. They don't take human frailties into consideration. Yes, because he asks for it. He talks a lot about what he's going to do. What it's all about is winning and losing and he's done a lot of losing. He thinks he's a genius, but he's not."

A local reporter, Steve Klein of the *Wisconsin State Journal,* was in the crowd of students despite the no-press request. His story—"RUSSELL PRAISES YOUTH, KNOCKS WILT"—appeared in the morning. The wire services picked it up. The "PRAISES YOUTH" part was not mentioned in the stories that went across the country. The "KNOCKS WILT" part was retained as the headline.

Wilt Chamberlain would not talk to Bill Russell for the next twenty-four years.

The final piece of the Boston celebration for the Celtics was a parade on Thursday, May 8, 1969, three days after the series-clinching win in L.A. This might be seen as a ho-hum event, eleven championships in the past thirteen seasons, parade every year, but it was not. This was a first. A parade never had been held for a Celtics championship.

This also might have been a first parade in the city for a champion in any sport. Nothing was held for the Red Sox in 1918 when they won their last World Series. (Not that anyone remembered.) Nothing was held in 1929, 1939, and 1941 when the Bruins won the Stanley Cup for the only times during their existence. (Not that anyone remembered.) Take away the Celtics and there hadn't been a lot of winning in Boston. Not in the first two-thirds of the twentieth century, anyway.

The players were seated in the backseats of convertibles, tops down on a cool and windy day that was troubled by intermittent rain showers. The route went past the State House, around the Boston Common and Public Garden, down Washington Street, to the new Boston City Hall. A platform for speeches and presentations with a large sign that said "Boston Celtics" stood in the shadow of the grim concrete building that was opened in the past year and was described as either a Brutalist monstrosity or masterpiece depending on the speaker.

The crowd was estimated at thirty thousand along the route, another three thousand at City Hall. Raincoats were worn by most of the people. A kid shouted to Auerbach, riding with Emmette Bryant, "Hey, Red, make the sun come out." Auerbach either did not hear or simply did not comply. Another kid held a sign that said "Russell For President."

Russell was not there. He had been in Auerbach's office earlier in the morning. Auerbach had told him about an interview a day earlier with George Sullivan of the *Herald-Traveler*. Sullivan had asked, "Are you happy with your coach?" Auerbach replied, "Happy with my coach? We just won the world championship." "Yes," Sullivan said, "but before that you finished fourth in the East." Auerbach cited this conversation to Russell as an example of how, Jesus Christ, sometimes you just can't win. Russell agreed. He would remember this conversation fifty years later. He played for the Celtics. He did not play for the city of Boston. No parade.

Larry Siegfried was also missing, probably to reattach body parts. Don Chaney was at a National Guard meeting. Don Nelson was in Florida. The rest of the team was there.

"Johnny Most once said, 'Havlicek stole the ball,'" John Havlicek said from the platform crowded with politicians and functionaries and fans. "Now we've got a new one—'Russell busted their balloons.'

"I think we've finally arrived as a symbol for the city of Boston. This year, I think we caught everyone with the way we won. Today has been terrific. I hope the enthusiasm continues."

A silver plaque was presented to Auerbach, another one to Russell in absentia. A Boston rocking chair, seal of the city on the back, was presented to Sam Jones because "at his age he needs this kind of chair in a hurry."

That was that.

A year later, much of the same script would be followed when the Bruins won their first Stanley Cup in twenty-nine years (and the piranha in John Premack's fish tank ate two goldfish for dinner). The organizers would use pretty much the same route and format, players riding in a line of convertibles, a reception at City Hall at the end. The difference would be the mayhem.

Over 125,000 people watched this parade, four times larger than the Celtics crowd. The weather was warm this time, temperatures near the eighties, a peek ahead toward summer. Bobby Orr and Derek Sanderson, respective star and teenaged heartthrob, never would make the stage, hidden in the mayor's office for their safety.

On the stage, Mayor Kevin White would be offered a chance to drink beer from the Stanley Cup by winger Johnny McKenzie. Accepting the offer, the mayor would be sloppy, spilling beer on McKenzie's hands and arms. Louise Day Hicks, an ever-grumpy member of the City Council, an anti-busing stalwart from South Boston, controversial just about every day, told McKenzie that he could wipe his hands on her dress. And—as Diane White reported in the *Globe*—he did.

Parades and receptions would become a Boston sports championship constant. (A classic Celtics moment happened in 1981 at City Hall. A fan in the large crowd held a sign that said "Moses Eats Shit," a reference to vanquished Houston Rockets center Moses Malone. Larry Bird spotted the sign from the stage and told the crowd that, yes, "Moses DOES eat shit.") Parades featuring the use of amphibious vehicles, duck boats, would become a feature of the twenty-first century, with twelve duck boat parades in eighteen years. Six Patriots. Four Red Sox. One each for the Celtics and Bruins.

The parade for the 1969 Celtics, though, modest as it was, was the first. History. The bright young man not only went and covered it, but also was a part of it.

The details have become murky with time. There was an extra car, maybe a couple of extra cars. Someone said, "Hey, why don't you come along?" The bright young man, again, was twenty-five years old. Would this cross the journalistic line? Would he be acting a little self-important? What the heck. Maybe it would be good for the story.

He sat in the back of the convertible, feet on the leather backseat, ass on the trunk, and waved to whoever was waving at him. There was little chance that anyone recognized him or confused him with any of the players or front-office executives (since there were only four front-office executives anyway), but he waved. Some torn-up newspapers or business forms floated down from the taller buildings on Washington Street. Not a lot, but some.

Everything is murky, except . . .

The thought went through the bright young man's head that this was how it must have been for Lindbergh when he came home from Paris. OK, Lindbergh might have had more ticker tape.

I do remember that.

Chapter 21

NEXT

Since 1943, when I first saw a basketball, I've played
approximately 3,000 games, organized and otherwise. I
think that's enough . . .
  Bill Russell
  Sports Illustrated
  Aug. 4, 1969

Bill Russell did retire. He made his announcement three months
later in *Sports Illustrated,* which reportedly paid him $10,000 for the
story. He said he had known from the beginning of the season that he
was done, but kept quiet and had told only Sam Jones on the Celtics
about his decision just before the final game in Los Angeles.

The bright young man was suitably upset about the announcement—"I asked him the question in the locker room and he lied to
me," TBYM said, quite too often to friends and relatives—but soon
accepted Russell's thinking. Take the money. Go ahead. Congratulations. The coach/player/columnist had more than earned everything
he received.

Russell later described how he left his marriage at the same time,
how he moved to California after the final championship and proceeded with the rest of his life. He never lived in Boston again. Miss-

ing his best player—himself—he did not find great success as coach of the Seattle Supersonics (1973–77) or the Sacramento Kings (1987–88). After a number of years out of public life, he became basketball's most recognized elder statesman for the past decade. He was awarded the Presidential Medal of Freedom in 2011. A Bill Russell statue was dedicated near City Hall in Boston in 2013. The Most Valuable Player Award for the NBA Finals is now the Bill Russell Award.

He was eighty-seven years old when this book was finished.

Wilt Chamberlain played five more years. Another seventh-game disappointment arrived at the end of the next season with the famous return of Willis Reed that led to a 113–99 loss to the Knicks. In 1971, the Lakers lost yet again to the Milwaukee Bucks and that Alcindor kid (soon to be Kareem Abdul-Jabbar), but in 1972 the world championship finally was put in the refrigerator in Los Angeles, the Jell-O jiggling at last. Wilt was thirty-seven years old when he retired a year later. He had dominated his sport for fourteen years, set records in assorted statistical categories that still stand, but had won only two championships.

His death in 1999 from congestive heart failure at the age of sixty-three was stunning to anyone who had watched him walk across a room, much less play basketball. He was physical perfection, an actual giant among us, an outsized man with great coordination. The best measurement of his talents is that no one, from Wilt's NBA debut until the present day, has been called "the next Wilt Chamberlain" or "a lot like Wilt Chamberlain." He was a unique basketball force, constrained only by his own insecurities and the imagination of Bill Russell.

Never married, he claimed in his autobiography that he had slow-danced with twenty thousand women. Like blocked shots, the NBA did not keep track of this statistic during his career.

The National Basketball Association is celebrating its seventy-fifth birthday this year. The league has thirty teams, as opposed to four-teen in 1969. There are twice as many players, more than twice as many coaches, much more than twice as much attention. The money involved has skyrocketed everywhere. (Except, perhaps, in the salaries of sportswriters.) The average valuation of an NBA franchise is $2.12 billion, according to *Forbes* magazine. The Knicks, Lakers, and Golden State Warriors all are valued over $4 billion. The Celtics are valued at $3.1 billion.

The league is in the sixth year of a nine-year, $24 billion television contract with ESPN and Turner Sports. The minimum salary for the 2020–21 season is $893,310. Steph Curry of the Golden State Warriors, the highest-paid player in the league, will earn $43 million for the season. Anthony Davis, six-foot-ten center for the Los Angeles Lakers, signed a five-year, $190 million contract at the start of the season. He was twenty-seven years old.

The league profile on the LinkedIn website says it has 1,001–5,000 employees.

The ***Boston Globe*** has been squeezed in size and influence along with every newspaper in the United States by the digital/Internet revolution. The weekday print circulation has dipped below 85,000, the Sunday circulation to 147,000. Digital subscriptions, seen as the future for newspapers, moved past 200,000 only in 2020. The newspaper's large headquarters at 135 Morrissey Boulevard were closed in 2017, editorial and business offices moved to Exchange Place in downtown Boston. The printing was moved to a site in Taunton, Massachusetts.

Money told the story best. John Henry, owner of the Boston Red Sox baseball team, bought the *Globe* from the *New York Times* in 2013 for $70 million, which was less than the $82.5 million he was paying nondescript pitcher John Lackey for five seasons' work. The *Times* had purchased the paper for $1.1 billion in 1993, only twenty years earlier. The age of the printed page had disappeared, just like that. The *Globe*'s final competition, the downsized *Boston Herald,* a tabloid, is on life support with a daily circulation of less than thirty thousand.

The *Los Angeles Times* has gone through similar contractions and upheaval, daily circulation down to 417,000 in 2019, staff reduced again and again. The paper left its iconic downtown headquarters in 2018 and now is located in El Segundo, California. The *Los Angeles Herald Examiner* went out of business in 1989.

Sports Illustrated was sold and then sold again, the last time for $110 million. Staff cuts were made in waves. The new owner, Authentic Brands Group, changed the magazine from a weekly to a monthly. Declining subscriptions and ad revenue indicate the final victim of the *SI* cover jinx might be the magazine itself.

Jerry West played four more years to complete a fourteen-year career. The 1972 championship (at last) was the high point. A three-year stretch as the Lakers coach, 145 wins, 101 losses, was followed by his greatest basketball success during eighteen years as the team's general manager. His teams won six NBA championships. He followed that with successful front-office stints with the Memphis Grizzlies, Golden State Warriors, and now the Los Angeles Clippers. His entire adult life has been basketball.

In his autobiography, *West by West: My Charmed, Tormented Life,* he told how his first marriage was falling apart during the 1968–69 season and playoffs. He also noted that he never returned to Boston Garden after he retired as a coach. The memories were too painful, even when the teams he built as GM were big winners. He was eighty-two when this book was written.

Elgin Baylor played two more full seasons before his knees forced him to quit nine games into the 1971–72 season, which meant he missed that one NBA championship shared by West and Wilt. He tried coaching for three seasons with the New Orleans Jazz (86-135), then became the general manager of the Clippers for twenty-two seasons. His legacy is the individual game played on every NBA court, the ability to run and fly. He died on March 22, 2021, at the age of eighty-six.

John Havlicek continued to play for the Celtics for nine more seasons. He won two more NBA championships with an entirely different cast of teammates, bringing his championship total to eight in fifteen years. Once he left basketball, he never returned, working every now and then as a corporate spokesman, mostly living off investment income from his playing days.

"Hey, do you want to go to lunch?" he asked the bright young man one day after some post-retirement press conference.

"This guy is the model for the modern retired athlete," the bright young man thought while he refused, already late for work. "They're all going to be set for the rest of their lives in the future. What a thing."

Havlicek died on April 25, 2019, of Parkinson's disease. The man who could run forever, the most durable Celtic of all time, was seventy-nine. Larry Siegfried, his Ohio State teammate, had died from a heart attack in 2010 at the age of seventy-one. Sam Jones was eighty-seven when this book was written. Emmette Bryant was eighty-two. Don Nelson was eighty, living on Maui, raising his own strain of marijuana for personal consumption, playing poker with Willie Nelson, Woody Harrelson, and Owen Wilson.

The Boston Garden was closed for business forever on September 29, 1995, one night before the $160 million Fleet Center was opened next door. Unlike Fenway Park, given a rebirth after the Red Sox were purchased in 2002 by John Henry and associates, the Garden never was viewed as a tidy little bandbox or quaint repository of history and dreams. The arena stood, vacant, for three years before it was torn down in 1998. The bright young man, assigned to do a story on the building's final days before it was dismantled, was escorted inside. It was a sad experience, like visiting an old friend at a rest home, everyone knowing what would come next.

The Fabulous Forum still exists, but in a reduced civic role since 1999 when the Lakers and Kings moved from Inglewood to the $375 million Staples Center in downtown Los Angeles. The building has been used primarily as a music venue. Prince played twenty-one straight concerts in the Forum in 2011. Five Finger Death Punch, the Eagles, Ozuna, and Sturgill Simpson were scheduled for dates in April and May 2020 that corresponded to the dates of the 1969 NBA finals. Performances were canceled due to the pandemic.

In March 2020 the building was purchased by Los Angeles Clippers zillionaire owner Steve Ballmer as part of a plan to build a basketball-specific palace in the neighborhood for his team. The Forum neighborhood already has experienced a sports resurgence with the opening next door of the $4.963 billion SoFi Stadium, home of the NFL Rams and Chargers.

There apparently is more money to be made in that macadam desert.

Seven Players from the 1969 Finals have been inducted into the Naismith Basketball Hall of Fame in Springfield, Massachusetts. Russell, Havlicek, Sam Jones, and Bailey Howell represent the Celtics. Chamberlain, West, and Baylor represent the Lakers. Both referees from the final game—Mendy Rudolph and Earl Strom—are in the Hall. Don Nelson was added as a coach, Tom Sanders as a contributor. Red Auerbach, the Celtics general manager, is included as a coach. Chick Hearn, the Lakers broadcaster, is a contributor.

It is an impressive list of people. Somewhere in the cosmos, Johnny Most is wondering—loudly—why Hearn is enshrined and he is not. Chick Hearn died in 2002 at the age of eighty-five. Starting on November 21, 1965, he broadcast 3,338 consecutive Laker games, a record sportscasting streak that will never be touched. Johnny Most died in 1993. He was sixty-nine years old.

Sportswriters older than the bright young man pretty much are all gone. Retirements were followed by deaths, sometimes the other way around, plans be damned. Jerry Nason, Herb Ralby, Jack Barry, Clif Keane, Jack Craig, Harold Kaese, the great Ray Fitzgerald (at the age of fifty-five, cancer), Bud Collins, Ernie Roberts, an entire layer of solid craft and knowledge was peeled away from the *Globe,* obituary by obituary.

Will McDonough went for a stress test on the morning of January 9, 2003, came home, sat down in his living room chair to watch *SportsCenter,* had a heart attack, and died at age sixty-seven. His wake was held in the new Boston Garden, the first—and so far, only—wake held in the building.

Eddie Gillooly died. George Sullivan died. Jim Murray died. Milton Gross died. George Plimpton died. Frank Deford died. There is a temptation to say that the entire business of sportswriting died somewhere, too, but it did not. It changed, with less appreciation of style, a larger reliance on instant Twitter information, less access, more opinion, but it did not die. It did become more boring. The anecdote, the mainstay of New Journalism, became an endangered species.

The Boston Celtics have won six more post-Russell world championships since 1969 with stars like Larry Bird, Paul Pierce, Dave Cowens, Robert Parish, and Kevin McHale. This gives them seventeen titles, but the last one was in 2008. The new generation of fans is getting nervous.

The Los Angeles Lakers have won twelve (TWELVE!!!) world championships since 1969 in successive eras that have run from Chamberlain and West at the start to Kareem Abdul-Jabbar and Magic Johnson and Kobe Bryant and Shaquille O'Neal and, in the 2020 bubble, LeBron James. Los Angeles basketball historians say that the Lakers now have accumulated seventeen championships, same as the Celtics. Boston historians point out that the first five Lakers championships were won when the team was in Minneapolis and really shouldn't count.

The basketball rivalry between Los Angeles and Boston endures, despite the long stretch of geography between the two cities.

The Bright Young Man went to sleep one night and when he awoke in the morning found that he was seventy-seven years old. He is not sure how this happened.

Coda

The year is 1992. The summer Olympics are being held in Barce-lona, Spain. The Dream Team is here, a collection of stars from the NBA wearing the uniform of the United States. These are interna-tional celebrities, players known by their first names alone—Michael and Magic, Larry, Charles—a representation of how big the sport has grown. The bright young man and Will McDonough also are here.

The bright young man is forty-nine years old, not so young anymore and certainly not as bright as he once thought he was. He works for *Sports Illustrated* full-time now. He is divorced after twenty-one years of marriage, two kids. McDonough, fifty-seven, divorced and remar-ried, still works at the *Globe*, but has become much more famous as a pro football expert and commentator on NBC television broadcasts. NBC has brought him to the Olympics as a reporter. He works often here with O. J. Simpson, another NBC voice.

On a night in the middle of the Games, McDonough and the not-so-bright, not-so-young man run into each other on the deck of a cruise ship anchored in the Barcelona harbor. *Sports Illustrated* has rented the entire ship for three weeks. One of the magazine's tradi-tional marketing ploys is to fly the fattest of fat-cat advertisers to both the summer and winter Olympics, put them up in a four-star, five-star hotel, treat them to three or four days of sports action, wine them, dine them, send them home, and bring in a new batch of fattest fat cats. The limited number of four-stars and five-stars in Barcelona, alas, had been booked by other enterprises, and *SI* scrambled with creative thinking to rent the entire cruise ship.

Part of the fat-cat package is a party, thrown on the ship. *SI* brings Olympic stars of the past onto the scene to mingle with the guests and the latest Olympic heroes, snatched from the victory podiums and the headlines. John Havlicek is here from the past, along with Mike Eruzione, Wilma Rudolph, Edwin Moses, assorted greats. Three of these parties are held during the Olympics, one for each group of fat cats, and TBYM is invited to all of them as part of the *SI* staff. Will McDonough is invited because he is part of the NBC coverage. O. J. Simpson is invited, too.

The night is warm. The full moon hangs over the Mediterranean. Nick and the Nice Guys, an oldies band out of Rochester, New York, imported only for these parties, bangs out the Alan Freed songbook. TBYM and McDonough enjoy a couple of cocktails. Fat cats in their country-club casual golf shirts and Palm Beach blazers are everywhere, accompanied by their well-tanned fat-cat wives or sleek fat-cat companions. Waiters slide through the crowd with expensive finger food. Glasses are refilled automatically.

"This is pretty good, huh?" TBYM says in a quiet burst of moonlit emotion.

"Yes, it is," McDonough says.

He becomes philosophical.

"You know, you get into this sportswriting business and you know you're never going to make a lot of money," he says. "The business doesn't reward people that way. You won't get rich. Money will always be a problem. You do, however, get experiences. You go places, see things. You have great seats. You get to be around people with money sometimes, too. Not often, but sometimes. You come to a thing like this and for a night, a couple of nights, you get to live the way they live. You eat what they eat, drink what they drink, see what they see. You talk with them. You get to live in their world."

(Pause.)

"You're right," the former bright young man says. "I guess we're a couple of lucky guys."

(No pause.)

"WE?" McDonough says. "I'm talking about YOU. YOU'RE the

lucky guy. I have this kind of money. I'm in television. Television pays a LOT of money. I am one of these people now. I live like this every day. I'm talking about YOU."

Hah.

The Former Bright Young Man (TFBYM) smiles.

Wouldn't trade it for anything.

Acknowledgments and
a Note on Sources

The biggest source—sadly—was my memory. I can't tell you how many times I wished that I had kept a diary, notes, some chronicle of those days in the long ago. My own and other people's stories from the *Boston Globe* were a great help in making me remember time, place, situations, people, but the little details are missing. I want to know where I had lunch, who was with me, what was our conversation. I remember a lot of things, but wish I remembered more.

(Note to next generation: write down a couple of lines every day: an anecdote, a joke, an opinion, the color of your favorite shirt, something about the high cost of living. Just because. You will be happy with the result in the not-so-distant future.)

The books in the bibliography that follows were further guides. The characters in the 1969 finals have talked and dissected the games and the outcomes for years. Bill Russell, alone, has written four books with four different collaborators. Wilt Chamberlain is chronicled in three books, Jerry West in two. *Sports Illustrated* ran assorted articles on the games and the participants, especially by Frank Deford and George Plimpton, a Hall of Fame combination. The July 1969 issue of *Sport* magazine, Tony Conigliaro on the cover, Elgin Baylor's playoff diary with Bill Libby on the inside, was a fine help.

The Internet, of course, is a modern researcher's dream. The *Los Angeles Times* appears, tap-tap on the writer's screen on newspapers

.com, followed by the *New York Times* and the *Philadelphia Inquirer* and assorted other publications. Google, tap-tap-tap provides other sites and other answers. The ABC television coverage of the fourth quarter of the seventh game of the 1969 Finals can be found easily on YouTube. Check it out, see if you think Wilt really was hurt. Count the bounces on Don Nelson's shot. Wikipedia, truth's controversial stepchild, also opens many research trails.

The greatest joy of working in the *Boston Globe* files was being reconnected with an assortment of characters—long gone—fellow workers and friends. Their preserved words brought the everyday past back to life, all of us getting something to eat from the cafeteria upstairs, sitting around and talking and talking (and smoking) when we were supposed to be doing work. This has become a lost art. Thanks to Tom Mulvoy, a fellow survivor of that time, for helping me remember. Thanks to Heather Stevenson, Janice Page, and Ed Ryan for their *Globe* help.

Thanks to Mal Graham, Rick Weitzman, Don Nelson, Jeff Cohen, and Jan Volk for their time and memories. Thanks to Celtics public relations director Jeff Twiss for his help. Thanks to Bob Sales, Nick Curran, Lyle Spencer, Steve Bisheff. Thanks to Matt Barton and Eric Graf, at the Library of Congress, and to John Miley, in his garage in Indiana, for help with old radio recordings.

Thanks to Jason Kaufman, my editor in these different excursions into the sports past. Thanks to Carolyn Williams, Ana Espinoza, and Nora Reichard, all at Doubleday. Thanks to Esther Newberg at International Creative Management, another traveler on these excursions.

Thanks to my grandson, Jackson Moleux, who asked if Wilt Chamberlain was "any good" when picking his NBA2K20 team during an afternoon of video hoop. (That was an inspiration for this book right there.) Thanks to his brother, Colin, another video game star. Thanks to their mother, my daughter, Robin Montville, and to my son, Leigh Alan Montville. Thanks and more thanks to Linda Finkle, who has not only kept the home fires burning but kept us sane during this pandemic.

Thank you for reading this effort.

Bibliography

Aldrich, Nelson A. Jr. *George, Being George: George Plimpton's Life as Told, Admired, Deplored and Envied by 200 Friends, Relatives, Lovers, Acquaintances, Rivals—and a Few Unappreciative Observers*. New York: Random House, 2008.

Auerbach, Red, and John Feinstein. *Let Me Tell You a Story: A Lifetime in the Game*. New York: Little, Brown and Company, 2004.

Baylor, Elgin, with Alan Eisenstock. *Hang Time: My Life in Basketball*. New York: Houghton Mifflin Harcourt, 2018.

Carey, Mike, with Jamie Most. *High Above Courtside: The Lost Memoirs of Johnny Most*. New York: Sports Publishing, LLC, 2003.

Chamberlain, Wilt. *A View from Above*. New York: Villard Books, 1991.

Cherry, Robert. *Wilt: Larger Than Life*. Chicago: Triumph Books, 2004.

Deford, Frank. *Over Time: My Life as a Sportswriter*. New York: Grove Press, 2012.

Deford, Frank. *The Best of Frank Deford: I'm Just Getting Started . . .* Chicago: Triumph Books, 2000.

Goudsouzian, Adam. *King of the Court: Bill Russell and the Basketball Revolution*. Berkeley, CA: The University of California Press, 2010.

Havill, Adrian. *The Last Mogul: The Unauthorized Biography of Jack Kent Cooke*. New York: St. Martin's Press, 1992.

Hearn, Chick, and Steve Springer. *Chick: His Unpublished Memories and the Memories of Those Who Knew Him*. Chicago: Triumph Books, 2004.

Luckman, Charles. *Twice in a Lifetime: From Soap to Skyscrapers*. New York: W. W. Norton and Company, 1988.

MacMullan, Jackie, Rafe Bartholomew, and Dan Klores. *Basketball: A Love Story*. New York: Crown Archetype, 2018.

Meschery, Tom. *Over the Rim: Poems by Tom Meschery*. New York: The McCall Publishing Company, 1970.

Murray, Jim. *Jim Murray: The Autobiography of the Pulitzer Prize Winning Columnist*. New York: The Macmillan Publishing Company, 1993.

Pluto, Terry. *Tall Tales: The Glory Years of the NBA, in the Words of the Men Who Played, Coached, and Built Pro Basketball*. New York: Simon and Schuster, 1992.

Pomerantz, Gary. *Wilt, 1962: The Night of 100 Points and the Dawn of a New Era*. New York: Crown Publishing Group, 2005.

Reynolds, Bill. *Rise of a Dynasty: The 57 Celtics, The First Banner, and the Dawning of a New America*. New York: New American Library, 2010.

Russell, Bill, with Alan Hilburg and David Falkner. *Russell Rules: 11 Lessons on Leadership from the Twentieth Century's Greatest Winner*. New York: New American Library, 2001.

Russell, Bill, with Alan Steinberg. *Red and Me: My Coach, My Lifelong Friend*. New York: HarperCollins, 2009.

Russell, Bill, with Taylor Branch. *Second Wind: The Memoirs of an Opinionated Man*. New York: Random House, 1979.

Russell, Bill, as told to William McSweeney. *Go Up for Glory*. New York: Coward, McCann Publishers, 1966.

Ryan, Bob. *Scribe: My Life in Sports*. New York: Bloomsbury USA, 2014.

Sullivan, George. *The Boston Celtics: A Championship Tradition, Fifty Years*. Del Mar, California: Tehabi Books, 1996.

Taylor, John. *The Rivalry: Bill Russell, Wilt Chamberlain, and the Golden Age of Basketball*. New York: Random House, 2005.

West, Jerry, with Jonathan Coleman. *West by West: My Charmed, Tormented Life*. New York: Little, Brown and Company, 2011.

West, Jerry, with Bill Libby. *Mr. Clutch: The Jerry West Story*. New York: Grosset and Dunlap, 1969.

Whalen, Thomas. *Dynasty's End: Bill Russell and the 1968–69 World Champion Boston Celtics*. Boston: Northeastern University Press, 2004.

Index

About the Author

Three-time *New York Times* bestselling author LEIGH MONTVILLE is a former columnist at the *Boston Globe* and former senior writer at *Sports Illustrated*. He is the author of *Sting Like a Bee, Evel, The Mysterious Montague, The Big Bam, Ted Williams, At the Altar of Speed, Manute,* and *Why Not Us?* He lives in Boston.